IN
SEARCH
OF
MR DARCY

IN SEARCH OF MR DARCY

Lessons Learnt in the Pursuit of Happily Ever After

CHRISTINA FORD

ICON

This edition published in the UK in 2024
by Icon Books Ltd,
Omnibus Business Centre,
39–41 North Road, London N7 9DP
email: info@iconbooks.com
www.iconbooks.com

ISBN: 978-183773-003-2

Typeset in Mrs Eaves by Marie Doherty

Printed and bound in Great Britain
by CPI Group (UK) Ltd, Croydon CR0 4YY

For my family, of course.

And in particular, Alan. You, more than anyone, would appreciate the irony.

A note from the author

This book is an account of my life ... so far.

It is drawn and crafted from memory, impressions, worn-out stories I can recite forwards and backwards, untold stories so fresh I can taste them, faded photographs, emails, texts, adolescent journals, and friends and family whose own memories have added light, texture and colour to mine. Some memories diverge and blend, and others burn so brightly it hurts my eyes to look at them. This is how we remember, and these are the tools I have used to render the events in the telling of my story.

Of course, in some cases, the dialogue is reimagined, inspired by the essence of the story, the emotion of what was said and how I remember it to be. Years have been compressed into sentences, tiny moments examined in forensic detail, single emotions teased over pages and entire years left unwritten.

Memory is imperfect and flawed. It ricochets like a pinball as you are squeezed through the wormhole of time. So, I recognise and respect that there is a personal lens from which others might view events.

Some, but not all, of the names in this book have been changed. Family and some friends are exactly who I say they are. But those men whose stories have overlapped with mine, well, their skins have been creatively reimagined. Their physical descriptions camouflaged, their careers and interests altered, and their names all inspired by Jane Austen characters, which I thought fitting, considering the title. So don't go looking for them.

This is my story. An honest recollection of my life, loves, lessons, and experiences ... as I remember it to be.

Contents

The Book of Blurry Men and Skinny Bitches

The Book of Edward

The Book of Christina

Epilogue

Prologue

How Did I Get Here, and Who Can I Blame?

*'I know not all that may be coming, but be it
what it will, I'll go to it laughing.'*
Herman Melville, *Moby-Dick*

I once heard that we are the sum of all our choices. If that's true, then I need to reflect on the plethora of men I've dated, loved, hated, tolerated, fucked, envied, liked enough, settled for, failed to understand, was unable to love, or loved too much. Because if that doctrine does stand true, I think I owe you guys a debt of gratitude, for your collective contributions have all added up to someone I'm pretty frickin' happy with: me.

When I look back at my life, I don't tend to remember exact years or what month something happened, I go by relationships. The Brandon years. The Jackson experiment. The Edward decade. You get the picture. I bet right about now you are thinking, *Is she really defining herself by the men in her life? And if so, what a lacklustre feminist*, but hear me out. It's not about the men per se, it's about who I was at that time, my choices, and, of course, the influences surrounding me.

So, permit me to unpack the one influence that has most continuously messed with my head, has confused my heart, and has set the bar so incredibly high when searching for that perfect man that one would need to be an Olympic pole-vaulter to clear that thing. I'm talking about the profound and super unsettling lifelong aftershock that comes from reading books. You heard me, readers. Let me be more specific. I'm talking about being lulled into a blissful, naive childhood sleep with classic fairy tales like 'Cinderella', 'Snow White' and 'Sleeping Beauty'.

We were told tales of handsome princes, fabulous castles and, well ... happily ever after. The heroines were beautifully illustrated with their impossibly tiny waists, perfect facial features and long, blown-out, big, bouncy hair. Often, amid their strife, they'd burst into uncontrollable songs of longing. Sometimes nearby friendly woodland creatures would sing along in perfect three-part harmony.

These fictional young women of disproportionate beauty believed that 'one day their prince would come', and would carry them off to new-found wealth and opulence. And guess what? It happened. Hell, they even looked daisy-fresh, despite having spent the day sweeping cinders from the hearth or gathering nuts and berries in a dark and scary forest. In my only attempt to clean my fireplace, I can honestly say I looked like a charcoal briquette with blonde hair, and strangely, not once did I feel the urge to break into song. And where the hell are her girlfriends during all of this abusive, domestic, unsanctioned labour? Are they also dipped in Disney, singing solos in rural isolation?

When I was a child, I had a disconnect with the heroine who always seemed to need rescuing. I wasn't dreaming of Prince Charming, white steed and happily ever after. Admittedly, a fairy godmother would certainly have come in handy on multiple occasions, and those enviable glass slippers were no less practical than some of the other fabulous footwear taking up space in my closet. But I could not identify with a girl whose sole source of happiness revolved around this one thing, being plucked out of her shit-show of life by a super-rich guy with great hair. I would be full-out lying, though, if I said that as I grew up, those romantic fairy-tale notions didn't plant an acorn of hope in my slightly jaded, well-used heart, one of enduring love, a financially solvent man with a full head of hair. Why? Because we're told over and over in books and movies that it can happen. It's the single girl's Holy Grail, the infamous brass (I mean gold) ring topped with a honking big, brilliant round-cut solitaire.

Not once did we, as readers, get a glimpse of that happily ever after ten years down the line. The story stopped in modern-day terms with handfuls of confetti thrown in the air outside the church. If we fast-forward a decade, the chances are that our beautiful heroine has had a messy litter of children. Her hips have spread. Her boobs, empty of any former life from breastfeeding, will be hovering just inches above that not-so-tiny waist of hers, and she'll be too tired to even think about having sex, or shaving her legs, for that matter. As for our Prince Charming, he's lost half his hair and no longer fits into his suit of armour. He'll probably be complaining that since slaying dragons and rescuing damsels are on the decline, they will have to have some serious cutbacks in the castle. The only heated action in the bedroom is the two arguing about the temperature setting on the thermostat because the doctor has just told our princess that she's perimenopausal. Where's that story, Disney?

As I got older, I started examining the books and movies that had deliciously lured me as a youth, the well-respected writings of authors such as Jane Austen or the Brontës – esteemed writers of literature whose books I'd devoured or their film adaptations I'd obsessively wept over. But at some point, the penny dropped ... DANG. There it was. These highly regarded literary works were fairy tales too, with an eternal romantic pursuit of the near-perfect man and 'happily ever after'.

In London, I have access to a private gated garden outside my flat in Marylebone – think Julia Roberts and Hugh Grant in the movie *Notting Hill*. It's picturesque and overgrown with dense leafy hedges and flower beds meticulously and lovingly tended. Inside gardens like these are often park benches. A functional romantic memorial, if you will, engraved with messages of remembrance and devotion, most often from a surviving loving spouse. Carved deeply into the wooden back or engraved on a brass plaque read messages like:

> *To the world, you might have been one person,*
> *but to one person, you were the world. Henry.*

> *Alice, come rain or shine, I sit here every day, so*
> *never am I far away. With all my heart, George.*

And this one really got me.

> *Remembering you is easy. I do it every day.*
> *But there is an ache within my heart*
> *that will never go away.*
> *I did not see you close your eyes*
> *or hear your last sigh.*
> *I only heard that you were gone,*
> *too late to say goodbye.*
> *For Daisy.*

Damn, that's sad.

Could this be it, evidence of the fairy-tale ending, a love so profound and transcendent it is worthy of a park bench? Or is it just the work of guilty poets and old lovers? I mean, did 'bench-worthy' Alice ever lose it so badly that she wanted to throw plates at George's head? Could a bench ever read, 'Max, you old goat, at least the room will no longer be filled with your night farts. Yours, Sue'?

So, let's discuss the fictional man who truly fucked with my romantic expectations. In what *O* describes as 'arguably the greatest romance novel of all time', Jane Austen's *Pride and Prejudice*, spunky heroine Elizabeth Bennet meets the wealthy, handsome and proud Mr Darcy. At first, the two are at odds and have outward disdain for each other. By the end of the story, they have not only discovered they have misjudged each other, but they have fallen madly in love (sigh). Mr Darcy marries Elizabeth Bennet, whisks her off to his incredible grand manor house in the English countryside, and, you guessed it ... they live happily ever after. I'd put big money on the hunch that Austen was read fairy tales as a child, and it might be significant to note at this point that Austen never married. Hmmm?

And to permanently tattoo this story onto my somewhat romantic, slightly jaded heart, *Pride and Prejudice* was made into a mini-series in 1995, with Colin Firth cast as the handsome Mr Darcy. Immediately I fell hopelessly, deeply and forever in love with Colin Firth, as did millions of women viewers and, I suspect, quite a few men.

Helen Fielding, the author of *Bridget Jones's Diary*, admits she stole the plot of *Pride and Prejudice* for her book. And she was so captivated by Colin Firth's portrayal of Mr Darcy that she insisted he played Mark Darcy in the film adaptation. The name is not coincidental. Side note: I take objection to how anyone could describe a young 30-something single girl like Bridget as a loser when she has an awesome group of friends, a career, and can afford her own flat in Zone 1. Goddamn it (I'm incensed here!), she's nothing short of aspirational! If that were a description of a guy instead of Bridget Jones, we'd be calling him 'marriage material'.

I can identify with so many Elizabeth Bennet types. In fact, if I had to pick one fictional woman to describe me best, I think it would be her. OK, I don't play the pianoforte, but that's not to say I couldn't learn. But does Mr Darcy exist? Are we, the practical and cautiously optimistic romantics, doomed in our pursuit of the unobtainable fabricated man, the modern-day Prince Charming? I have to say, maybe. But that doesn't stop us from searching for Mr Darcy, does it? And it didn't stop me.

I'll admit my search hasn't exactly gone the way of Austen or Disney, and the only thing my mirror assures me with blasted regularity is that I'll not be shimmying into my skinny jeans any time soon. In fact, I've found myself on more than one occasion brushing off the dust and gravel from some unfamiliar road asking myself, *How did I get here, and who can I blame?* But whether I measure my relationships in years or hours, something wonderfully unexpected has occurred, a surprising discovery that taught me about life, love and, most of all, myself. So, to all the men whom I've stumbled upon in my search for Mr Darcy, thank you.

The Book of

Alan

CHAPTER 1

Thick-Skinned Children

*'If you're not embarrassing your children, you're missing
out on one of the ultimate pleasures of being a parent.'*
My father, Alan Dixon

Before I delve into my assorted stories of love, men and
seriously questionable behaviour, I thought it might be
prudent to provide you with a bit of background on me and
the most unusual, unorthodox influence on my life, my father.

There is some nugget of theoretical wisdom floating around
out there. It says that girls marry their fathers. Women subconsciously are drawn to guys who remind them of their dads, with
similar traits, good, bad or socially frowned upon. Well, I don't
think that's what happened in my case. In fact, it's a little more
dramatic than that. I didn't marry my father. I became him. This
snuck out of nowhere. I was so busy not becoming my mother
that this just slipped under the door like smoke. One day all is
normal, and the next, I'm quoting the Marx Brothers, Steve
Martin and Oscar Wilde.

Of course, I'm not exactly like my dad. There's a bucket-load
of things about him that I never understood or even attempted
to understand: his left-wing politics, why he refused to attend
my wedding, or his reasons for kicking me out of the house for
getting my ears pierced, even though I was eighteen – at an age,
I reminded him, I could've been called up to the army if we'd
been at war or had the draft. But where he does reside in me is
in my passion for writing, my love of fashion, and the absolute

joy I find in a side-splitting, knee-slapping, tears-rolling-down-your-face laugh. If this book is a thank-you letter to all the men who taught me something incredible about myself, then of course I'd have to acknowledge my father, Alan Dixon, an unusual, introverted man of wit, poetry and disarming charm.

I was born exactly nine months after my parents were married, leading my father to cite my conception to my three younger sisters and me as a warning about the frequent failings of contraception. My mother, reframing the story, called me her honeymoon baby. As a young girl raised in the seventies, I wanted the same things that other girls of that generation wanted: embroidered bell-bottom jeans, to marry David Cassidy, and the right to burn my bra (once I required one). Fun was simple, uncomplicated and could last all day. I never tired of the pure pleasure of running through the sprinkler on our front lawn on a hot day, an orange popsicle split in half, or finding a full day's worth of imagination in a box of coloured chalk. I was utterly content with my two main modes of transportation, my CCM banana-seat bike or skipping down the street. Friends would show up at my house after dinner and wait on the front lawn until I'd finished mine. There was no texting, no tracking locations, no social media showing us how inadequate our lives were compared to everyone else's. There was no 'everyone else'. The only people I knew were the ones who were waiting on my lawn to play hide and seek.

I believed in the magic anticipation of shaking a Polaroid picture, creating forts with secret passwords out of large appliance boxes, and in the summer, I could stay out until the street lights came on. I also imagined a fabulous career, reminded by Gloria Steinem and my mother that 'girls can have it all'. I dreamt about having two adorable babies, one boy and one girl, that always smelt of Johnson's Baby Powder. This all made perfect sense to me, and I never questioned it … Well, maybe the David Cassidy bit as I got older, but that was just to make room for Rick Springfield.

We were one of a small handful of Gentile families in a predominantly Jewish neighbourhood. The Yiddish term for us was *shiksa*, which I had no issue with, although in general it wasn't meant to be flattering. I always assumed I'd marry a good Jewish boy, which both my parents were completely fine with. As for the parents of the Jewish boys I came to know – that was a whole other kettle of gefilte fish. We *shiksas* were acceptable to date, sleep with and even introduce to the family, but when it came time to marry: 'You, my son, are marrying a Jew.' My Jewish friend Benjamin, who was in love with me from early high school, reassured me he'd get me on his second marriage, when his parents would be dead or simply have given up. Looking back, I think that might have been one of my earliest lessons about men: sometimes there are other factors at play.

Alan and my mother, Elena, were like most parents who made up my youth's colourful tapestry. Optimistic immigrants, a British journalist and a Russian beauty queen, a first-generation family who'd come to carve out a better life than the one they had left behind. They raised four daughters in a comfortable middle-class neighbourhood, and to the best of my knowledge, there were no epic parenting fails. We weren't sold into white slavery, we still have all our limbs firmly attached, and we managed not to kill each other during our homicidal, hormonal teenage years. Extra kudos to Elena, for as my sisters and I were raging, hormonal teenage nightmares, with few, if any, likeable qualities, Elena was standing on the threshold of Hell, dealing with puberty's evil older sister, menopause. A hormonal shit-storm if ever there was one, slamming hard against the walls of a split-level bungalow on Castlefield Avenue.

Alan gleefully and rather chauvinistically supported the Prince Charming fairy-tale concept. He repeatedly declared to me and my sisters, 'Girls, it's just as easy to fall in love with a rich boy as it is a poor one, maybe even easier,' and suggested to my sister Victoria that she might want to forego university to become a stewardess, so she could find herself a businessman husband.

There was a particularly twisted torture my father seemed to thrive in, and the verbal comedic spew he'd fire off to the unsuspecting was nothing short of legendary. If you hadn't developed a 'thick skin' – and show me a ten year old who has – those scars could be borne for years, leading to hours upon hours of well-justified talk time with a therapist. To give you what I'd consider a tidy example of the thick skin required, I share this one parenting story with you. As small kids out shopping at some store or mall, my father frequently said, 'Now, girls, hurry up, or you'll be left behind like Little Freddy.'

'Who's Little Freddy?' we inquisitively and innocently asked, the first time we heard his name.

'You don't remember Little Freddy?' my father replied. 'Well, Little Freddy was your brother, and we were out years ago, someplace very much like this. And I said, "Little Freddy, if you don't hurry up, you'll be left behind …" and we've never seen Little Freddy since.' This was my father's idea of street-proofing us.

Years later, I told Benjamin the Little Freddy story, likely to try and prove my father was weirder than his — an argument he'd have to go pretty far to beat. The first time Benjamin met my dad, he reached out his hand to shake my father's, smiled and said: 'Nice to meet you, Mr Dixon, I'm Freddy.' My father, without missing a beat, pulled Benjamin into his arms and, with joyous exuberance, said, 'Freddy, you've come home.' From that day forward, and for years to come, Benjamin sent him Father's Day cards.

Alan's humour, both weapon and armour, had its highs and lows, particularly when boys and dating were introduced. We were the only girls whose father had a 'Hit Wagon'. This was Alan's dark green convertible Cadillac Eldorado – a tank of a car. The Hit Wagon was basically an assassination tool at the ready any time a boy did one of his daughters wrong. My dad's solution for teenage heartache was simple and effective, although I don't recall that car ever being deployed for that reason.

It must've been challenging for my father during that time. My sisters and I were shedding our childhood skins, entering the world of boys, drinking and overall atrocious (a word my father favoured) behaviour. If Alan hadn't had a sense of humour, a parenting tool that's as essential as a Swiss Army knife on a camping trip, I believe he would've run from the house screaming. Perhaps we all would have.

CHAPTER 2

What Would Wonder Woman Do?

'All grown-ups were once children ... but
only few of them remember it.'
Antoine de Saint-Exupéry, *The Little Prince*

Teenage years are such a unique time in our lives. Never again will so many of us be single, with the same rudimentary experience, lined up together at the starting gate, looking to bust out of the paddock. With the youthful confidence supported by every fairy tale and Judy Blume book I had ever read, I was optimistically looking for that special guy ... You know, 'the one'. The strong, athletic boy who runs track, or the dark, misunderstood artsy guy brooding in theatre studies; boyfriend material, a first love, and for many of us, our first broken heart.

I had two serious boyfriends in high school, Cam Sheppard and Dave DeCarlo. I'm using the high-school definition of 'serious', meaning anything lasting longer than a semester. Cam was the first, and, much to his frustration, I never slept with him. He was a tall, lanky sixteen-year-old boy on the school swim team. He had a blond feathered shag haircut and sported the fashionably required white puka shell choker. He was a year older than me and reminded me of the teen heartthrob of the day, Bobby Sherman. Dreamy, as my girlfriends and I used to say.

Cam discovered my father's unique brand of teenage-boy torture early on, after escorting me home after one of our first dates. Trying hard to be quiet, we stood in the dark hallway of our split-level bungalow, coats still tightly fastened and still wearing our winter boots. Cam was coming in for our very first kiss, which I had been eagerly anticipating. *This is the moment*, I thought.

'Shhhhh,' I whispered, moving my body closer to his. 'My parents might hear us. They're right up those stairs.' I nodded to indicate the five steps leading to my parents' closed bedroom door. Cam made his move and awkwardly kissed me with all the skill of a teenage boy who knew little about the subject. His lips were still warm on mine, my eyes were closed shut just like I had seen in the movies. Suddenly, I heard my father's voice from behind their closed bedroom door. It rattled the small hallway walls like a sonic boom.

'No tongues,' he yelled. That was followed by the clear and unmistakable sound of my mother hitting my father. 'Alan … don't.' My father exploded with laughter. I wanted to kill myself, but first him.

My second and more serious boyfriend was Dave DeCarlo, who I started dating in Grade 11. He was my first real love and the young boy for whom I'd eventually give it all up. He was raised by a divorced Italian Catholic mother and lived with his younger brother and his *nona*. There would be many a conversation between me and Mrs DeCarlo around their small Formica kitchen table about the importance of waiting until marriage to have sex. If I listened close enough, I could hear Dave banging his head against the wall in the other room.

Scattered throughout my teenage years, there were dubious make-out sessions with a variety of boys. Even with a gun cocked and pressed against my temple, I'd be hard-pressed to come up with more than a handful of names. Time has mulched and blended them into a pubescent potpourri of a Levi's-wearing, pimple-faced teenage boy tasting of Juicy Fruit gum. And all were drunk into existence with one or more of the following: Mateus, Molson Export, peach schnapps or something called Purple Jesus. Purple Jesus was a vile concoction that only teenagers with little previous drinking experience could successfully consume. It consisted of whatever anyone could steal from their parents' drinks' cupboard, all poured into a collective plastic bucket then capped off with a healthy dousing of Welch's grape juice. With such an insalubrious start to my lifelong consumption of alcohol, I do wonder how I ever came to love it, to worship the ritual of cocktail hour, which had started off in such sick-making infancy.

Most often, these drunken teenage mixers took place in a dank, smoky basement of someone's absent parents' house, often accompanied by Led Zeppelin wailing at near-eardrum-splitting decibel, or *The Best of Bread* when snogging demanded a more befitting soundtrack. Of course, back at school on Monday, you completely ignored whomever it was whose tongue you'd granted permission to enter your mouth that weekend. Often spotted on one's neck was a souvenir hickey the size of a hockey puck, which no amount of concealer could successfully hide.

My basement of choice belonged to a cute dark-haired boy named Pete Walsh. Pete had a mischievous smile that always gave you the impression he was up to no good. I think that's likely because most often he was up to no good. Pete's basement was perfumed with the aroma of stale beer, damp carpeting, cigarettes and hash oil, all clinging like a sticky film to the fake-wood-panelled walls. Pete had made the most of Mrs Adams's science class, as evidenced by the fine array of handcrafted water bongs made from empty plastic Coke bottles. A single black lightbulb often lit his basement, making anything white glow like plutonium, including your teeth. Kiss, Aerosmith, Queen and The Police posters plastered the walls. And, of course, the iconic dream girl, Farrah Fawcett, with her skimpy red bathing suit, her big, bouncy blonde hair and just enough nipple protrusion to be the subject of regular discussion.

It was a time painted with adolescent hormones, a little foolishness and a lot of curiosity, coupled with the overwhelming desire to fit in, or at the very least not stand out. So those basement snogs weren't so much selective as they were educational. Or, to paraphrase Springsteen, we learnt more from a three-minute record than we ever did in school. It was not the end goal to have a rotating roster of boys making it to first base and sometimes stealing second; this was the bullpen. We were warming up and doing what young people have been doing since the dawn of time: rushing to become adults.

My father taught me many things, big and small, influences over the years that have really stuck with me, giving me a slightly unconventional lens through which I view life. I was no older than six when I first heard his lifelong toughening-up mantra of 'Don't let the bastards get you down,' a phrase I can't tell you how often I've chanted. He indoctrinated me into what is now a commonly held belief that clothes do make the man, and to always check out his shoes because everything you need to know about a guy is reflected in his footwear. I still do this today, and have dismissed some guy's flirtatious overtures solely on the basis of his tragic Clark's Wallabees.

A unique, inspirational motivation or call to action was born from when I was about fourteen. It was my first introduction to the power of the superhero stance, and a new catchphrase, 'What would Wonder Woman do?' There was something about Wonder Woman, this beautiful, statuesque superhero warrior that my father was inexplicably obsessed with. Added to this, by the time the TV world was introduced to Xena Warrior Princess (another full-figured, iconic fascination of Alan's), he told my sisters and I that he would willingly sell off any one of us to watch Wonder Woman's Lynda Carter take on Xena's Lucy Lawless in a wrestling match. I held confidently to the belief that it would be my sister Susan he'd sacrifice over me.

Mimicking my father, hands on my hips, feet slightly apart and head proudly held high, just like Wonder Woman, I'd stand in front of our television.

'This is what Wonder Woman would do,' my father would say. 'Just before she takes down the villain … she psyches herself up.' So, there we both would be, standing heroically still, my father and I channelling our inner superheroes as my mom, a mere mortal, nonchalantly walked by with clean laundry. Decades later, I saw a TED Talk about summoning your inner superhero, just like my dad had taught me to do while watching *Wonder Woman*. He was ahead of his time, my father, but as we know, timing is everything.

My father died four months and thirteen days before my mom. They were married for 56 years. After he died, I found numerous old boxes that held his writing: neatly bound poems and manuscripts of toiled words and immense love, trapped, unread in cardboard coffins. Almost all of it was a declaration of love to my mother, Elena, as if loving her was no more of a decision than breathing. And even though our love stories couldn't be more different – my father's love of one person that endured a lifetime, and my many loves, which did not – what they had in common was an incredible desire to express in words something essential to us, our definition of love.

We learn a lot about men and love from our fathers. I mean, it's the first relationship most girls have with a man, and it can define what we are inexplicably drawn to or repulsed by when it comes to searching for love. But perhaps, instead of searching for the qualities I loved most about my father in man after blessed man, I have taken on a few of those qualities within myself, so I am never without them. I can't speak to how my sisters feel about their relationship with Alan. Nor can I say with any confidence that they would interpret my father's social behaviour or idiosyncrasies with the same nostalgic fondness that I do, nor am I aware of what superhero powers he thought to bestow on them, but I feel I may have got the best of him. After all, here I sit writing, recalling the laughter, with my closet unapologetically busting with many a pair of fantastic shoes.

The Book of

Brandon

CHAPTER 1

You Had Me at 'Hello'

*'There are many things that we would throw away if we
were not afraid that others might pick them up.'*
Oscar Wilde, *The Picture of Dorian Gray*

O nce upon a time, long, long, ago in the 1980s, before the
internet and way before online dating, there was a magical
place where cocktails were exchanged for coins, and music was
so electric it could spontaneously move your body like a gyrat-
ing puppet on an invisible string. There, many a young person
would sip their cocktail elixir, which bestowed upon them great
courage to make small talk with a handsome stranger. Then, as
the clock chimed midnight, you'd hear those four magic words,
'Your place or mine,' and think, *Ya, I'll shag you,* for this could
just be the beginning of … happily ever after.

This enchanted place was called a singles bar.

What dating apps are to the 2010s, singles bars were to the
nineties, eighties, and, well, I don't know how far back they go.
The seventies were all about discos, and I'm too young to know
where people in the sixties were hooking up. Maybe it was during
an anti-war protest, or at a Beat-poetry reading while snapping
their fingers in praise. I can't be sure. But whatever the decade,
all this is to say that sex has always been the alleged road to love.

At nineteen, I worked as a cocktail waitress at an insanely
popular singles bar called Brandy's. This is where I met
Brandon. I was engaged at 23, married at 25 … and divorced
at 26. Damn.

Brandy's holds the dubious distinction of being the only job I've ever been fired from. This was a direct result of me sleeping (*what's the plural of sleeping?*) with Jonathan Taylor-Woods, the live-in boyfriend of one Theresa Garcia, fellow Brandy's waitress. Jonathan was the only 'bad boy' I had ever been drawn to, as evident from his obsession with what he liked to call 'the magic of serial killers'. He was exceptionally charming and possessed stalker-like qualities, waiting for hours in his white Stingray outside my parents' house for me to get home. I mistook this as devotion. Ten years my senior, Jonathan was only the second guy I had slept with, and a massive pendulum-swing from fellow virgin Dave DeCarlo. I guess that's what made him exciting, and I think that's also what made me interesting to Jonathan: I was the closest he could come to having sex with a virgin without being brought up on charges.

Theresa, Jonathan's girlfriend, discovered a love letter I'd written to him while on vacation with my family in Rome. In what could best be described as a 'hell hath no fury' moment, she tacked my letter to the Brandy's bulletin board to expose my traitorous liaison(s). She campaigned with blinding ambition to get me fired. When I returned from Italy, the manager sacked me. I can't say this was one of my proudest moments, sleeping with someone else's boyfriend and then getting fired for it, but it wouldn't go down as my worst.

I might have no longer been working at Brandy's, but it was still the place to go, so one night, out with my girlfriend Amy, we went to the back entrance to try and bypass the exceptionally long queue. The door opened, and there stood an unfamiliar six-foot-one strawberry-blonde moustache-sporting human barrier between us and the bar. From what I could tell, underneath his porn-star moustache he had a friendly smile. He was athletic-looking, and I remember noticing that each of his massive thighs were the size of my torso, and wondering if he had to get custom-made jeans to fit those burly legs. He was new and cute and delayed my quick entrance and speedy warm-up tequila shot. I went to introduce myself – you know, to make sure he knew I had the necessary clout/reputation to secure me and Amy access, when he smiled and said, 'Hello, Christina, come on in.' I smiled, surprised, and thanked him, but resisting asking his name, since if he knew who I was, maybe I was supposed to know who he was too. Up at the bar, I asked Steve, one of the bartenders, 'Who's the cute new bouncer with the 'tache?'

'That's my friend, Brandon. Brandon Clutterbuck. He started last week.' Clutterbuck! The name blasted out of Steve's mouth like a car backfiring. *Clutterbuck? What kind of a name is Clutterbuck?* I thought, with a certain amount of judgemental horror. It sounded like a torture device from the Dark Ages. But what instantly followed that cerebral surname gut-punch was something so immediate, so bold, not to mention utterly insane, that I cannot come close to understanding it even to this day. With a White Russian in hand, surrounded by the sounds of loud chatter fighting to be heard over 'Boogie Wonderland', a wave of complete certainty hit me: *Wait ... I am going to be Christina Clutterbuck?*

It took a little time for my 21-year-old life and Brandon to catch up with the divine flash 'aha' moment I'd experienced that night at Brandy's. *But why not marry Brandon?* I thought. Without exception, he was one of the most well-meaning people I had ever met. He was the kind of gentle giant who, at weddings, would have a little girl standing on his feet dancing as the DJ played 'Total Eclipse of The Heart'. *What a great father he'd make,* I thought. Plus, it was time to settle down. I mean, everyone I knew was getting married, so shouldn't I?

Brandon had played professional hockey in Sweden, explaining the thighs. This, for many girls, especially those growing up in Canada, would be the equivalent of dating a rock star. But the celebrity of athletes was lost on me. Since a particular demographic of women (whom I affectionately call 'puck buddies') would unabashedly throw themselves at their skates, most of the hockey players I knew were cheating dogs and scallywags (my father's words, not mine). A collection of men I'd further describe as walking, living Petri dishes of questionable cold sores and transmittable diseases. So athletes, as a rule, held absolutely no interest to me. Except for Brandon. He was different.

Having just retired from Sweden, Brandon had joined his father and his three brothers in the family-run aluminium door and window manufacturing business — an industry I contentedly knew zero about. As a naturally gifted athlete, he had an uncanny ability to pick up and master any sport instantly. The sum total of my athletic ability and/or interest could be neatly summarised as squat-diddly-do. Brandon's all-consuming love of sports was so intense he'd tear up watching the opening of the Masters, just like I do now watching Ryan Gosling in *The Notebook*. There was also the time he burst into an inconsolable girlish weep when Canada's 1984 Olympic men's hockey team lost a deciding game, relegating them to fourth place and so just outside of medal contention. These were emotions I didn't understand or share. I was one of five women and one primitive metrosexual man living in one fashion-forward household, and we liked it that way. We didn't know of Bobby Orr, Phil Esposito or Jack Nicklaus. We knew of Gucci, Baryshnikov and Klimt. It was a Herculean effort for Brandon and my father to find much in common to talk about. That was also my challenge. We had absolutely nothing in common.

For a while, and maybe because I was young and didn't know better, I convinced myself it didn't matter. He was good. Better than good, he was great, the perfect potential loyal husband, devoted father, lover and friend. He had a solid job and had just bought his first house. He was a total catch. Everyone said so. Yet inside of me, why wasn't this 'love' making me weak in the knees? Were my youthful, romantic notions of love as told by Austen, Disney or Judy Blume unfairly sabotaging Brandon? Did I just need a little more time? I shook off those damaging, unrealistic expectations and told myself to grow up. I was almost a quarter-lifer. It was time to shake off my sophomoric adolescent lifestyle. Get a job, or better yet, a career. Settle down, get married, host couples' dinner parties with food that wasn't ordered in, and serve wine that didn't come out of a box. Move to the suburbs and start spitting out those kids. *What more is there, right?* I asked myself with the frequency of children on a family road trip, asking, 'Are we there yet?' The problem was, I was not there yet.

CHAPTER 2

Sorry I'm Late, I Didn't Want to Come

'Victory was within our grasp! And then the game started!'
Charles M. Schulz

I t was a cold, wet Christmas Eve. We were getting ready to visit Brandon's brothers and his mother, Ruby, at her condo. I had all but officially moved in with Brandon and his two roommates. We'd been dating for well over a year, and I enjoyed the blissful escape from my parents and sisters.

'Let's go sit by the tree and exchange one gift before we head to Mom's,' Brandon said, calling from just outside the bedroom door. I was in the bathroom dabbing on my lip gloss when a prickly sensation washed over me. The tiny hairs started to rise on the backs of my neck and arms.

'Crap,' I said out loud to myself. 'Crap, crap, crap.'

Now I think this might be as good as time as any to confess something to you. Because this will come up again, and this is just how my weirdly wired brain sometimes fires or, in some cases, misfires. Some might call it intuition, a sixth sense, gut feeling or ESP. Hell, you could even call it an overactive imagination that you've moulded into reality. But the bottom line is that I have unexplainable flashes of clarity in which I'm able to see instant glimpses of the future. They aren't all-encompassing or even broad in scope. I can't forecast elections or see dead people. It's rather like that immediate spark you feel when you meet a person, and somehow you instantly know they will be a fabulous friend. I can't explain them, these white-witch flashes.

They're something I just feel. So I guess it wasn't too surprising that I knew right then what Brandon was trying to do. He was planning to give me a gift I wasn't ready to receive.

'Brandon, let's do this later ... tomorrow,' I said as casually as I could while I anxiously re-dabbed my lip gloss. 'We don't need to open a gift now, plus we need to leave soon, and I hate what I'm wearing.' I looked in the mirror and yelled, 'I'm going to change.'

Brandon called back in frustration, 'You look great, really, you don't need to change.' I pushed back just hard enough for him to back down.

'OK, let me know when you're ready. I'll wait for you downstairs by the tree,' he said.

'Thanks, babe,' I said. I closed the bathroom door, reminding myself to breathe.

I came downstairs after a while, apologising for taking so long. 'Sorry, Brandon, nothing was working,' I explained as I looked for my coat.

'You looked fine twenty minutes ago,' he said.

'Thanks,' I smiled. 'You ready to go?'

Reluctantly he looked at his watch and said, 'Ya, I guess we better.' We gathered our assortment of wrapped parcels and some gingerbread cookies I had made earlier that day, and we headed out, me believing that I had at least for the moment avoided any unwanted gifts.

We were in the car, halfway to his mom's place, somewhere between one dreary suburban strip mall and another. Gazing out the window, I was reminded of how miserable the suburbs were, even with the addition of twinkling Christmas lights. I watched the 24-hour doughnut shops, gas stations and giant box stores repeat themselves every block or two, all devoid of charm. Even the snow took on an insipid grey hue. *How could anyone choose to live here?* I thought. We stopped at a red light. As I brought my attention back inside the car, there it was. In the palm of Brandon's outstretched hand was a small velvet box tied with a blue satin ribbon.

Wait! He's not planning on proposing to me here?! I screamed inside my head. Stopped at a traffic light ... in the Volvo ... in front of a Home fucking Depot? Hell no! This had all the romantic charm of a Do-It-Yourself car wash.

'Hey, Brandon, I thought we weren't doing this Christmas Eve gift thing,' I said anxiously.

'I know,' said Brandon, 'but I want to give this to you tonight before we get to Mom's.' With the small box still in the palm of his outstretched hand, waiting to be received, he smiled and said, 'Merry Christmas, Christina.'

'Brandon.' I remember sounding like I was pleading. 'Are you sure you don't want to wait until tomorrow? This can wait. We're almost at your mom's.'

'No,' he said with conviction and sounding a little hurt. 'I've wanted to give this to you for a long time. Go ahead, open it.'

The light turned green. Brandon was reminded to drive from a blast on the horn by the guy behind us. I reluctantly took the small velvet box tied with a blue satin ribbon and slowly, very slowly, opened it. There it was. A sparkling round-cut diamond sitting on top of a gold band. Brandon was driving and looking at me, driving and looking at me. I was thinking, *Shouldn't you at the very least pull over?* The car's interior briefly filled with a reddish illuminating glow thanks to the massive adjacent 7-Eleven sign, making Brandon's already-ginger complexion take on a somewhat radioactive sheen. 'What's this?' I asked, with complete knowledge that it might be the dumbest question of all time. Brandon's red face beamed, all the while maintaining the legal speed limit, and he asked: 'Christina, will you marry me?'

I looked up from the ring to see Brandon's face naturally radiating brighter than any outdoor commercial signage ever could do, the car still meandering through the snowy suburban streets. That face, that happy, hopeful face of his, is burned onto my brain. Even all these years later, I can recall every detail of how he looked. I stared at the ring and then back at Brandon, who was waiting for me to respond.

How could I say, 'I know this is what you've been planning for a long time now, but this is what I've been trying to avoid for the same length of time'? How could I ask, 'Why are you proposing while driving your Volvo through the dreary industrial streets in Markham in probably the most unromantic marriage proposal in the history of the world that didn't require a shotgun?' But most of all, looking at his face, how could I say, 'I don't love you enough, Brandon, to want to marry you'? I stared at the ring and back at Brandon. I smiled and exhaled, letting the unanswered question between us sit for just a second longer. 'Of course I'll marry you, Brandon.'

And just like that, somewhere between the 7-Eleven and Bumfuck, Nowhere, I was engaged.

CHAPTER 3

There's No Business
Like Show Business

'Give a girl the right shoes and she can conquer the world.'
Marilyn Monroe

The decade of our twenties comes with a crazy amount of change. Not only are many of us settling down into what is most likely our first adult relationship, but we're now paying bills, shopping for furniture and optimistically diving into the world of full-time employment. My dive came at 23, recently engaged, when I was baptised into the world of television commercials at a midsize production house called Wilde + Partners Productions. This would be more than just the place where I'd start my 30-plus-year career. This would be where I'd learn first-hand about men behaving badly, sexual harassment and the tremendous power they could wield.

My friend Marianne put in a good word with her husband Charlie, who was one of the executive producers at Wilde. Be it rumour or fact, there was something about the world of advertising and production that made Brandon uncomfortable about me working there. It had a reputation as a bad-boy industry, a Wild West frontier with very few rules or codes of conduct. If Brandon had had his way, I'd have been safely behind the Lancôme counter selling lipstick and eyeliner. But regardless of Brandon's objection, he wasn't the one in charge of that decision.

The job I was offered was the glamourless job of production assistant. The lowest rung of the production house's long, gruelling ladder. PA meant the first one in, the last one out. Endless grunt work of striking sets, loading and unloading trucks, getting cigarettes for directors, coffee-and-doughnut runs for client meetings, and any other menial, filthy task. Now, perhaps I'm sounding a little princess-like, but this newly offered steel-toe-boot-optional job wasn't exactly playing to my strengths, although I was unclear what those strengths even were at the time.

The day before I started at Wilde, my mother told me something that to this day stands alone as the best career advice I've ever received. 'Christina,' she said, as if she were channelling Coco Chanel, 'dress for what you want to do, not for what you're doing.'

So, armed with that nugget of wisdom, I entered Wilde + Partners on my first day as a PA with the confident sound of my Aldo patent-leather slingback heels clicking across the shiny poured-concrete floor. I was wearing a cream silk blouse I'd borrowed from my mother, a black linen skirt and my new DKNY camel-coloured linen blazer, which at that time was the most expensive wardrobe piece I owned. I can't be sure what career choice I was dressed for that day, but I was pretty confident that no one was getting me to load a truck.

I was immediately 'redirected' to the wardrobe department, thus effectively giving me the shortest career ever in the history of production as a PA. They got me working as an assistant stylist alongside the in-house wardrobe stylist, Felipe Torres. I was sent out shopping for wardrobe to dress a family of four for a Duncan Hines commercial. Let's take a moment here to recognise that I was hired to shop for clothes. This, *this* I was super qualified to do. Felipe was a temperamental gay twenty-something, with a colourful Boy George fashion flair and a PMSing Mariah Carey attitude. 'I'm better than this shitty commercial company,' Felipe would rant frequently, usually with some foot-stomping action to accompany his genuine outrage.

'I trained at Parsons, for fuck's sake,' he'd say, flailing his heavily ringed black-nail-polished fingers in the air. In his rarer, less pissed-off, entitled moments, he'd spontaneously break into a bold Ethel Merman-like style of singing, with an ironic chorus of 'There's No Business Like Show Business'.

I hadn't been at Wilde for more than eight weeks, and I'm not exactly sure what happened, but they fired Felipe, the Parsons-schooled stylist. In a diva-like tantrum about something or another, he'd told one of the executive producers, Cecilia Obermeyer, to go fuck herself. So I, Christina Ford, following the brilliant advice of my mother, Elena, was now Wilde + Partners Productions' new in-house wardrobe stylist. *This is more like it*, I thought. I was shopping for a living. Some weeks, as payday rolled around I'd find myself actually owing the company money, for spending one's time in stores all day can be dangerous for a fashion-loving consumer like myself. But I didn't care. I was in. I was working, I wasn't loading trucks, and I was almost making money. I was happy, and God knows I was well dressed.

Now, if there were a moral and ethical centre of the universe in which all minorities were respected and treated equally, advertising would be the furthest planet from that centre. Furthermore, the production business would be merely a dark moon orbiting around that outpost planet, perhaps where they sent their criminals. Although Wilde was owned by a fabulously flamboyant gay man, who had more in common with Cher than De Niro, make no mistake: Wilde was rich with testosterone-loaded alpha men. Toxic machismo I called it. Being one of the few women at Wilde who didn't wear sensible workplace footwear or answer the phones, I came up hard against the frontline of sexist, macho men of advertising. My day was often filled with an endless litany of offensive pick-up lines, ass-grabs, close-talking confessions of lust, and language that would make a sailor blush.

The most overt of these offensive offenders of men behaving badly was the crew. This was a conclave of middle-aged, over-weight, cigarette-smoking, burping, farting man meat. It wasn't unusual to hear catcalls from the gaggle of grips and gaffers with oh-so-clever quips like: 'Hey, darling, if those pretty little legs of yours get tired, you can always come over here and sit on my face.'

As a young woman with no brothers and a metrosexual father, I was unaccustomed to what I can only describe as disgusting male behaviour. I'd never been surrounded by that before. This must've been what my father had meant about 'bastards'. They were like bullies on a playground who picked on the weak and vulnerable. And I was not weak, my father saw to that. I apologise now to the camera department as those guys were more evolved, more sophisticated and were further up the evolutionary man-chain. I also want to state that, of course, not every man I came across, be it crew, the management or otherwise, performed these Neanderthal mating calls (#notallmen). But here's the thing, it was rare that a male bystander would shut down the offensive banter in those early formative days, even if they weren't partak-ing. Some days, I'd just brush it off, vent to a few friends after work over a couple of beers, and that would usually be the end of the conversation. But on occasion I pushed back, all five-foot-seven of me. I knew I had to learn to handle these bullies if I had any chance of survival in this new playground. I earned a weird respect for not letting them visibly upset me, and eventually they learnt not to mess with the wardrobe stylist.

The only woman in management at Wilde was just as crass and offensive as the crew, executive producer Cecilia Obermeyer, the one responsible for firing Felipe. Cecilia was in her mid-fifties, as well as I could guess. Who knows, perhaps she was younger, and the unrelenting hours and often-gruelling business of making television commercials had prematurely aged her. I have to say, her outdated bright coral Revlon lipstick did her no favours. Looking at it objectively, I could make an argument that back then it was necessary for her to be more masculinely aggressive. After all, it was a boys' club, and to succeed you needed to play by their frat-house rules, talk the talk, tell a deeply offensive joke or two, develop a taste for Cohibas and Macallan. But Cecilia had crossed over. She had become an honorary, card-carrying knuckle-dragger in style and mannerism. Only she was doing it in chunky heels and a particularly large kaftan. She possessed the swagger, style and class of a longshore sailor on leave as she strode onto set, swearing at the crew. 'Shoot it now, light it later, you lazy pricks,' she'd frequently bark, to announce she had officially entered the studio.

For the most part, I loved working at Wilde, cutting my baby teeth inside a creative den of ambitious young production types. I sometimes worked fourteen hours a day, six or seven days a week. It was the finest example of the 'work hard, play hard' ethic I had ever seen – elastic young twenty-somethings working with blinding focus and then crawling in totally hungover after partying all night. God bless the recovery time of your twenties. I was learning at the rate of an expanding infant brain, drinking in everything new around me. I overcame the pressures of tight deadlines and tighter budgets, getting an education on how to handle the explosive, volatile tempers that often went hand-in-hand with the stress of delivering on million-dollar budgets. I discovered a vast variety of exciting jobs I'd never known existed before walking in that first day. I knew I was on the bottom rung (or half a rung higher now, perhaps), but I was charged. It was the most exciting place I had ever seen. I was in the stream, and the stream was exhilarating and swift. I had not settled on a final career, but I thought, *Don't fight the current, Christina. Let's just see what ocean this stream empties into.*

CHAPTER 4

Hurricane Charlie

'What happens on the road stays on the road.'
Cheating men everywhere

I don't know what naive part of me thought that my friendship with Marianne, Charlie's wife, would shelter me from the executive producer known to the entire office as Hurricane Charlie. I believe he was negotiating a little quid pro quo. Yes, I think, that's how I'd describe that night in the elevator, the night everything changed. During my time at Wilde, I'd learnt that if you had a problem, you either kept it to yourself or told your therapist. Cecilia dealt with grievances like Louis Gossett Jr would handle Richard Gere in *An Officer and a Gentleman*. A humiliating berating, the sole purpose of which was to destroy your will to live.

'Suck it up, cupcake,' or 'Grow a pair,' you'd hear her tell some poor sod as they left her office in tears.

This was a time before most of the world used terms like 'sexual harassment', 'sensitivity training' or 'political correctness'. There were no HR-generated interoffice dating protocols or codes of conduct. I had been working at Wilde for about eighteen months and had been promoted from wardrobe stylist, a position I had outgrown, to producer. The role of producer was exhilarating, terrifying and heavy with stress. But it came with a euphoric rush, a thrill that a skydiver must feel both from free-falling through the sky and then being yanked upwards as their parachute successfully unfurls. Producing itself was much like being one of those jugglers at the circus spinning plates. Someone keeps throwing items their way, and they just incorporate it into the routine, making sure nothing hits the ground.

The first time I heard the life-changing doctrine 'What happens on the road stays on the road', I was on my first big location shoot. Charlie flew in to stick-handle the job. His role, as far as I could see, was to make sure the clients were well looked after and entertained. Charlie was a slight man, willowy, with long, thin arms and legs that seemed to flutter like branches in the wind. He had a finely groomed beard, which he seemed exceedingly proud of, as noted by the frequent stroking of his chin, like it was a cherished cat. When he got angry or nervous, his voice would stutter, like a repeating skip on a worn old record.

Charlie's temper and unorthodox reactions to the daily office problems fully warranted his gale-force nickname. He was rumoured to have once climbed under the boardroom table, mid-meeting, and forcibly removed the shoes of a cocky young director he disagreed with. Cranking open the second-storey office window, he supposedly threw the shoes out of the window, one at a time, then excused himself from the boardroom, saying in a light tone, 'I'll be right back.' A minute later, the long blast of a car horn was heard from outside the office. Charlie was in his Jaguar, running back and forth over the shoes. He parked his car, picked up the flattened shoes, and returned to the meeting, placing the damaged shoes on the boardroom table directly in front of the director, and calmly said, 'I'm sorry, what were you saying again?' I managed to get along with Charlie despite his notorious reputation, and up until this particular job, all was well.

It was our last day of shooting and, as was customary, there was a wrap dinner. I'd arrived late as I'd been tidying up some of the job's final loose ends. I walked into the crowded Japanese restaurant where our team, approximately twenty of us, sat around two large tables. Charlie motioned that he had saved a place for me beside him at the table, indicating the empty chair. Dinner, from what I can remember, was pleasant. Charlie made attempts to include me in conversation with the clients. He was boisterous, loud and often amusing, with his big hardy laugh, and I remember thinking that I could see how he was good at his job. He had a charismatic charm, and the clients seemed to like his jokes and his ability to tell a story.

After dinner, back in the hotel lobby, Charlie motioned to me to hang on, like he had something further he needed to discuss. I waited as he said his goodnights to the clients and received praise for a job well done. Charlie smiled at me and said, 'Come on, let's go,' and with that, I followed him into the empty elevator.

Some basic animal instinct lets us know we are in danger. That prickly feeling your skin gets, the rapid acceleration of your now-audible heartbeat. I felt all of that the moment the elevator door closed on me.

'Christina,' Charlie grinned, standing so close I could smell his sour breath – an unpleasant blend of soy sauce, sake and cigars. 'I can catapult you to the top of this business. I've done it for others,' he boasted.

I glanced at the elevator buttons; only one floor was pushed, mine. There was a look in his eyes that scared me, icy yet somehow fiery. I started digging my nails hard into the fleshy palms of my tightly clenched fists, as if the discomfort I was causing myself would distract me, protect me.

'I have some girls in the office,' he continued. 'I call them Charlie's Girls.' Then he went on to list the names of about three or four women in the office whom he 'took special care of', for whom his door was always open, day or night. *Charlie's Girls*... I thought. *There are others*.

Starting at my shoulder, Charlie slowly traced his long, twig-like forefinger down to my wrist, drawing a line down the inside of my arm. He was grinning widely with the implied invitation, his well-groomed beard inches away from my face. I dug my nails deeper into my palms.

'Christina, you're aware that what happens on the road stays on the road?' Charlie moved even closer, trapping me in the corner of the elevator, becoming a sort of man-flesh barricade. He grinned. 'Why don't you and I get to know each other a bit better, shall we?'

In situations like that – and by 'that', I mean men in positions of power coming on to me – my default is to play dumb and cheerful, and hope, really hope, they give up and go away. So I did what I do: I played dumb – cartoon super-blonde, dumb as a box of hair. I babbled nervously in one long, rambling, run-on sentence about anything other than what Charlie was saying, like there was a chance I hadn't heard it, understood it, or picked up on exactly what he was overtly communicating to me. If I hadn't heard it, perhaps it would just disappear. *Oh God, please make this disappear.*

The elevator stopped at my floor. Charlie's eyes pierced through me like daggers, his sickly breath coating my skin, his slimy grin now eradicated from his ruddy face. With frightening force, he barked, 'What are you, fucking stupid? I'm asking you back to my room.' There was no room for misinterpretation, no retreating to my default defence of dumb. Trying very hard not to damage the salacious ego of my boss, and as gently as I could muster, I said, 'I'm flattered, Charlie. But I'm engaged to Brandon, not to mention friends with your wife.'

That's all I remember coming out of my constricted throat, past my lips and into the atmosphere that reeked of foul-smelling Charlie. He jerked his body away from me, releasing me from the corner. Unable to breathe, my trembling body rattled, jarred and jolted, as I quickly escaped through the open door; he angrily and rapidly pushed the button as the elevator closed behind me. I let out an intense, audible sigh. I slowly opened my hands, looking down to see the deep red crescent shapes my nails had carved into the flesh of my palms. I rubbed them gingerly, observing the unintentional pain I'd just caused myself to distract from my emotional pain as I returned to my room. I shut the door, my legs rubbery, barely holding me, and dissolved into tears. I thought of calling Brandon, but somewhere in the back of my mind, I knew this would just give him added ammunition to get me out of a business he'd never liked in the first place. He'd want me to quit, to walk out the door immediately and never look back. But I wasn't ready to do that, not yet.

The wrath and punishment that was to ensue painfully taught me that one can never underestimate the fragile male ego's depth. Charlie stopped speaking to me entirely, shunning me like a petulant child. He even refused to reply to the casual 'good morning' I'd throw his way most mornings. Immediately, he reversed any progress I had made as a producer. It all stopped dead. I was back to my life as a wardrobe stylist. I did wonder what excuse Charlie gave Cecilia to demote me. My guess was none. She would have been told, and she would not have asked why. She knew we were all disposable, even her. I did the best I could under the circumstances. I tried hard to project an even perkier disposition than usually required to sort boxes of discount department-store clothes. I lived in fear that at any moment I'd be summoned into Cecilia's office, as Charlie would not have had the nerve himself, and for reasons she may or may not understand, she would fire me.

I curiously and cautiously observed the other women in our office. Those women Charlie had declared were 'his'. I'd watch as they went about their day, their jobs, in what looked like a carefree, unencumbered manner. No one looked damaged, compromised or scared. One of 'Charlie's Girls' was a beautiful, statuesque young production assistant named Sophie, who had just been promoted to casting director. *Is this how it works?* I thought. Had she indeed slept with Charlie for the professional privilege of wrangling talent, a little quid pro quo?

The next few months were unbearable. I tried hard not to let it show at work. However, at home, I'd walk through the door and instantly Brandon could see it etched into my face. With nothing more that a raised eyebrow, all the hurt, pain, humiliation, anger and frustration I had to camouflage in the office would uncontrollably spill out of me. Brandon and I would argue, as he couldn't comprehend why I hadn't just walked out the door and said, 'Fuck you, Charlie.' I figured if I just worked hard, kept my nose down, rode this out, that eventually things would go back to how they were. My career would be back on track, and all would be well again. That never happened.

After about six months of steely silence, a permanent and unwarranted demotion, and the most uncomfortable of work environments, with absolutely no hope at all of things changing, I quit. I had no job to go to, and for fear the folks at Wilde would sabotage any future employment prospects, I didn't ask for a letter of recommendation.

That night in the elevator pushed me onto a new path. It spun me around and knocked me clear into a different lane. It led me to find my next job, working for a woman, and that job led me to start my own company. One could maybe argue that had it not been for Charlie and his unforgivable, disgusting behaviour, effectively forcing me to work elsewhere, perhaps I wouldn't have gone on to the career and success I had. But I will give him no such credit. Charlie was merely the horrible car accident blocking the road, stopping the traffic. And I, well, I found a way through and I went around the damage. When I got over being scared, I got angry. I'm still angry that men like Charlie can lord their power over women in the most salacious, disgusting way imaginable. I never worked for a man again.

I saw Charlie multiple times throughout my career, often crossing paths at award shows or industry functions. I worked hard to avoid him, except for once. About a year after I became an executive producer at the new company, I saw Charlie at a cocktail party held by the elegant, successful ad-man, Morton Laufer. Standing in the grand living room, looking out of the two-storey glass windows, I saw Charlie walk in. Even with my back to him, he was unmistakable in the window's reflection as he floated towards me like a ghost. Seeing me, he stopped dead a few feet away from where I stood. I watched his reflection immediately turn and walk in the opposite direction. I could smell his fear. He was fleeing. Quickly, I followed Charlie as he made his way into the next room. With the stealth-like movement of a cat-burglar, a moment later, I was in front of him, grinning.

'Hello, Charlie,' I smiled confidently. He looked at me and nervously started scanning the room. His eyes were rapidly moving from side to side, like an animated cartoon villain looking to make a run for it. I don't recall him saying 'hello' back. All I heard was Charlie stuttering, 'How do you ... you ... you know Morton?' Inserting subtext here, I believe what he was asking was, 'Who the fuck let you in?'

I wanted to say something clever yet surgically cutting. You know, go all *Pretty Woman* on his ass. 'Big mistake ... BIG ... HUGE!' I would rave about my great new job as executive producer – a job title we now shared. I needed him to see for himself that had neither broken me nor made me. I was successful despite declining his generous offer of his penis penetrating me. Then, something unexpectedly wonderful happened. A deliciously scented midnight-blue crushed-velvet arm came around my shoulder and hugged me warmly to say hello. It was our host, Morton. His timing was impeccable.

'Christina, so glad you made it, welcome,' Morton said. I looked around at the opulent room and joked, 'So this is the house Home Hardware bought you, Morton? Nice.' Morton humbly laughed, agreeing he had been fortunate. Charlie stood awkwardly and uncomfortably, with no boisterous laughter or animated stories. His silence was brilliant, rewarding, freeing. Morton and I chatted for a moment or two, and after suggesting I refill my champagne, he kissed me on both cheeks and then moved on to greet the next guest. I turned back to look at Charlie, feeling strong, confident, like at the end of a movie when justice has been richly and rightly restored. In the unholiest of churches, I'd been ordained by the almighty Morton Laufer, Church of the Latter-Day Sinners of Advertising. Grinning at the man who had inflicted so much pain, and recognising a perfect show-stopping ending, with the swagger of a total badass, I exited the scene.

I find it so interesting to look back at moments that require no nostalgic prodding or photographs to flush them out. Memories that effortlessly float to the surface of your mind like vivid scenes from a movie you've watched a thousand times. Decades later, that tiny sliver of my life, that fraction of a moment with Morton that couldn't have lasted longer than three minutes, still stands out today as one of the sweetest career and moral victories of my life.

CHAPTER 5

Miss Moonshine's Warning

'It is only with the heart that one can see rightly;
what is essential is invisible to the eye.'
Antoine de Saint-Exupéry, *The Little Prince*

B randon thought it would be nice to take my parents out for Sunday brunch to announce our engagement. The Old Mill was one of those quaint faux-Tudor restaurants, with a massive stone fireplace burning birch logs and oiled timbers set into white plaster walls. It was bustling with multi-generational families, dressed smartly, looking like they were there to celebrate something important like a milestone anniversary or a grandparent's birthday.

Now, had I even had an inkling that this would be one of those horrific, life-scarring moments that would be seared into my memory forever, I would've foregone the crowded restaurant, slipped my parents a note under their bedroom door and beelined back to Brandon's. We waited until coffee and dessert before settling into the real purpose of our meal, me keeping my left hand on Brandon's knee to conceal my engagement ring.

'Mamma, Pappa,' I started, 'Brandon and I have some very exciting news. Brandon asked me to marry him.' With that, I brought my ringed hand into view.

My dad quickly looked at me, deadpan, and said, 'So … what did you say?'

'Father,' I said, still smiling, 'you can see the ring. You know what I said.'

Elena, lovely and jubilant, jumped up and gave Brandon and me genuine hugs of love and congratulations. That, however, was not my father's reaction.

'Christina, I'll give you the money it would cost to pay for the wedding. Use it for a down payment on a house. Fly to Vegas, or get married at City Hall.'

Although my father's advice was practical in nature, he wasn't trying to secure me a jump-start on the housing market. That wasn't his motivation. As I excitedly discussed the traditional wedding we wanted – a big puffy dress and the pride of him walking me down the aisle – my father, as if I was fifteen and trying to renegotiate my already extended curfew, pushed himself up from the table and said, 'No. Out of the question.'

I don't have to look back far to gather evidence of this man's unreasonable behaviour. After all, I was the legal adult he kicked out of the house for piercing my ears. But this, this I couldn't wrap my head around. What kind of father wants his daughter to elope? Elena took my hand to look at the ring, and I felt its weight grow heavier as my body started to sink into total and complete sadness. My throat tightened, with that first swell of emotion telling me my tears weren't far behind. Alan stated again, in his bold, authoritarian father voice, 'If you want to have a wedding I can't stop you, but I will have nothing to do with it. Nothing!' With that, he said, 'Elena, get your coat.'

This conversation marked the beginning of a period where my relationship with my father was the worst it ever was. He was a man I had always loved, respected and tried harder than most to understand. Now the only emotion I had for him was pure, unapologetic loathing. The months went on as plans started taking shape for an August wedding. I decided that the best way to navigate this potential minefield of my life was to avoid being alone with my father. As a result, I avoided some family gatherings altogether. The idea of my father coming around was losing more and more of its appeal. As each day rolled by, I cared less and less. I was hurt, I was angry, but most of all, I was totally confused. I can't even imagine what my mother and father's dialogue on this issue must've been like behind closed doors, but I'm confident there were some severe matrimonial blasts between my parents.

I reminded myself that this was not just my drama unfolding anymore. It was Elena's too, and my unmarried sisters'. My dad was standing completely alone. Not a single soul could understand or empathise with his position. So I don't know what would've happened if I hadn't felt the complete need to stand up and push against my father, not only for me but for my sisters as well, for there was an unmistakable voice inside my head that I was actively ignoring: the one telling me I shouldn't marry Brandon.

Six weeks before the wedding, and with no evidence to suggest my father's position weakening, I asked my Uncle Geoffrey, my dad's older brother, to fly in from England to give me away. Geoffrey was pleased to be giving me away, but he too was utterly baffled by his brother's inability or lack of desire to perform such a wonderful fatherly tradition.

Though not as monumental as my issues, Brandon's mom Ruby also added her own unique brand of personal chaos to this special occasion. Ruby had not been in the same room as Brandon's dad, Joe, since their divorce hearing years before, where they'd painfully extracted their pounds of flesh. I can't remember how many years that had been, but in my mind, it was long enough that Ruby should have got over it. Of course, that was from the ignorant position of a quarter-lifer who had never been brutally betrayed. With all the focus of a politician seeking re-election, Ruby was actively campaigning to get Roberta, Joe's new wife and former secretary, banned from the wedding and any adjacent activities. Ruby was unsuccessful. However, it did support my father's idea that eloping had unforeseen benefits.

Now, had this been the only 'Ruby issue', it would hardly be worth mentioning. It would be just another typical anecdote of planning a wedding with divorced parents. However, Ruby's upset led her to seek spiritual guidance from her psychic, someone who called herself Miss Moonshine. As it turned out, Miss Moonshine had very little to say about Joe and Roberta. She did, however, have plenty to say about me.

Communicating to her through soggy tea leaves, Miss Moonshine's spirit elders warned Ruby that I'd unduly shatter her son's heart into so many fragmented pieces it would take years for the sensitive Pisces to recover. So, like Moses did with his Ten Commandments, Ruby brought forth Miss Moonshine's spiritual prophecy to her son, suggesting he stop the wedding, or at the very least put it off for a year or two.

As you can imagine, Brandon was upset and annoyed with his mother and, of course, with Miss Moonshine. He immediately dismissed it, ordering his mother to forget what her quacky psychic had said and fully get behind supporting our wedding. From then on, every time I hugged Ruby, her arms would fall by the sides of her bird-like frame, and she'd welcome me like a lipstick-wearing old bag of twigs might. This would be the closest I'd ever get to her.

Although Brandon dismissed the psychic reading as nothing more than cosmic bullshit, there was something about Miss Moonshine's warning I couldn't shake. It felt like I had covered up the perfect airtight crime, and she was that first thread pulled. That unforeseen surprise piece of evidence that materialised out of nowhere from which the whole thing would start to unravel. Not a single soul knew the emotional conflict I was battling marrying Brandon, mostly because I was trying to deny it with all that was holy; it could not exist if I didn't speak of it. Surely these were just wedding jitters, I'd tell the negative committee meeting inside my head, with the added instruction to calm the fuck down. He was everything any girl could want, and maybe, just maybe, when we were married and had kids, I would fall madly in love with him, just like any sane, normal girl would do.

It was here: the big day. The day every little girl dreams of, right? My sisters and I were up early with the buzzy, frenetic energy usually reserved for wedding days and beehives.

'You nervous?' Victoria, my sister, asked.

'Strangely, no,' I answered honestly. I was remarkably chill and happy, considering. With my hair in giant hot rollers, my mom entered the room that was filled with joyful girl chatter.

'Christina, when you have a moment, your father would like to see you.'

That silenced the room immediately. Up until that point, my father had been out of sight. Like some endangered species, there had been no spotting him. I looked at my mom and raised a desperate eyebrow, 'Please, please, please don't make me go,' I begged.

My mother continued. 'He's in his room. He's asking to see you.'

Victoria jumped in: 'Why can't he come here?' Elena looked at Vic but didn't bother to answer her.

'Can you please go and see him … for me?'

Damn. I hated when she added, 'for me'. My mother had done so much for me, especially around this wedding. It was impossible not to do what she asked, especially when she added those two words. So, reluctantly (and I do mean reluctantly), I stood up, hot rollers in my hair, took a couple of deep inhales, and walked up to my parents' bedroom, where my father was waiting.

As I stood in the doorway, my heart was thumping hard, reverberating through my body. *Don't let him upset you*, I told myself on repeat.

There were several complete sets of clothing neatly laid out on his bed. Three suits, three shirts and multiple ties lying on top of the shirts, wrapped in a way that a high-end men's store might display them for a customer.

'Hey, Alan,' I said, as casually as I could, deliberately calling him by his first name in a kind of offspring retaliation. 'Mamma said you were looking for me. I don't have much time – what's up?' I could see that my father was nervous, more so than I had ever seen him before. He wasn't making eye contact but instead busily moving around the pieces of his wardrobe on the bed like he was studying a chessboard.

'What should I wear?' he asked, pointing to the fashion combos he had carefully laid out. Before I could answer, he asked, 'It isn't black-tie, is it? I have a tux if it's black-tie, is it black-tie?'

'No, Alan, it's not black-tie.'

I think it's important to note here that this dialogue was the first and only conversation I can recall having with my father since our Sunday brunch when Brandon and I had announced our engagement.

Alan continued, 'I was thinking the navy YSL with the Turnbull & Asser white shirt. Or there's the grey Gucci suit, or is that a little too sombre?' he asked. 'I could brighten it up with this Hermès tie. Or if you want something more understated, the navy striped tie with the fine lines of yellow could work.'

Here he was, Alan Dixon, my father, discussing his wardrobe choices with me roughly 45 minutes before I/we were leaving for the church.

'Alan,' I said, still hovering in the doorway, 'whatever you want to wear is fine with me.'

'No,' he said, sounding a little hurt. 'You choose Christina,' pointing down to his perfectly displayed clothes. Again I repeated, 'It doesn't matter to me what you're wearing. Just pick whatever you want.'

Again, it might be worth mentioning that never in this exchange about clothing did my father indicate or say outright that he was planning on coming to my wedding. He would think it was implied. He often used this term when he didn't want to change his position on something: 'It was implied.'

I looked at my dad, his fine clothes, and stepped into his bedroom and pointed. 'This and this ... with this,' I said.

I turned to walk out the door and he asked, 'Christina, how are we getting there? Do I need to order a car?'

'No, Pappa, it's all taken care of.'

I walked out of his room, noting that I had gone from calling him 'Alan' to 'Pappa' without conscious thought. I exhaled and smiled: it seemed my father was coming to my wedding after all.

Outside my parents' home sat two black stretch limos, and a silver Bentley with a giant satin bow stretched across its bonnet. The plan, or the plan we'd rehearsed, was that Uncle Geoffrey and my mom would ride with me in the Bentley, and the rest of the wedding party would be in the limos. My sisters were helping me as I came out of the house, holding my train to keep it off the ground as I approached the Bentley. The driver opened the car door, and my Lady Diana-inspired puffy dress and I backed into the spacious backseat. I guess I was more preoccupied with my dress because it wasn't until I was all in and the driver had shut the door that I even noticed that there, sitting beside me, was my father.

It's interesting the thoughts that go through a young girl's head on her wedding day. I think mine were more unusual than most. About an hour previously, my father had not even been coming to my wedding. Shortly, in the company of friends and family, I would be promising to love and cherish 'till death do us part', a lovely man I was not quite in love with. I optimistically thought I could make this work. It was the same kind of optimistic determination with which you might try to squeeze yourself into a fabulous one-size-too-small dress you find on the final sale rack at Harrods. *Although it doesn't fit now, it's too good a deal to pass up,* you think. *And maybe with a little work, I'll eventually make it fit.*

You've got this, Christina, I repeated in my head over and over again, like a professional sports coach psyching their team up before a big game. This, all of it, would be fine.

The car pulled up to Timothy Eaton Memorial Church, the same church my parents had married in exactly 26 years earlier. The last of the guests shuffled inside, and I noticed the gentle hushing of the quiet conversations as the small chapel picked up on our arrival. My sister Victoria straightened my train behind me. My bridesmaids, all dressed in unfortunate *Little House on the Prairie*-inspired dusty rose dresses with white lace collars, lined up in front of me, bouquets in position. Still standing by my side, my father had not said a word. Uncle Geoffrey kissed me on the cheek. 'I'm going to take my seat now,' he said, and disappeared into the church.

I looked at my mom beside me, radiant in her lavender silk dress, and my father in his navy YSL suit with the white Turnbull & Asser shirt. They were a beautiful, stylish couple.

The familiar opening notes of Wagner's 'Wedding March' boldly filled the chapel, officially announcing us.

'That's our cue,' I said.

My mother threaded her arm through mine. I smiled at the clear physical declaration that she, too, would be walking me down the aisle. In all of this, Elena had had a contingency plan. Whether it be with Geoffrey, my father, or on her own, she had attended enough Jewish weddings to know that the mother of the bride had every bit as much right to walk down the aisle as the father did.

I turned to my father. 'What about you, Pappa? Are you ready to do this?' My father did not reply. He was as white as the lilies that filled the church, and for an almost-translucent Northern Englishman, that was a new level of whiteness.

'Pappa, are you OK?' I asked with growing concern. 'Mother is here,' I said, 'and apparently she's not letting you do this without her.'

I honestly thought at that moment his eyes would roll back inside his head and, in a well-dressed heap, he'd crash to the ground, creating another fascinating talking point I could share with my future children about my wedding. My father leaned into me, and ever so faintly whispered, 'I'm afraid.' His voice croaked, 'What if I trip on your dress? I don't … don't … want to embarrass you.'

And there it was. Right there. In that one sentence, everything became clear: his fear of crowds, expectation, dis-appointment, of everything. All of it had left my father almost paralysed. Without my father ever once saying, 'I'm sorry,' every-thing was forgiven. My anger and frustrations were released like those white doves used to announce the newly wedded couple to the world.

Looking at him, I smiled. 'You've got this, Pappa.' I turned to my mom and then back to my father's terrified face. 'We've got this.'

The three of us walked towards Brandon, standing proudly in his rented black tuxedo, red bow tie and cummerbund, and sans moustache, at the bride's request. His face emitted a wonderful, dreamy look. You know, the one that says, 'I'm the luckiest man on the planet,' as the best man proudly places his hand on the groom's shoulder as if to say, 'Way to go, buddy.' I was rocking my big puffy dress and my hair was similarly big and puffy, all of it screaming the Bananarama eighties. Brandon took my hand and whispered, 'I love you so much.' I offered him a bright smile in return, and then turned my attention to the minister, who immediately began, with 'Dear friends and family ...'

Looking straight ahead, I drank in every meticulous detail of that moment: the chapel filled with fragrant white flowers, the minister's strong yet friendly voice, the warm feeling of my hand tight in Brandon's. *This is my wedding day. I'm standing in front of everyone in my life who is special to me, and some who aren't.* But as my senses absorbed my surroundings, there was only one thought, screaming at me with the din of a speeding freight train barrelling through a small village, one that I could not silence. Smiling brightly, as Brandon stared deep into my very soul, as I said, 'I do,' to this wonderful, wonderful man, my heart cried out with unrelenting confusion and despair, *What the fuck am I doing?*

My marriage to Brandon lasted fifteen months and four days. I have pantyhose that survived longer. There was not one part of my soul, conscience or mortal being that didn't know I should not have been marrying Brandon. Yet there I was. Brandon was there for all the right reasons, and me, well, I was nothing more than a smiling, big-haired, ecru-silk-taffeta-wearing imposter. So, I went about the painful task of disentangling myself from this man who loved me, an exercise I called 'How to leave a good husband'. I worked late, I retreated, I detached myself physically and emotionally. I thought that maybe if he didn't love me it would be easier on him, so I went through the unkind undertaking of making myself entirely and utterly unlovable. Get him to leave me, not the other way around. He couldn't have won. I didn't want him to.

It is said that no experience is ever wasted if you learn something. Well, I certainly learnt something. Lessons that only naivety and the misplaced optimism of youth can tolerate. Easy lesson: never again would I marry someone I was not completely, fully and passionately in love with. It can't just look like love. You can't hope that it will magically emerge somewhere in among tax bills, mortgage payments and colicky children. If it doesn't fit, much like that Harrods sale dress that's still hanging unworn in your closet with the price tag on, leave it on the rack for some other girl, someone who's the right size, and let her take it home and cherish it.

Harder lesson: I was the problem, not Brandon. I was the one that needed fixing. I deliberately ignored the voices in my head, allowing them to drown out what my heart already knew. And when I alone couldn't silence those voices, I knowingly dragged Brandon, two families and all my friends along like the orchestra on the *Titanic*, all ordered to play with deafening volume while the ship filled up with water. From the tender age of 26, I'd have to be ticking the horrible 'divorced' box for the rest of my living days, declaring to the world my failed marriage on something as trivial as a Visa card application form.

Of all the relationships I've had in my life, never were there more white witch flashes than with Brandon, and I can't tell you why. Perhaps it was the unspoiled lens of youth that permitted me to see well beyond what I could explain. But even as recently as a few summers ago, and over 25 years later, I'd had an overwhelming feeling I was going to run into him, and sure enough, I did. We spoke for a few minutes. He was warm and friendly, with his lovely wife standing a few feet back, neither introducing herself nor leaving his side. But if youth granted me this ability, then age has given me the wisdom to not stand in its way. For what good is instinct if ignored?

I think it's a little like arguing with your GPS. Your heart is clearly telling you which road to take, what direction you should follow, and you, and that nattering noise between your ears, override the message, and *bam!* you miss the off-ramp. But if I was given just one invaluable lesson from this relationship, it is this: the answers are always, always there inside of me. I just have to shut my eyes, ignore the noise, and trust.

The Book of

Jackson

○┄┄•┄┄◍┄┄•┄┄◍┄┄•┄┄○

CHAPTER 1

Cruella

'When a man of forty falls in love with a girl of twenty,
it isn't her youth he is seeking but his own.'
Lenore Coffee

'**M**y work here is done,' Dr Keene said as he stood back from his chair, precisely 55 minutes after I'd sat down. 'Good luck.'

Wait, was that it? Really? After nearly two years of weekly therapy sessions searching for emotional salvation, of weepy run-on monologues, ones that most often left me drained and socially catatonic (you know, in a Bette Davis kind of way), that was it? Over? Was Dr Keene content, at peace, legally free to let me loose on the world again, to the unsuspecting, unprepared world of men?

He smiled at me in a congratulatory way, much as if I had successfully found my way out of an escape room. Honestly, I wasn't exactly sure what science my therapist had used to determine that I was now free to stroll among the living. Maybe he was just worn out with my excessive drivel. Nonetheless, with the added reassurance of a warm handshake, Dr Keene had graduated me to the land of the emotionally available, the unencumbered, eligibly single.

Since my split with Brandon, which was almost two years ago, my youngest sister, Jennifer, had moved into my apartment. I don't recall asking her to move in. She just showed up, and I found myself months later discussing new paint colour options for her bedroom. I adopted two adorable silver-haired tabby kittens, Madison and Max. To replace the affection of a broken marriage with the unconditional love of a pet, as one does. Jennifer quickly renamed Madison Yoda after the *Star Wars* Jedi Master, whom she unfortunately resembled. Renaming my pets was another sign Jen was in there for the long haul.

On those evenings when I wasn't on set placating a temperamental director, or honing my social talents with trite small talk at a client dinner, I was super content to stay at home. I'd eat a carefully balanced dinner of Orville Redenbacher microwave popcorn and Häagen-Dazs coffee ice cream straight from the tub, delightfully paired with a few chilled glasses of Jacob's Creek Chardonnay. I'd then curl up with Jen, Max and Yoda and blissfully watch *Cheers*. The four of us were all living our Zen-like, man-free existence on the second floor of a brownstone walk-up in the quaint upscale Toronto neighbourhood of Forest Hill Village, situated beside a lovely park I'd played in as a child.

I was working as head of sales at McWaters Film Company. Without the extraneous distractions of boys, I'd thrown myself hard into my new career, much to the delight of my new boss, Rosanne McWaters. I'd quickly made myself indispensable, and had been rewarded after only five months with a promotion to executive producer. I was sitting clearly and comfortably in the number-two seat behind my illustrious leader at the second-largest production company in the country. This was more than good. This was fucking awesome.

This is a period in my life when I can't recall one sassy single-girl story, disastrous date, one-night stand or even sloppy drunken snog worthy of sharing. If the back end of my twenties wasn't about dating men or pushing out babies and swapping casseroles recipes like it was for some of my friends, at least I was nailing my career. I don't remember feeling lonely, horny, or in want of a boyfriend. My career was my full-time narcissistic, demanding lover.

Rosanne, not yet 40, was a tall, attractive woman with fine, wispy white-blonde hair which she often piled on top of her head, creating a little water fountain effect, reminding me of a mature Pebbles Flintstone. The nickname she'd been given, however, was Cruella, after the evil Disney villain famous for her pursuit to use dead Dalmatian-puppy fur to make a coat. In the mornings, as she was spotted approaching the office, you'd hear the receptionist warn all by way of the office intercom, 'Cruella is on the bridge. I repeat: Cruella is on the bridge.' If there were foghorns or colourful spinning sirens, they too would've been regularly put to use.

It's easy to assume, based on her pet name alone, that not everyone liked Rosanne. She could be downright mean, scary, and God knows she didn't like most people, nor did she suffer fools. But I liked her, and weirdly she liked me too. I welcomed working for Rosanne, especially after working for that piece of human garbage, Charlie. She was a strong, successful woman, and I believed much of the noise or dislike surrounding her mainly had to do with the fact that she was a ballsy, smart, take-no-shit kinda woman, and I, for one, admired her for that.

Despite being a powerhouse and a super-successful production house owner, at a time when few women had that kind of success, Rosanne grew reclusive, seeming almost afraid to interact with people she wasn't familiar with. This I didn't understand. She kept herself sequestered in her office, out of sight of clients, and rarely did she do any of the entertaining that was usually required when you own a large production company. It was Rosanne's hiding herself away that quickly pushed me into the front lines, a role she unintentionally and slowly vacated.

As executive producer/head of sales, my job in part involved cold-calling producers, copywriters and art directors. I'd invite them for lunch, or to screenings of the company's recent genius television commercials. I was to get to know as many agency folk as possible and convince them to shoot their next television commercial at McWaters. It was a super social job, often leaving me flying off on shoots around the world, throwing lavish wrap dinners in high-end restaurants, and making frequent sales trips to LA, New York and Cannes.

The less talked about, or let's call it the 'implied', part of my job was where the real work began though. I was there to clean up the messes or dispel the cloud of rumours that surrounded my illustrious team leader like a foul-smelling fog. I was to break down the doors of agencies that had bolted Cruella out, and Leo Burnett was one of those agencies. For reasons I was not aware of (but I'm sure Rosanne could have told me if she'd been honest with me), Burnett had blackballed her. During a weekly sales meeting, Rosanne said, very matter-of-factly, 'Christina, dear, I need you to get us back into Burnett. The creative director, Jackson Tilney, is so unreasonable. Take him for lunch. He won't return my calls.'

'What's the issue?' I naively asked, like I was expecting an honest answer.

'Christina, he's just one of those guys, and trust me, you will run into them yourself soon enough.'

Rosanne's vague answer led me to understand I'd have to surrender to the idea of going in blind, with no heads-up on where the landmines were buried. Rosanne was optimistic as she dismissed me, letting me know, 'Darling, that's why I have you. So you can go in and straighten everything out.' I left her office tasked with the uncertain piece of business of convincing Jackson Tilney, hater of Cruella, to have lunch with me.

I left several messages with Jackson's secretary that all went unanswered. Then I remembered a trick I'd been told about how to get someone who's avoiding you on the phone: call them at lunch. Of course, this was a time before voicemail or caller ID, when pink message chits, once read, were harpooned on a silver spike sitting prominently on one's desk. High-powered type-A personalities often worked through lunch, while their secretaries were off on their break, leaving them with the task of answering their own phones. In doing so, they were taking a calculated risk that people like me, whose calls they'd been actively dodging, thanks to their secretaries, might call. So I tried again, this time at lunch.

'Hello? Jackson Tilney,' said a smooth voice on the other end of the phone. *Holy shit,* I thought. I had only half prepared for getting him on the line. I dived in quickly.

'Hello, Jackson Tilney, it's Christina Ford from McWaters Film Company. I've been unsuccessfully trying to get you on the phone, so I guess today is my lucky day.' Continuing quickly, so as not to give Jackson a reason to hang up on me, I said: 'Jackson, I've heard some great things about you, and I'd very much like to take you for lunch.'

Working in sales in the advertising industry taught me early in the game that few have ever failed when pandering to the creative ego. But Jackson stopped me there.

'Christina, is it? Can I call you Christina? We don't work with McWaters, and I don't do lunch.'

I thought for a second and retaliated.

'Jackson, is it? Can I call you Jackson?' I said in a light-hearted way. 'I'm not looking to change your opinion of McWaters overnight, but I would like to learn more about what the prob—'

Jackson interrupted. 'You work for a tough lady, Christina. You know that, right?'

'I know I do, Jackson. So I need you to carefully think about what she might do to me if she hears that I could not convince the famous Jackson Tilney to have lunch. The consequences might be a heavy burden for you to bear. Blood … there might be blood.'

That got a slight laugh.

'Listen,' I continued, 'lunch, just one lunch, then I'll never darken your unguarded phone again.'

'You're persistent, aren't you, Christina?'

'Indeed I am, Jackson. Just tell me when and where.'

There was a long pause, during which I thought I could hear his mind shifting gears.

'OK, Friday, Fenton's, 1pm.'

With that I hung up the phone, walked straight into Rosanne's office, and said, 'Tilney, Friday at Fenton's.'

She looked up from signing cheques and smiled. 'Good girl.'

As always, I was early for our lunch on Friday, having adopted the personal credo that if I wasn't five minutes early I was five minutes late. Rosanne's instructions to me had been simple. Keep him out as long as I could, order whatever he wanted to drink, and most importantly, make him trust me. I loved that this was my honest-to-God work directive: eat, drink and repeat. A few minutes later, and right on time, in walked a tall, stylish, attractive man. He was wearing pressed jeans, a pale blue linen shirt, a suede bomber jacket, ostrich cowboy boots and carried an Hermès man-purse. His dark hair that sat just above his shoulders screamed that he didn't work at a bank or sell insurance. I immediately thought, *Gay: thank Christ. Gay is good. Gay men love me, I love them, I can so work with gay*. But I was surprised to learn that Jackson wasn't gay. This was the uniform of the well-paid creative man.

He was clacking down hard on a wad of gum when he reached out his hand and smiled. 'Christina, thank you for coming.' He sat down and immediately ordered a double vodka on the rocks. Knowing that one cannot let a client drink alone, I ordered a white wine spritzer, which he gently teased me about in comparison to his vodka. Until I got to McWaters, I didn't realise lunches like these existed, let alone that they could be someone's actual career. I mean, an accurate measure of my job was going drink for drink with my clients.

Jackson was easy to talk to, a charismatic storyteller with plenty of stories to share. I can't remember all we chatted about, but I remember the impression the lunch left on me. He was engaging, witty and far more attractive than I'd been prepared for. His age surprised me – not that he told me during the lunch, but I looked into him afterwards. He was 44, which to a 27-year-old girl was ancient. He had no grey hair, and no lines on his face to give away any signs that he was older than in his mid-thirties. Clearly, there was a portrait ageing in his attic, I thought. I was honestly surprised just how well we got along and how much we seemed to have in common, despite the seventeen-year age difference. As I enjoyed profiteroles, he ordered green Chartreuse for both of us. It tasted vile, like thick, syrupy mouthwash, and I politely sipped the green liqueur as our lunch stretched to almost three hours. *Rosanne will be thrilled,* I thought: *a three-hour lunch with Jackson Tilney and me coming back to work half in the bag.* In my head, I could see my enthusiastic little happy dance, as I said under my breath, 'I'm a fricking advertising dam-breaker.'

Now, if you'd told me that afternoon at Fenton's what was coming next, what was around the corner, I'd tell you to your crack-smoking face that you were high, insane, not fit to operate heavy machinery. But as crazy as it seems, as mad as it was, seven weeks after that lunch, 49 sunrises and 49 sunsets later, I was moving out of my brownstone walk-up, surrendering Max and Yoda to Jennifer's temporary custody, and moving in with Jackson, bringing new meaning to the term 'nailing the client'.

CHAPTER 2

There's Nothing So Dangerous as a Man with Charm

'If I loved you less, I might be able to talk about it more.'
Jane Austen, *Emma*

To say it was a whirlwind romance would likely stand out as the world's most mammoth understatement. I've taken more time deciding between the chicken or the veal than I did moving in with Jackson. My relationship with him certainly put an end to the drought of McWaters working with Burnett, although I don't think Rosanne had quite had this in mind when she'd insisted I met him. Then again, knowing Rosanne, I couldn't entirely rule it out.

Jackson was so different from anyone I had ever dated. He was worlds away from Brandon, with his wicking clothing and his ESPN lifestyle, and in my head I thought he a much more logical match. Aside from the chewing gum, Jackson reminded me of my father. In fact, Jackson was closer to my father's age than he was to mine. My parents didn't seem remotely bothered by the generational age difference. They loved Jackson, he was genuinely likeable, and they had a lot in common. It was as if they had made a new friend who could share their own time-stamped throw-back stories, like where they'd all been when Kennedy was shot, or nostalgically recalling the first time they'd seen a colour TV. Jackson, in short, was the first man I had ever been with. Until then, they had all been various degrees of 'boy'.

Jackson's pristine Yorkville apartment was so meticulous and glorious that it too supported Jackson's metrosexual image. The trendy neighbourhood with its upmarket cafes and expensive boutiques made it a finely feathered nest for super-successful singles, power couples, champagne socialists and early retirees with money to burn.

When one moves in with someone at the heightened pace of a six-part mini-series, you have to surrender yourself to the notion that there will be more about that person that you don't know than what you do know. OK, I get that, I do. But I think some fundamentals should take priority and rise higher on that list of 'personal sharing'. For instance, where in priority do you think these life-story moments should fall in terms of 'need to know'?

A) The emotional trauma you went through at four when your parents brought your new brother home from the hospital.
B) The make and model of every car you've owned, starting from sixteen.
C) The names of all your childhood cats.
D) The fact that you have a child the same age as the other partner in the relationship.

Take a moment. Think about it.

Yes, there was indeed a lot about each other that was slowly, oh so slowly, unfolding. In fairness to Jackson, I'd never asked if he had children. I'd just assumed that he didn't, as there was absolutely no evidence in his pristine Yorkville world that one existed. His daughter, Mary, my age minus a few months, was a souvenir from high school, an unplanned pregnancy when Jackson was seventeen. After Jackson and Mary's mother had split and other men had entered the picture, they'd taken on the role of dad, thus effectively removing Jackson from the daily life of his daughter. I don't know if this was a traumatic time in Jackson's young life, letting another man raise his daughter, or if it was completely freeing. As I said, there was a lot we didn't know about each other. I further learnt (and this nugget required sedation by way of a 90-minute massage and a bottle of Chateau St Jean) that Mary had three children, making the man I was living with a grandpa.

Everything was great for the first six months. Well, mostly great. The sex was erotic, passionate and, at times, frightening. It was much more complex and layered than I ever knew sex could be. The boys I had been with, and there hadn't been many, had all had the same limited sexual experience I'd had, like we were two equally matched novice tennis players, never improving their game but confident by their own limited standards that they're ready for Wimbledon. This sexually seasoned man added new chapters, books and volumes to my small library of sexual experiences, and would come to demonstrate an intensity and appetite for sex I had never encountered, nor had expected to.

Sexuality is so interesting, so complex, so personal, and with Jackson, there was a dark underbelly to it. Of course, you generally don't see it at first, or at least I didn't. The kink, the bent, the unusual fetishes, they are awakened with time and trust. They are foreshadowed with whispered innuendo and ultimately explode from a complete and total inability or desire to contain them. Up until Jackson, I had only ever tasted vanilla. I didn't know much about the other flavours: dark chocolate, wild cherry, fudge ripple, red velvet. It was presupposed that I would replace any vanilla tendencies and embrace the variety of what was being fed to me. Not all flavours were welcome or appreciated, but it was assumed that all must be tasted.

The first time I experienced Jackson in the way he really was, not who he thought I wanted, it was months into our relationship. Getting ready for bed, he asked me to go into his closet and return with all the contents I found in the bottom of one of his drawers. In the drawer, I found black satin ropes, padded handcuffs, a black blindfold and a large bottle of lubricant. I obediently picked up the items, knowing some but not all of the ways they could be used. Jackson drew me towards him, undressed me and lowered the blindfold over my eyes. Cuffing my hands above my head, he led me to the ladder which reached to the loft above his bedroom. A feeling of unfamiliar excitement and aberrant fear ran through me. With my arms high above my head, he attached my wrists to the ladder. I was quiet. I had no idea what to say.

He left and returned shortly. I could hear the familiar sounds of the shutter and the slow gears as his Polaroid camera rolled out photograph after photograph. Even with the blindfold covering my eyes, there would be a pop of light as the flash lit my naked body. I was now upset, as my acute vulnerability was being archived. Over my clear vocal objection, he took photos, ordering me to stay still and be silent. While I was still attached to the ladder, he left the bedroom, and I could hear a porn film coming through from the living room. He came back occasionally, when he was concerned that my yelling to be untied might cause the neighbours to suspect he was holding me captive. Spanking me once, hard, he requested I be a good girl and stop making unnecessary noise. I remained quiet, but inside I was feeling that same kind of panic as when a rollercoaster moved away from the gate. You are strapped in (literally), ascending to a place that you know will scare the crap out of you, uncertain if it will make you sick or have you queuing up for more.

I don't know how long I was left there uncomfortably dangling, naked. It seemed like time had stopped, forgetting me completely. I had never before felt that kind of intense vulnerability. It was the most naked I had ever been. When he returned to the bedroom, I thought he had come to release me, but Jackson spun me around, my hands still high and whispered, 'I need you to relax now, Christina.' His calm, authoritative voice gave me the immediate impression that something else was coming. I heard a click as he opened the bottle of lubricant, and seconds later, my skin was slick, wet and a little sticky. He wrapped one arm tightly around my waist, one hand between my thighs. 'Shhh', he whispered. An intense, unfamiliar surge hijacked my body, weakened my legs and forced the air from my lungs, as Jackson entered me like Marlon Brando in *Last Tango in Paris*. A loud, primal noise escaped from my lips; foreign, intense, impossible to control.

'Quiet,' he demanded. 'You'll get used to it.'

I guess Jackson was right, I did get used to it, or maybe I thought this must be what an adult sexual relationship was really like, having only previously mastered three basic sexual positions, none of which were utilised that evening. I can't recall a lover I ever learnt so much from. I guess coming into that relationship with such little experience, I had a lot to learn and I was so eager to please him, make him happy. But even if I wasn't entirely certain what I was doing, I'm pretty sure that my sex life with Jackson was a lot like boxing: unless both people are consenting, one of them is committing a crime.

Jackson was an immensely talented writer. He wrote poetry of such romantic depth and passion that it was as if he were holding a mirror up to his tortured artistic soul while bleeding onto the page. He'd stand up at a restaurant or dinner party and, with the delivery of Laurence Olivier, propose a toast or recite a poem so passionately he'd silence the room, leaving all those who heard him silent and captivated. It was like the enduring romantic Colonel Brandon had stepped off the pages of Jane Austen's, *Sense and Sensibility* and I was his young heroine. And if swooning had been a 20th-century thing, I'm sure that's what I would've been doing.

Equally intense and as unpredictable was his anger, an explosive, volatile temper I had never experienced before. I'd heard many rumours of his legendary temper within the ad community. There were so many stories of Jackson in fits of rage, not dissimilar to a toddler kicking and screaming in a grocery aisle when denied a sugary breakfast cereal. There were tales of him picking up a large potted palm and with Hulk-like power hurling it across a room when told by some account exec that the client did not approve his ad campaign, or throwing his desk chair through his glass office wall. I took these stories to be nothing more than advertising folklore, rumours, the creative ink pumping through the veins of the world of advertising.

The first glimpse of such tendencies that I recall, the first red flag I willingly ignored, was at a pub, The Madison, one night after work. Jackson was at the bar, several drinks in when I arrived. We were casually catching up on each other's day, chit-chat, nothing important, when I suggested we play a game. You know the one where you share the name of some celebrity that you'd want to spend one night, one month and a lifetime with? I can't remember who my three choices would've been back then, but I have to say that since 1995 and *Pride and Prejudice*, Colin Firth has done a spectacular job of holding on to my lifetime position.

It was a benign little nothing of a game. However, this is not how Jackson interpreted it. He glared at me, stiffened his back, and out of nowhere spat, 'Do you think I'm just one of those boys you can play your little games with?'

I immediately assumed Jackson had misunderstood the playfulness of the game. He started at me again, this time loud enough to catch the attention of a few people around us. Tightly squeezing my upper arm with one hand and slapping the other down hard on the mahogany bar, he barked, 'Don't you dare confuse me with all the others.'

My confusion immediately gave way to the realisation that he was furious. His eyes were dark, intense, frightening, and I felt the blood drain from my face. With weak legs, I stood up from the bar. 'You,' I said with a shaky, rattled voice, 'you're never allowed to speak that way to me. Never! It was just a stupid game.'

Picking up my purse, I quickly left the pub. A man followed me outside, asking if I was OK and if I needed any help.

'No,' I said. 'I'm OK, thank you.'

I'd walked no more than 50 feet when I heard Jackson calling after me. I kept walking, but now I slowed a little, finally turning around to let him catch up with me.

'What the fuck was that in there?' I screamed.

'I'm sorry,' Jackson said. 'I was out of line. It touched a nerve. Please, I'm sorry. I didn't mean any of it. Let's just go back inside ... please.'

It was like a poltergeist had passed through him, in one side and out the other. Quietly and sheepishly, I returned with Jackson to the pub, turning a few of the heads of the people who had overheard his outburst. Their faces were painted with looks of judgement or pity, or maybe I wasn't reading them correctly. Perhaps that's what deep concern looks like from strangers. He ordered me another pint, and with a calm, composed demeanour, Jackson asked, 'So, that man you were talking to outside, you didn't tell him any of our business, did you?'

I took an uncomfortable deep breath, exhaled and quietly answered, 'No. I didn't say anything to him.'

'Good,' he said, patting my hand in approval. 'You're never to do that, do you understand?' And he smiled.

Months went on, and for the most part, things were good. The poltergeist who had briefly inhabited Jackson was lying dormant. Business was booming and Jackson's guidance and insightful ideas on advertising were invaluable. I'd been given a rare and coveted behind-the-scenes glimpse inside the often-twisted creative mind, as though I had pulled the curtain back on the great and powerful Wizard of Oz. Professionally, I was killing it, and not just with Burnett. I was landing massive jobs worldwide. World-class directors were now reaching out to me by name. Jackson's belief in me pushed my thinking, taught me new problem-solving skills, and, most interestingly, opened me up to a notion I hadn't even dared to dream about: starting my own company. With incredible frequency, he'd encourage me to think beyond McWaters. He saw something in me I had yet to see in myself. Brandon had often tried to pull me out of this world. Jackson convinced me I could own it.

Jackson had a passion for travel, and, unsurprisingly, it took on all the style and glamour of an old 1940s Hollywood movie. The charming tuxedo-dressed Cary Grant with the spunky Katharine Hepburn. All that was missing were the impractically large Louis Vuitton steamer trunks, which I'm sure if the airlines had allowed, Jackson would've had a complete set of. I was willingly swept into another world as we travelled to Cannes, Monte Carlo, St Barth, Paris, Saint-Tropez and wherever else the Condé Nast Gold List said you had to see before you die.

I was romanced on tropical beaches, feasting on baskets filled with buttery foie gras pâté, warm baguette, French cheeses and chilled Cristal. We lay naked on private beaches, jumped in and out of the surf, made love anywhere and everywhere we could. He wooed me with Wilde, Yeats and Kipling's unbelievable power with words. Until Jackson, my comprehensive education from lovers could be pinpointed to accurately calling, 'Icing!' or 'Offside!' in a hockey game, or knowing the difference between a putter and a sand wedge. I'd never known a man like that existed outside of classic literature. I can't remember at the time if I thought this was forever, that he was the one, but I adored how he possessed those romantic traits that would've inspired Jane Austen. I was enamoured, enchanted, besotted … I was in love.

We decided to buy a house together, a finely restored old Victorian townhouse on the more artsy and affordable side of town. Jackson didn't grasp the fundamental idea of savings accounts, tax-free products, or the concept of investing in anything that couldn't give him immediate pleasure. He believed in living life in the grandest of styles, 'the luxuries and necessities of opulent living', he'd call it. So when we bought the house, I had more money saved than him, even though I made a fraction of what Jackson earned. But this all worked well for us as long as the balance of power stayed as it was, Jackson the master and teacher, and me, the dutiful and grateful student. But as they say: change is inevitable, growth is optional.

I'd lived somewhat of a naive, sheltered existence before Jackson. Not in some hayseed, life-on the-farm way, but rather that I was unexposed to a world that extended beyond the edges of what I knew. Travel, art, sex, literature and even love had now been redefined, all a sensory explosion blasting open a door into a new vibrant world. But with the romantic poet came the tortured demon.

I had seen waves of his temper, like a storm gathering strength, perhaps forewarning me like a distant foghorn warns ships of impending rocks. I was beginning to see it more frequently in more random situations beyond that night at the

Madison. Jackson's frightening fits of temper could ignite like dry grass on a hot day. He could argue with the hotel's front desk if the room wasn't perfect, although I had rarely seen a problem. Or sometimes, arrogant with rudeness, he'd unnecessarily return a bottle of wine. I'm not saying he wasn't right to if the wine was corked or there was some fundamental issue with the service, but it was the belittling, unkind way he sometimes dealt with it, and the rude, curt tone he'd use to address the staff that I had issues with. On various occasions of discord, he'd use the most clichéd line of the super-elite, and with a diva-like attitude he'd blast the classic 'Don't you know who I am?' as though anybody, and I mean anybody outside his tiny microcosm world of regional advertising, would have a clue. Even within the industry, some introductions might be required. His foot-stomping, hands-on-hips persona did beg a bigger question in my mind: *Who does he think he is?*

I also noticed that there was never a time when Jackson wasn't drinking. The sound of ice cubes crackling in a glass would act as a warning that the evening could hold no promises of protection. Every night I'd hear the *clink-clink* from the kitchen as they hit the bottom of his Old Fashioned glass, the sound of the long, languid liquor pour, the rumbling of the ice cubes moving closer as he tilted the glass and took a long sip. Then they would fall back, crashing to the bottom of the glass. I never knew the sound of someone drinking could be so deafening. At 29, I had never once used the word 'alcoholic' to describe even the most casual of acquaintances, and during our two-year relationship, that word was never spoken, not once. Not even whispered like my mother used to do with the word 'cancer', and I can't tell you why.

Memory can be imperfect and flawed, often leaving us to fill in the gaps. But not that night. There are moments too powerful to be faded, distorted or eradicated by the passing of time. All who were there that night remember exactly what happened, with no detail lost, no nuance blurred. My sister Jennifer and her new boyfriend, Theo, were coming over to spend the evening. We had a nice dinner, and like he often was, Jackson was eloquent, funny and charming. Looking for a little fun, we decided to play a game of Pictionary, boys versus girls. With his natural creative flair, Jackson figured the boys had a clear team advantage. We had all been drinking, but he was far ahead of any of us. He always was. The girls had a commanding lead, and this was not sitting well with Jackson. That guy hated to lose, even a drunken game of Pictionary. It was Jackson's turn to draw, and as Theo kept guessing incorrectly, he was getting more and more agitated.

'Moon,' Theo guessed. 'Is that a set of lips …? Someone waving hello …? God, I don't know,' Theo laughed. '*Bye Bye Birdie!*' he blurted. '*Bye Bye Birdie!*'

And with that, the timer went off. And so did Jackson.

'*Gone with the Wind*,' Jackson yelled. '*GONE WITH THE* FUCKING *WIND*. How did you not get that, Theo? Only an idiot would miss that.'

I looked at the drunken scribbles that were supposed to be the illustrated version of that movie.

'Ohhhhhh,' we all laughed.

'For sure, I see it now,' I lied.

Jackson became uncomfortably quiet, like an eery calm before a storm. I heard a methodical tap, tap, tap, as he evened out the pencils on the table. Lifting them dramatically over his head, he snapped the pencils in half and threw them in the air. Then he picked up the game pieces, and with fiery force hurled them across the room. With that, he marched upstairs. I lowered my eyes in silent shame. Now, there were witnesses.

There was genuine heart-tugging remorse after every storm. Almost like Jackson was someone else, looking around with seismic shame at the damage he had caused. He'd often weep in my arms, begging for forgiveness, and isn't that what I was supposed to do, forgive? I loved him, I mean, I was swept-off-my-feet in love with this romantic contradiction of a man, a paradoxical mash-up between dark and light, joy and pain, Jekyll and Hyde. Empowering in some areas and oh so damaging in others. I'd let it go, move past it, and try not to look too closely at the rubble that was starting to surround me, like a house that was damaged from a nearby bomb blast. I didn't know how to defuse Jackson. I didn't possess the skills needed, if they even existed. But with every earnest apology, every tender hand-written note of forgiveness left on my pillow, another blast would shatter windows. I felt uncomfortably isolated, like I was a small plane flying through heavy fog, looking for any sign of runway lights. The warning he'd given that night at the Madison, not to share our business with anyone, was icy and thick with unspoken threats, like an emotional non-disclosure agreement I'd naively signed, uncertain of the consequences but not blind that I didn't know they'd be big and unpredictable, like the man himself. I would make excuses, I'd protect his loosely guarded secrets, but I could speak to no one.

I needed help, and she was on her way. The greatest gift Jackson ever gave me came in the form of one Marie McDonald, and she couldn't have come at a more perfect time. Marie was an agency producer and an ex-girlfriend of Jackson's, and he suggested she'd be a good in for me at Saatchi. I liked that Jackson remained friends with his exes, which I thought boded well for the most part. Although I'm guessing that Jackson would never have imagined how hand-holding, secret-sharing, blessedly tight we'd become.

We met after work at a midtown bar called Noodles, a popular ad hangout renowned for its pink neon room and its fancy cocktails. I loved Marie instantly. An outgoing petite blonde whose laughter could rattle windows, surprising for her wee frame. I relished meeting someone who had survived Jackson's captivity. We barely spoke of him, not really, not yet, but she knew the demon I was facing, the secrets I could tell no one. It was the way she looked at me, something in her eyes that dimmed just a little when his name was spoken. We were members of the same small sorority, the sisterhood of Jackson Tilney. As I hugged her goodbye that first night, I knew Marie would be my person. She would know better than anyone how I could escape.

CHAPTER 3

The Devil Is, and Always Will Be, a Gentleman

'Behind every exquisite thing that existed,
there was something tragic.'
Oscar Wilde, *The Picture of Dorian Gray*

I t's always one thing that destroys a relationship, that last straw that pushes you beyond the point of no return. Something impossible to recover from, which severs those last remaining slivers of justification you've been desperately protecting, clutching to like a buoy at sea. In my relationship with Jackson, that one thing nearly killed me.

McWaters had just wrapped up a large job for one of Jackson's clients, Bell. We'd flown in a famous music-video director for the campaign. His main claim to fame was having been the lead singer in a British pop duo in the seventies. Our sixteen-person wrap dinner was in the private dining room of a modern Italian restaurant called Centro. In between courses, Pop Star Director, with the aid of the client's Montblanc pen, would roll and pass around the longest rock star spliffs I had ever seen. A rocker's palate cleanser, if you will. Everyone seemed too loaded to worry about Pop Star Director lighting up in a restaurant; everyone, that was, but me. I was still working, staying two drinks behind the crowd, making sure everyone was looked after, the bill got paid, and all got safely poured into cabs.

Jackson ordered another double Chartreuse, a drink that I've never seen anyone other than him even contemplate ordering. He stood and raised his glass. Going round the table, which was littered with red wine rings and coffee cups, Jackson personally acknowledged everyone's contribution with a humorous and eloquent toast. He reminded me of Dean Martin and his boozy roasts, back in a time when the television world glamorised alcoholics. Still standing, Jackson turned his attention to me.

'Last but not least ...' he started. 'As you all know by now, Christina is the brilliant executive producer responsible for the flawless execution of this campaign, and for that, I thank her.' There was a drunken round of applause, and a few loud whoops around the table. Then Jackson started to get emotional, as he was sometimes prone to do. His glassy eyes edged with tears, he emoted, 'And I love her with all my heart, and I don't deserve her.'

There was the collective 'Aaah!' with smiles from some of the women, as if to say, 'What a lucky woman you are, Christina.' He composed himself, but not before inviting everyone back to our place.

'Yee-haw!' I heard the copywriter yell, totally hammered. 'Afterparty at Jackson's.'

I looked up at Jackson and smiled, raising my glass to signal to him, *That's enough, please sit down,* when I noticed something odd about him. Maybe it was the mega party joint that had made it around the table several times, as Jackson rarely smoked weed. He was swaying in an anti-clockwise motion, the drink in his hand sloshing around its bright green liquid like a tornado gathering momentum. My first instinct was to protect him. Funny, it never occurred to me that there was a greater need to protect myself. I stood up and gave him a tight hug, thinking he might be about to hit the ground.

'Thank you for the lovely toast, Jackson,' I said.

With his arms tight around my back, I felt a warm wetness on my leg. At first I thought it was the swishing Chartreuse. Oh, how I wish I could blame the Chartreuse. Jackson Tilney, elegantly dressed, the enviable poetic leading man, in the middle of a private dining room, in front of clients, colleagues and Pop Star Director, had relieved himself all over the front of his finely pressed Italian linen trousers.

'Jackson,' I whispered urgently, still holding on to him, 'you need to sit down now.'

He took his seat to a round of jubilant applause, with no one the wiser. I placed my hand on his thigh and dug my nails into his flesh so hard that he looked at me sharply and angrily. With only my cold eyes, I directed his gaze to the wet mark on the front of his trousers. I removed my hand from his thigh as I didn't want it to be interpreted as an invitation. It was anything but that. I wanted him to feel pain. I needed to draw blood to make him feel just a sliver of the intense agony I felt just looking at this damaged human being.

In the cab that I insisted we take alone, I could smell him – a unique combination of homeless vagrant infused with light tones of Aramis, his jacket draped across his lap. Annoyed, I said, 'You shouldn't have invited everyone over, Jackson; not without asking me first.' Jackson didn't respond. He just gazed out the half-open cab window. I didn't have it in me to say anything more. Jackson changed his clothes while I greeted our guests as they arrived. I put out some cheese and crackers, directed all to the vicinity of the drinks cabinet, then quietly slipped upstairs. I had nothing more to give. I was officially off the clock.

It was just before four o'clock in the morning when I heard the piercing ringing of the smoke alarm. The shrieking sound penetrated deep into my ears and chest. Opening my eyes from an uneasy sleep, I looked around the room; the bedding on Jackson's side was still taut.

'Jackson,' I called out. 'Jackson?'

I quickly got out of bed, still unclear what was going on and where Jackson was.

'Jackson!' I screamed, trying to be heard over the piercing sound of the alarm. I threw on my bathrobe, unsure who was still in the house as I started to make my way downstairs. 'Where are you?'

There, at the top of the stairs, Jackson was sitting on the floor. Legs stretched out in front of him, leaning against the wall, struggling to pull his jumper over his head.

'Jackson, is that the fire alarm?!'

Jackson was oblivious to both me and the alarm as he continued to struggle to find his way out. He was trapped inside an Argyle cashmere jumper. I looked down the stairs and saw the living room was filling with a blue-grey smoke.

'Jackson!' I screeched. 'The house! Fire!'

Rushing down the stairs and into the smoke-filled living room, I stood terror-stricken in the middle of a grey toxic storm cloud. My heartbeat was pounding in my ears, dampening the deafening screech of the alarm. The silvery smoke billowed out from the kitchen as I covered my nose and mouth with the sleeve of my dressing gown and rushed in. The stove was engulfed in six-foot-high flames that licked the ceiling. The melted plastic knobs, like tar, oozed onto the floor. Running for the fire extinguisher under the sink and praying to a god I didn't believe in, I pulled tight on its trigger, the force surprisingly pushing me back and setting me slightly off-balance. The extinguisher sprayed white foam over the stove and the adjacent countertops. In the distance, even with the sound of the alarm ringing in my ears, I could hear the sirens. Around me, everything was smouldering, hissing, dampened under the thick, wet foam. The fire was out. Coughing, I tried to clear the smoke from my throat and lungs, as the firemen pounded on the front door. Wrapping my bathrobe tightly around my waist, I made my way to let them in.

We walked around the smoky, smouldering kitchen, three firefighters and me.

'You did a good job containing the fire, Ma'am,' one of the firefighters said, surveying the damage. 'This could've taken the whole house down.'

Another firefighter stared at the stove more closely. 'Here's the cause of the fire,' he said, pointing to a broken plate sitting on top of one of the burners. 'Looks like someone turned on the element to light a cigarette and left the pack on top of the plate.' He looked around the smoky room. 'You alone in the house, Ma'am?' he asked.

'No,' I said, sheepishly. 'My boyfriend is asleep upstairs.'

'Asleep?' he asked, in shock. 'He slept through this?'

I was silent. I didn't answer, nor did he ask any more questions.

I thanked the firemen as I let them out, the harsh smell of smoke and burnt plastic tangled in my long, thick hair. I clearly remember the sound as I turned the deadbolt on the front door. Funny what you remember, how the simple sound of a deadbolt turning was deafening to me. Every bit as loud as the smoke alarm or ice cubes falling into a glass. It was in that instant that it came to me, a reality I couldn't see before. I was locked in, living in a cage that smelt of smoke, burning plastic and vodka – my cage with the urban dimensions of a beautifully appointed Victorian house, with high ceilings and generous rooms. A cage I could have died in that evening. Very slowly, I made my way up the stairs, and there was Jackson, my captor, the gatekeeper, passed out on the floor, exactly where I'd last seen him, his cashmere jumper tangled around his neck. He looked like a marionette puppet whose strings had been cut and limbs lay lifeless. He hadn't heard the smoke detector, the sirens, the heavy banging on the door by the firemen. He hadn't smelt the smoke of the fire he had started by lighting a cigarette. He couldn't even manage his way out of his jumper.

I stepped over him with more anger at myself than at him, and don't misunderstand me, I was livid with him. With a white-hot intensity, I hated him. I walked into the bathroom, shut the door and stared into the mirror, the smudge of soot on my forehead suggested a rudimentary religious cross. *How telling,* I thought, *the devil is and always will be a gentleman.* I don't know who said that. *Maybe this is what hell looks like.* Leaning against the bathroom door, like a scene from *Girl, Interrupted*, I slowly slid down it and completely, totally shattered into a thousand million pieces.

My tears hit the tiled floor as my arms wrapped around me tightly like I was wearing a straitjacket, and I rocked myself back and forth. My sobs were heavy, guttural, primal, thick with an excruciating pain that I had never come close to experiencing before. For a moment, my mind flashed back to Brandon. This would've never happened if I had just stayed married to him. I was so confused and disoriented with the choices in men that I'd made. How was it that I could love the sinner but not the saint? My mind screamed in abhorrent judgement, *What the fuck is wrong with you, you stupid girl?*

I don't remember how long I was in the bathroom, my exhausted body and tear-stained face lying pressed against the cold tiles. Eventually, picking myself up, I splashed cold water on my face and gazed in the mirror again. Transfigured, scarred, damaged, I did not recognise my reflection. Mortified, I thought, *Who is this woman with eyes and cheeks smeared with tears? I mean, who the fuck is she?* I returned to the empty bed, pulling the blankets up against my chin to warm my shivering body. At that moment, I understood that I couldn't save him, so I needed to save myself.

The end never comes when you think it will. Untangling myself from Jackson was not as simple as me picking up and leaving the next day. Rarely is it. Someone told me it is never at the lowest moment of your relationship when you leave, it's six things after that. Maybe I was hoping things would get better, or perhaps it was just about formulating a solid exit plan. I don't remember my reasons at the time for not walking out the door immediately. If there were hours of painful conversation or explosive arguments rendering me hoarse, or pleas for forgiveness, or perhaps a punishing silent treatment, I don't remember. It's like someone has *Eternal Sunshine*d me.

What I do know is that something switched off in me that night. I didn't love him anymore. It was like I had been standing in the middle of a large, empty stadium as, one by one, Jackson's actions had shut down the banks of lights that once were blindingly bright, leaving me standing in the dark alone. The lights weren't coming back on, they never do. I now had to find my way out of the arena in the dark, without disturbing the gatekeeper.

CHAPTER 4

My Shawshank Redemption

*'It's no use going back to yesterday, because
I was a different person then.'*
Lewis Carroll, *Alice's Adventures in Wonderland*

It was just before my 30th birthday. Marie had nuzzled her
way into my life as and was now a very important friend – she
was like the Piglet to my Winnie-the-Pooh. She was my trusted
confidant, my primary source of unfiltered laughter, and my
co-conspirator as together we plotted how to Shawshank my ass
out of my gilded Victorian cage.

A few weeks had passed since the fire, and as I'd been known
to do, I had thrown myself deeper into work, keeping busy,
working late nights and weekends. It was my distraction, my
therapy. I was gathering my strength. I was getting ready to leave.
Jackson could see I had checked out emotionally, and he had
been on particularly good behaviour.

In fact, Jackson was throwing a surprise birthday party for
me, about which, of course, I had been well briefed by Marie.
Inspired by a trip to Punta Mita, the party was to have a Mexican
theme, including a five-piece mariachi band, a taco bar and, of
course, tequila. The night of the party, the house was packed
with what seemed like every single person I had known since the
age of eight: old friends, new friends, family, employees and
clients. Bouquets of pastels balloons filled the house, and where
there weren't balloons, vases were dripping with spring flowers,
all bearing cards conveying best wishes for my 30th birthday.

Conversations were drowned out by those deeper into the Margarita pitchers, and I could hear some of the wasted party guests accompanying the band singing 'Volare'.

'Surprised?' Jackson asked, putting his arm around my shoulder.

'Very,' I replied.

'Liar,' he smiled, 'but you will be ... Come.'

Jackson took me by the hand, leading me into the living room. Clinking his tequila-filled glass, he asked the band to stop playing.

'Can I have your attention, please, everyone? I have a special surprise for the birthday girl.'

I anxiously watched as people gathered around Jackson and the large TV he had positioned 'just so' for the occasion. Some were making themselves comfortable on the floor, as if they'd been instructed that this might take a while, so I did the same. The crowd hushed, much like those final seconds as the conductor lifts his arms into the air to ready his orchestra. Someone dimmed the lights as Jackson hit 'play' on the VCR. A title card came up, 'The Birthday Girl', and an edited montage of photographs filled the screen, with Jackson's recorded voice singing 'You Must Have Been a Beautiful Baby'. My life, literally flashing before my eyes. Had it been another time, a better time, I would have thought this gift lovely, a wonderfully romantic gesture. But as it was, I was embarrassed and uncomfortable as I sat cross-legged on the floor. This could not finish soon enough. As my life story was brought up to its current-day conclusion, Jackson asked for the lights to be turned back on. *Phew,* I thought, *OK, that wasn't too bad.* Then I heard someone in the crowd gasp, almost like some air had escaped from one of my pastel birthday balloons. I looked up, and there was Jackson on one knee, an engagement ring in his hand. The room was now painfully silent. He looked at me, and lovingly said, 'Christina, my dove, will you marry me?'

It felt like someone had just thrown a brick at my head. *For fuck's sake, what is he doing?* As a self-proclaimed amateur part-time psychic, this was an epic fail on my part. He could not be serious. I looked at him holding a cocktail-type ring in the shape of a tiny wing, encrusted in diamonds and coloured gems. The room was filled with palpable joyous excitement as the crowd waited for my answer. I was standing at the threshold of Hell. I wanted the floor to open up and swallow me whole. I mean it. I wanted that more than anything. I saw Marie looking at me from the corner of my eye. I couldn't return her gaze for fear that at that very second, I'd grab her hand, and we'd run from the house like Thelma and Louise and willingly drive the car right off a cliff. A viable option, all things considered.

Looking at Jackson, I thought how well he was playing this. He knew I'd never knowingly embarrass him in front of all these people. In fact, he was betting on it. Had he proposed in a quiet restaurant, or anywhere else where it was just the two of us, my response would have been honest and unwavering. But he'd needed to enlist the power of every single person I had known since fourth grade to be part of this moment, a hundred other voices supporting his. This was my stadium, filled with my people, and there was Jackson with his well-played jumbotron proposal. *Damn him,* I thought. I could feel the tightening panic set in. *Think, Christina, think. You need a plan.* One that perhaps didn't involve the awkward, abrupt shutdown of what had been, up until that moment, a pretty good party. A plan that would not be gossiped about and creatively retold for months to come. And one that didn't flatten the man who was still kneeling in front of me, winged cocktail ring in hand.

There's a saying in war: 'In the absence of a plan, move towards the sounds of gunfire.' So, with some uncertain *Art of War* credo, I looked at Jackson and squeaked out the word, 'Yes.'

People rushed in to congratulate us, hugging me tightly, voices in unison: 'We're so happy for you.' I looked anxiously for Marie, but I couldn't see her. *Stay strong,* the voice inside my head said. *Help will be here soon.* After all the well-wishers made their way back to their tacos and tequila, and the band resumed playing, Marie made her way to me.

'So ...' she said in a lilting sing-song voice, 'let's see the ring.'

She lifted my reluctant hand to take a closer look at the ring that was sitting heavily like an ACME anvil.

'Well, have you had enough now, Christina?' she asked, still holding my hand in hers.

I looked up at her, her green eyes digging into mine. 'Yes,' I nodded.

'I mean, really had enough?' she asked again, with the understanding that only we could share.

'Yes,' I answered again. 'Yes.'

'Good,' she smiled. 'Tomorrow, we will fix this, but as for tonight, let us not waste all this mighty fine tequila.'

'You know, Marie,' I said, 'just once, when someone proposes to me, I'd like to be happy about it.'

She smiled. 'You could have worse problems.'

Ten days later, I was unpacking the last of my boxes in my new brownstone flat, in the comfort of my old familiar neighbourhood in Forest Hill Village. I was returning not as a single girl, but as a single woman, one with confidence, experience, and an inspired belief in myself that allowed me to open my new company, Imported Artists. That was Jackson's parting gift to me, teaching me to believe in myself as he believed in me.

I returned to the familiar, but it was me that was changed forever.

♥

Graham Greene's novel *The End of the Affair* opens with a quote from Léon Bloy, that I remember at the time of first reading not fully understanding: 'Man has places in his heart which do not yet exist, and into them enters suffering, in order that they may have existence.' I understand it now.

The complex man I fell in love with, through the simple act of being who he was, shone a light on a part of me that I'd had no awareness of before him. My two years with Jackson were transformational: I was like the caterpillar, surrounded, encapsulated and trapped in her chrysalis, unaware of the world waiting for her to emerge into, as a butterfly. I know it's a schmaltzy, clichéd comparison, but I felt a little like that butterfly.

I'd possessed a youthful naivety about love, sex and the world before I'd met Jackson, like a child who had never ventured beyond their quiet neighbourhood streets, who always made it home by the time the streetlights came on. He took me beyond my tidy little world and shared its remarkable beauties and its frightening horrors. Maybe it's a little like seeing New York City for the first time, if all you'd known previously were pastoral farmland and friendly neighbours who greeted you by name; it's a rush of adrenaline coupled with an overwhelming fear that the world is so much bigger than you'd first imagined. It's an extraordinary gift that someone gives when they believe in you, almost like a superpower. Sure, there were things from the relationship I'd sooner not have been given, but overall the good outweighed the bad.

The night of my 30th birthday party, after everyone had left, I asked Jackson why he had proposed. It wasn't like I was the only one in that relationship who knew it wasn't working. He wasn't happily dancing with the druids while I lay there in complete isolated misery. He told me that he had to try everything he could, and that it was his Hail Mary pass. I learnt later that the advice had been given to Jackson by my mother. The two of them had sat together on a Sunday afternoon, sifting through old photos for my birthday video. She hadn't told him to propose, nor had she used the term 'Hail Mary pass', as my mother would have been the last person to use a sports metaphor accurately, but she'd said he should try everything he could, and for Jackson, that was all he had left.

Although we were technically engaged for a couple of days, I refuse to count it as an actual engagement. It was a stalling strategy, an act of mercy, nothing more. However, I did take a painful lesson from it, a vow I promised to uphold. I would never again enter into a relationship with an addict. Relationships are hard enough on a good day, but to add the volatility and the destructive behaviour that comes from loving an addict, well, that just sucks your soul straight out of your chest, leaving the remnants of you unrecognisable to those who love you most. Had I been a lesser person, and by that I mean not believing I deserved anything more than what I was being fed, I think Jackson's alcoholism would have eventually destroyed me, as it was destroying him, or trapped me in his dysfunctional way of life, leaving me to forever pick up the pieces of his shattered existence, instead of nurturing my own.

Jackson and I remained friends, kinda, just like he managed to do with most of his exes. He showed up from time to time as a client on a few of my jobs, would walk directly past reception, right into my office and greet me the way he always had, with a friendly and affectionate, 'Hello, my dove.' His drinking and uncontrollable temper eventually left him without a job, as the world of advertising was reluctantly growing up, leaving no room for outbursts and toddler-style temper tantrums. I lost touch with Jackson after that. I heard he lived alone in a small studio apartment, with a cat he named Marilyn, not after Marilyn Monroe but Marilyn Chambers, the porn star.

Maybe twenty years after the last time I saw Jackson, I received a phone call from his brother Oliver in Seattle, telling me Jackson was in the hospital with liver failure and didn't have long to live. Oliver said Jackson was asking if I'd come and see him. I hadn't had any real contact with him in decades, and now he lay dying from his drug of choice.

I gathered up some old photos, although there weren't many from our time together, and made my way to the palliative care unit of East York Hospital. My head was dizzy with decades of unanswered questions and millions of fragmented memories. Could he be looking to apologise, make amends for the abuse, the fire? I've heard that's what people do, lying on their death-bed, they ask for forgiveness from the people they have hurt, the people they have tragically loved.

I nervously walked in. Jackson was lying awake in his bed, his skin and eyes the colour of a cantaloupe.

'Hello, my dove,' he said in a soft, familiar voice.

I smiled, looking down at the man I'd once loved. He still didn't look his age, and once again, I wondered where he was hiding that Dorian Gray portrait of him, and what it must look like now.

'What the hell are you doing in here, Jackson?' I joked, gazing around a depressing, sparse hospital room, not a flower anywhere.

He managed a slight laugh. 'They tell me I'm dying, my love.'

I smiled sadly, 'Not a chance, Jackson. Don't they know who you are?'

'Apparently not,' he said.

We looked through the faded photos I'd collected, playing in the surf in St Barth, barging through Burgundy, and a Christmas Day at my family home, Jackson elegantly dressed in a tuxedo and me in a dress with Pat Benatar shoulders. He'd come dressed as Mr Darcy, but that was never who he was. These were memories of a life that had disappeared so long ago that it didn't seem like it had ever belonged to me. Jackson Tilney had become a distant dream, that as I reflect now, seems so totally disconnected to me, yet hugely significant to the pages that tell my story. I often look at old photographs, happy images and feel guilty, as I know something that the people in the photos don't … how the story ends.

Jackson asked if I could check with his neighbour that Marilyn the cat was OK. 'I miss her,' he said sadly, about his cat and no one else.

There was no apology or touching moment of self-reflection. Jackson was dying alone, and I just think he knew that, if asked, I'd still be the one person who would manage to do the right thing and not disappoint him. I'd tried to persuade Marie to come with me. After all, we were part of a set. But even Marie was able to handle her goodbyes with just a phone call. She hadn't been 'summoned', she reminded me. To my knowledge, he wasn't visited by his daughter or his grandchildren, and Oliver cited some excuse for not boarding a plane to be by his dying brother's side. Jackson's karma kicked him hard in the teeth. He was dying alone.

As I sat in the chair beside his bed, Jackson asked, 'Why do hospitals paint their walls such a putrid colour of green? If you weren't sick, the colour alone could kill you.' I found it amusing that even when dying, Jackson's desire for beauty had not diminished. Looking at the painted walls and paraphrasing Oscar Wilde, he said, 'One of us has got to go.'

Fours days later, Jackson died.

I quietly wept when I read his obituary weeks later, for there I was. It was a beautiful, romantic tribute to a faded relationship, undisturbed for decades. How I even got mentioned was the one thing I found the most heartbreaking, even more tragic than the man who'd drunk himself to death. For from his death, I had to sadly conclude that Jackson's life must have been resoundingly absent of love.

There is a quote I love, and I think it's intended as a warning: 'The world is full of monsters with friendly faces and angels full of scars.' If I think about it, it might just sum up Jackson, a complex man of contradictions, who, I believe, loved me the best he could.

The Book of

John

CHAPTER 1

How I Met Your Mother

'All the world is made of faith, and trust, and pixie dust.'
J.M. Barrie, *Peter Pan*

It was the evening of the Imported Artists Christmas party. The company had rented out a small grungy bar in Little Italy called The Orbit Room. It was about 11pm, and the party was in full swing. Clients, employees, crew and plus-ones were happily overindulging as the 1960s-style R&B band had the small dance floor spilling over to any and all available floor space. I was standing at the bar with Marie when they arrived.

'Good God, sweet Jesus, over there,' Marie gasped.

I looked up to see two women standing motionless, as the light from the spinning disco ball bounced off their shiny, reflective attire. One was short and round, with slicked-back lacquered hair, and the other, and the more striking of the two, was tall, with a fiery mane of bright copper hair that hung heavy and straight between her bare shoulder blades. Both were wearing matching black latex skirts and corsets, with thigh-high stiletto boots that hugged their legs like high-gloss paint. Their faces were painted heavily, with severely contoured cheeks and matte blood-red lips. If one could struggle to see beyond the harsh, garish makeup, both girls looked no more than twenty.

Two things crossed my mind immediately. Firstly, and most obviously, they had got lost looking for a stag do, where a room of drunken, randy middle-aged men were eagerly anticipating their arrival. My second thought, which was quite plausible, was that someone from my staff had hired them as entertainment, and that at any moment they would hit play on a loud boombox, and I'd be forced down onto a chair where I'd be immediately surrounded by the two dark mistresses lip-syncing to something like Van Halen's 'Spanked' or 'Where There's a Whip There's a Way' by Faster Pussycat.

I very much expected to see the women realise their mistake, and quickly leave, as neither one of them seemed to be carrying any obvious audio equipment. I watched as the eyes of the tall, fiery redhead, whom Marie took to calling Dom 1, scanned the crowded bar. It was then, parting the dance floor, that my husband, John, came bounding towards them. I watched in bewilderment and honest confusion as Dom 1 politely shook off John's attempts to get the girls a drink. They weren't there long, maybe six or seven minutes. They never left the illuminated glow of the red exit sign, until they turned on their exception-ally high, spiked heels to leave. As I watched Dom 1 turn, there was the slightest touch of her hand to John's, like a soft breeze. His little finger ever so lightly brushed hers, then gently and gracefully pulled back. I took a painful breath.

There could have been no way, regardless of whatever creative imagination I could've magically summoned, that I could've ever been able to predict that moment and all that it meant. Yet there it was. Illuminated by shiny hits of a mirrored disco ball, by the glow of a red exit sign, it was that night, for the first time, that I saw my children's future stepmom.

Eight Years Earlier

The receptionist apologetically asked me to wait in a small boardroom in Limelight's Hollywood office, as Alexander Helford, the executive producer, was running late – very late. Outside the boardroom was a frenzy of activity. People scurrying this way and that, as the longest anyone seemed to stand still was to sign for a package. Limelight was one of three production companies I'd signed when I'd first started Imported Artists. It was a sexy company producing music videos for superstars like Madonna and Michael Jackson. While I sat waiting, Adam Ant, who had graciously held the door open for me when I walked in, was somewhere combing the hallways.

Waiting for Alexander, and to kill some time, I began screening a two-foot-high stack of ¾-inch director reels sitting on the floor. I prioritised the names I knew first: Simon West, David Fincher and Steve Barron. Barron was one of the partners at Limelight, and his video for A-ha's 'Take On Me' was hailed as a creative masterpiece. As I got to the end of the long stack of notable directors, Alexander Helford still nowhere in sight, I pushed the last remaining reel into the video deck. A director I had never heard of before, John Bertram.

I remember so clearly looking at the unknown director's work, finding it fresh, raw and unexpectedly funny. There wasn't a single superstar video on it like the other directors I'd just screened, but I knew enough to know that those directors would require day rates that would rival the price of a new Honda Civic. There was something intangible about this Bertram guy. I had a rare, remarkable gut feeling. This director had potential. As I excitedly scribbled down his contact details off the reel jacket, Alexander walked in, apologising, citing some production crisis for his tardiness, which certainly wouldn't be unusual for this business.

I try not to spend too much time thinking about the *Sliding Doors* aspect of that chance screening of John's reel, but I later learnt that his reel wasn't even supposed to be in that pile. All the many variables that had to occur for me to see it have crossed my mind, including the extreme delay of Alexander Helford, for had he come in just three minutes earlier, I would've never met the man who would become the most prominent director in my company, my husband and the father of my children.

Bounding towards me in the lobby of the Royal York Hotel two weeks later was a tall, slim, attractive man. I had called John Bertram after seeing his reel, and he'd been eager to meet. His multi-coloured pea jacket contrasted brightly against the businessmen shades of grey and navy that surrounded him. There was almost a spring in his step, like a cantering young colt as he reached out his hand and smiled.

'You must be Christina. So great to meet you.'

He was one of those all-American handsome guys from New York who looked like you could find him playing touch football on the Kennedy compound lawn on the weekends. His dark brown hair was lightly gelled back, and he sported impressive Elvis Presley-inspired sideburns. During lunch, we worked out a deal that signed him to Imported Artists, and within three weeks, I had booked him his first commercial. John exploded onto the scene, and within six months he was cherry-picking from potentially award-winning television campaigns. I was 31 years old.

John was extremely outgoing and a master at putting people immediately at ease. He was confident without being arrogant. He killed on client pitches, expertly threading and disguising client ideas into his own voice. 'If the client said beige, I say ecru,' he'd joke. After every shoot, he'd go up to absolutely every last person on set, shake their hand and thank them for their excellent work. He made everyone feel instantly like they had been friends for years. In short, he had the most extraordinary way of getting what he wanted or needed from everyone, all the while making them feel honoured just to be part of his team. John was on his way to being one of the most sought-out storytelling directors in the country. And as for his effect on me, well, I had never felt more like a kick-ass, genius rainmaker.

CHAPTER 2

Don't Shit Where You Eat

'He could see the honey, he could smell the honey,
but he couldn't quite reach the honey.'
A.A. Milne, *Winnie-the-Pooh*

There's a wise old adage that goes something like this: 'Don't shit where you eat.' The gist of it is that it might be a tad unwise to date co-workers or colleagues, as it could very well come back to bite you hard in the ass when it most likely goes kaboom. Before interoffice romances were all but made extinct, illegal or frowned upon by HR departments, and well before Tinder and Bumble, I read that about 70 per cent of people met their partners at work. I get it. I had previously dated a few guys I met through work.

Of course, there was Jackson; you know all about him. And then there was Christopher Emerson, a client I was dating when I first met John. But I didn't share an office with either of those guys. We were eating and shitting in different places, to continue with the metaphor, and there was little chance of Aaron Sorkin-like drama when these relationships eventually ran their course.

Christopher Emerson was an intense advertising whiz-kid, and with his blonde hair, severe cheekbones and Nordic features, he resembled a young Nick Nolte. Likely due to his inability to play well with others, in his mid-to-late twenties he had started his own advertising agency that would slay come award time. John would often join Christopher and me out for drinks or dinner. It wasn't unusual that after one too many cocktails, Christopher and I would get into inane heated debates, as he'd passionately defend his two favourite topics, extreme left-wing politics and his strict Pentecostal beliefs.

That first year of working together, John claimed he was single. However, I'd get conflicting reports from his on-again, off-again girlfriend, Lilith, a pint-size outspoken blonde who on occasion accompanied him from New York. Finding Lilith equal parts annoying and obnoxious, I had zero qualms about actively setting John up with all my single friends, even floating him by my sister Jennifer. And although Jen was keen, John never took the bait with any of them. Maybe Lilith was right. Maybe they were more on than off.

Almost one year to the day we first met, John moved to Toronto from Manhattan, with his personal belongings stuffed into his Ford Bronco. He settled into an urban second-storey apartment in a neighbourhood he described as 'full-service' due to the easy accessibility of hookers and drug dealers – a gentrifying neighbourhood in the West End of Toronto. Between hearing the details of his long drive and informing him his utilities had been installed, I said something that changed everything, although I wasn't aware of it at the time. I casually blurted, 'Oh, I don't know if you've heard, but Christopher and I broke up.'

There was a bit of a pause and then the expected, 'Oh no, I'm so sorry ...' etc. What I didn't know, was that in that split second of silence, John's 'heart dropped into his stomach', as he would later go on to describe it. John had moved countries, was going to be full-time at Imported Artists, and now with Christopher gone, in his mind nothing was standing in his way, between him ... and me.

Firmly planted in Toronto, John mounted a pretty flattering and exhausting campaign to get me on board 'Team Johnny', as someone tagged it. He recruited friends and colleagues who casually and frequently dropped his name with the intent to get me to agree to go out with him. Shasta, John's line producer, used honest, unfiltered candour more than once, walking straight into my office, completely fed up, saying, 'Christina, can you please just go out with him, for fuck's sake. He's driving everyone crazy.'

I'd look past Shasta to see John smiling in the hallway, checking to see if she was making any headway. That was John all over. He'd charmingly erode any barriers between himself and what he wanted. And let me add, he was brilliant at it.

This went on for three months. John's relentless love-bombing campaign was slowly creeping into my consciousness, much like a song you keep hearing over and over again, and then one day you find yourself humming it. It's not that I wouldn't have been into John had he not been a director at my company. Sure, he was attractive, charming and a good friend. He made me laugh, and I wholly and thoroughly enjoyed being with him. But the ginormous staggering truth was that he was my busiest, top-billing director. So why, with my stellar track record with men (sarcasm), would I shit where I ate and sleep with my best director, only to have the whole thing implode, billings and all? If I was contemplating letting him so much as hold my hand, I had to be so sure. I mean John-loves-Yoko certain.

It was a chilly July weekend when my life changed forever. My friend Lauren and I had rented a small rustic cottage for us and our friends near the tiny town of Bolsover, or Blue Balls-over as it was forever known after that weekend. Lauren, an enthusiastic cheerleader of Team Johnny, believed I needed a gentle shove in his direction, so she invited him to join us without telling me. Although I might have outwardly objected to Lauren's well-meaning meddling in my life with a spluttering, 'You did what?!' secretly I was pleased, as if my heart knew something my brain did not.

I can't remember who sat around that July bonfire drinking wine and beer, as their faces all faded into the darkness of that summer night. John was standing alone by the fire as I came over with two more unnecessary drinks, oblivious to the late hour or others' whereabouts. The embers were dancing and swirling from the log John had just thrown onto the fading fire, and the air was sweet and earthy. I had lost count of how many times John and I had been alone together. We were friends, colleagues, confidants, and had closed out many a lobby bar of a random hotel after gruelling location jobs. But by the glow of the fire, I noticed his hands for the first time, his long fingers, and I let my mind wander, just for a second, to what they would feel like gently moving across my skin. Flickering flames, dancing and sparkling with hope, were reflected in his dark chocolate eyes.

Now, if I could, I'd blame what happened next on the wine. I mean, wine has been responsible for many questionable decisions I've made over the years. So legitimately, as wine was healthily consumed that night, I could set blame where blame was due. But it wasn't the wine. It was John. It was his perfect smile, his laughter, his undying, charming persistence. John must've seen the silent permission I was finally granting as my caution dissolved like sugar in tea. While I was still questioning whether this would be the stupidest business decision of my life, John kissed me like he had been training all his life for that moment. In that kiss, I knew. I was 100 per cent ... John-and-Yoko ... done.

CHAPTER 3

Who Are You Wearing?

'You can have anything you want in life if you dress for it.'
Edith Head

Looking out the window as the plane was making its final descent into Toronto, I thought I would throw up. My heart was beating so hard, my mind somewhere on the other side of the arrivals gate. I must have been either hyperventilating or looking some unusual shade of pale because the woman sitting beside me asked with concern, 'Are you OK, dear?'

'Yes,' I answered, mustering a slight smile. 'I'm just about to get engaged.'

Marie knew the plan. She'd been instrumental in getting me this far, and now she only had one last task: to make sure John left the editing suite on time. I mean, of course I needed a plan. A creative way to finally say yes to John, after he'd proposed over 100 times.

'You can't just say yes to proposal 104,' Marie said, jokingly. 'You need to knock it out of the park.'

'I love you, Ford,' John had said two days after that cottage weekend and immediately after we'd had sex for the first time.

'Nope, that doesn't count,' I said playfully. 'Saying "I love you" during or after sex.'

From then on John would weave it enthusiastically and seamlessly into his everyday conservation, as one might talk about the weather.

'I love you, Ford, and I don't care who knows,' he trumpeted, standing on a chair in my crowded office.

'John, get down. You're going to hurt yourself,' I said, trying to deflect the attention that was on both of us.

He remained remarkably unbothered with me not saying it back, confidently repeating, 'When you're ready, you will say it back to me, and not before.'

Again, John was seemingly unshakable, just waiting for me to catch up to him.

I've never told anyone I loved them if I haven't. I honestly don't see the point. Plus, I'm the world's worst liar. My face is transparent, a visible transmitter of my every thought. I guess it has safely kept me out of any high-stakes poker games or super-competitive rounds of Old Maid. If I fell in love with John, and I was certainly hoping I would, only then would I tell him. In the meantime, I did my best to endure his playful and consistent declarations. This went on for a while.

Two months after we'd got together, on a drizzly, lazy Sunday morning lying in bed, something rushed over me, almost electrifying me into full consciousness. I would go on to have this body-awakening jolt only one other time in my life. Billy Joel's 'Captain Jack' was softly playing on the radio. Something warm and wonderful washed over me, like a euphoric wave, making me feel like I was falling, flying and floating, all at the same time. I looked over at John, hair messy, and both of us a little hungover from the night before.

'John. Hey, Johnny,' I said, gently shaking his shoulder. 'I woke up this morning in love with you.'

John smiled that huge, brilliant smile of his. He pulled me tight, and without a moment of hesitation, he said, 'Marry me.'

I didn't agree to marry John, well, not that morning, but true to form, the campaign of wearing down did immediately commence. His proposals were frequent and inventive, and he didn't seem concerned about who might be watching. In Montreal, while crossing Rue Sainte-Catherine, I turned around and there he was on one knee in the middle of the busy street. Unbothered with the oncoming traffic, blasting horns and curious onlookers, John's arms stretched wide, as he said, 'I love you, Ford, marry me.' When I told him to get up, and that he was going to get us killed, some woman said something to John in French. She then threw a scowling glance my way, which I interpreted as, 'Young man, you can do better, let her go.' In the kitchen, stirring the tomato sauce over the stove, 'Ford, marry me.' Grocery aisles, on set, in front of friends, in front of strangers. I watched as people around us in a busy, loud restaurant went into an excited, anticipatory silence seeing him kneeling beside our table. Taking my hand, John shared his enthusiastic and romantic proposal with the crowd. This was followed by the crushingly awkward stares of sympathy cast John's way when I jumped in to say, 'Don't worry about it, folks, he does this all the time.'

On her way out, a woman put her hand on John's shoulder and politely suggested he might want to try it with a ring next time.

I don't know if I could adequately describe my stupefaction when I heard John squeal one night while making dinner. I mean *squeal*, like a little girl discovering a basket of kittens. An ad for *Speakers Corner* was on; a weekly 30-minute TV show where random people recorded 60-second videos outside the local television studio. It was a sort of early precursor to YouTube. Every Sunday night the station would broadcast the best of the *Speakers Corner* videos. So not only did John and his buddies singing a chorus of The Partridge Family's 'I Think I Love You', followed by what was now his signature, 'I love you,

Ford, marry me,' make the weekly show, but the network ran it as a promo all week.

John showed no awkwardness in asking this same question over and over. A question most men would find nerve-wracking asking once. No pride was damaged, or ego bruised, nor did my casual 'John, please stop' or 'Can you get up, everyone is staring' seem in any way to decrease his enthusiastic pursuit. Nor did he get discouraged by the lack of any affirmative responses. He'd defend his proposals and their frequency, telling everyone gleefully the same thing, 'She hasn't said yes, but ... she hasn't said no.' This was true.

I think it's essential to add here that I wasn't trying to be a dick or mess with his head or play impossibly hard to get. But my failed marriage to Brandon had taught me the excruciating lesson that never again should I get married unless I was categorically, without-a-shadow-of-a-doubt certain. I would absolutely not be the girl with two failed marriages. But I could feel what was happening inside of me. With John's charming, determined and inventive proposals, I was being romantically eroded, à la John Cusack and his boombox in Say Anything, and I knew it.

The idea of the 'Yes' T-shirt was born out of John always trying to tie even the most banal of my actions into an affirmative 'Yes, I will marry you.'

'You took a bite of my doughnut. Does that mean "yes"?'

'You're playing The Cure. I love that song. Does that mean "yes"?'

I'd answer all his inane stretches with, 'No, that does not mean "yes". "Yes" means "yes".'

When I finally decided that I loved this man so much that I wanted to be with him forever, the idea of creating a T-shirt with the word 'YES!!!' ten inches high across my chest seemed like a good one. Marie was right. I couldn't just respond to one of his many random marriage proposals with 'Enough already, get up off the floor, I will marry you.' As I was in LA for a shoot, the wardrobe stylist was only too happy to help me get the T-shirt made, especially when I told her its purpose. So that morning, when I boarded the plane from LA to Toronto, I was wearing black jeans, a linen blazer and a white T-shirt with the word 'YES!!!' most prominently displayed in large bold black capital letters.

Coming out of the arrivals gate, I nervously looked around for John. My blazer was buttoned, my computer bag and hand-bag were slung over my shoulder, and I was pulling my carry-on. For all the ways John kept looking for the answer 'yes' in everything I did, I thought this was perfect and unmistakable. I'd throw open my blazer, and I wouldn't have to say a word. He'd see YES, and he would immediately grab me by my waist with both hands. He'd lift me high in the air and spin me around in a euphoric celebratory twirl. As he would slowly lower me back to the ground, one leg stylishly kicked up behind me, I'd notice a tear in his eye. There would be an unrivalled airport kiss. The kind of kiss that would make people surrounding us cheer and a random woman need to enviously dab away happy tears uncontrollably rolling down her cheeks.

But that's not exactly how it went down. What I didn't count on at the time were two things. The first: Canada was preparing for a nationwide referendum about whether Quebec should separate from the rest of the country. There was heavy campaigning and signage everywhere, representing both sides, with slogans like: 'My Canada Includes Quebec, vote NO.' Or 'Vote Yes or *Oui* for Quebec leaving Canada.' The country was filled with signs that just read 'Yes' or 'No'. The second: I didn't count on John taking me for a political spokesperson.

My heart rate tripled as I walked through the sliding doors at the busy arrivals gate. My mind flashed backed to our first meeting at the Royal York Hotel. Could that have been only eighteen months ago?

'Ford, Ford,' he said, waving his arm like he was hailing a cab. 'Missed you,' he said, kissing me and lifting my heavy computer bag off my shoulder.

I looked at him, almost paralysed where I stood. This was it. The big moment, the massive reveal. He started to make his way towards the exit when I stopped him by gently tugging on his sleeve. Very nervously, I said, 'Wait! I have a gift for you. Actually, it's something for both of us.'

He looked around, waiting, like maybe I had something to pull out of my pocket. Slowly I unbuttoned my blazer and nervously revealed the message on my T-shirt. My heart was pounding so hard I was convinced it was making my T-shirt flutter rapidly. There it was, 'YES!!!', exclamations marks and all, in ten-inch high letters across my chest. Impossible to misinterpret.

There was a blank expression on John's face, as if he was still waiting for the surprise.

Silence. He looked confused.

Crickets. If we'd been standing in a field, we'd have been drowned out by crickets.

I looked straight at him and then lowered my eyes to my T-shirt and then back to him again. *Come on, John, you can work this out,* I thought in nervous bewilderment … and in that second, his face started to change. A cautiously optimistic smile took over, his eyes widening, sparkling like that night by the fire. Slowly, carefully and for what would be the very last time, he asked, 'Wait … does this mean "yes"?' Overcome with what seemed like the most prolonged, cavernous moment in my whole existence, I burst out with complete happiness, 'Yes!!! "Yes" means "yes".'

As we both immediately burst into tears, I asked emotionally, 'What took you so long to get it?'

He beamed and cried, 'I thought you had gone all political.'

We bought a fantastic run-down rooming house a few months before our June wedding, which we started restoring. It was the kind of place you'd expect to find Nancy Drew cautiously creeping around with a flashlight. It had incredible floor-to-ceiling wood-panelled rooms, and five ceramic mosaic fireplaces that had likely not been used in half a century. Phantom rug shadows, which lay dark against the quarter-cut oak floors, reminded me of police chalk outlines indicating where a dead body had lain. After a long day at the office, we'd come home, order Chinese or Italian, often eating directly out of the containers just to save time. We'd change our clothes and resume scraping off layers of century-old wallpaper. I'd climb into bed wiping away the grit and plaster from the bottoms of my feet like sand from the beach, too tired to bathe or shower. It was a magical year.

We quickly became *that* couple. Super annoying, believed we had invented sex, scoffed at Byron, Keats and Shelley for not being romantic enough, and criticised Leonard Cohen thinking he had nothing on us when it came to passion. All that was missing was a sappy musical soundtrack and we'd look like almost every rom-com movie montage of two lovers first discovering each other: walking dewy-eyed, hand-in-hand in the park, or a sickly cute eating scene where ice-cream or froth from a cappuccino gets playfully dabbed on someone's nose. We were that obnoxious. We glowed in the dark. It's the kind of happiness one doesn't feel worthy of, when it feels like at any moment, with a stroke from the great equalising universe, all could be taken away.

Within seven months of the 'YES' T-shirt, we were married. It was a small gathering on Nantucket, where John's mother, Lynda, and stepfather, Michael, had a little beach house. I was 33 years old, getting married for the second time. This time I didn't have that feeling of *What the fuck am I doing?* as I walked towards John. Nor did my father have any issue walking me down the cobblestone 'aisle' in John's mother's lovely backyard. I confidently walked towards John as the happiest of brides. *I love him, I love him, I love him,* I thought, *and he loves me.* I turned to Annie, John's stepmother, at some point during the day and, with complete conviction said, 'If I can't make it work with John, I can't make it work with anyone.'

Something I do wonder now, looking back, is if maybe that earnest statement was an inadvertent dare to the universe.

Everything was fantastic. Our intertwined careers were soaring, and I could not recall a time in my life when I'd been so happy, so in love, and so entirely and utterly content. I had everything I'd ever wanted. Well, almost everything. This brings me to what I can only describe as a magical moment in my life, that second bolt of electric awakening. I was hit with a surge of energy so intense, so extraordinary, that it woke me up like an earthquake in the middle of the night. My eyes snapped open, and with the confidence of an evening news anchor, a voice inside my head said, *I'm pregnant.* John was ecstatic, we both were, and as you might imagine, he devised many creative ways to celebrate. By far the most memorable came six months later in Las Vegas, when John surprised me with a second wedding after a shoot for Diet Pepsi.

Now, if anyone wants a fantastic, perverse glimpse into America's underbelly, may I suggest an Elvis-themed wedding in Vegas. In the most unfortunate dress, which took, I believe, its inspiration from flesh-coloured tensor bandages and a surplus supply tent, all 500 pounds of me waddled towards John in the Graceland Wedding Chapel. John was beaming from the altar, standing beside a justice of the peace as old as Jesus and looking like Tammy Faye Bakker. An Elvis impersonator, clearly channelling Elvis's latter years, walked me down the aisle, singing 'Can't Help Falling in Love'. John's face radiated the kind of love I could physically feel bouncing around inside of me. *My life will never be boring with this man,* I thought. I was almost 34 years old, pregnant, in what would likely go down as the most unique wrap party the Pepsi clients had ever attended. I wasn't sure if I believed in soulmates, but how could John not be mine if I did? I was off-the-charts happy, madly in love, and unlike Jackson, the only thing John seemed addicted to was me.

'I plan on marrying you over and over again,' John said as I reached his side. 'I'm thinking someplace really tacky next.'

'Tackier than this?' I laughed, looking around at the surreal Elvis-inspired chapel.

'Ya,' he said. 'I'm thinking glamour shots, the Mall of America and Taco Bell.'

I laughed. I knew he was serious.

I think that's the last time I remember John loving me like that. In three months, everything would change. We would be three, a family, and that's when it all started to fall apart.

CHAPTER 4

God Is a Nerdy Man Who Never Got Laid at Uni, or Shit Nobody Tells You

'Anything you think is wrong with your body at the age of thirty-five you will be nostalgic for at the age of forty-five.'
Nora Ephron, *I Feel Bad About My Neck: And Other Thoughts on Being a Woman*

Suppose one ever needed evidence that God is not a woman. In that case, you'd have to look no further than what happens to a woman's body after it acts as a host to a foreign parasitic entity we call a baby for nine months, one that is forcibly pulled, pushed, cut or ripped out of what once was your tight, beautifully maintained, Brazilian-waxed vagina. Sure, as women, we have the incredible experience of creating and growing life in our bodies, and once you get past the likelihood of morning sickness, adult acne, haemorrhoids, raging heartburn, crippling fatigue and uncontrollable flatulence, one might even start to enjoy it.

As the female body goes through irreversible changes, including sagging empty breasts, loosening vaginas, vanishing waistlines and little white scars that criss-cross our bodies like a city roadmap, one must look at the total injustice. That men have actually burned calories with their whole contribution to the 'miracle of life'.

I was raised in a household that celebrated beauty. Let's start with my mother, a former beauty queen and fashion model, who went on to have a stupendously successful career as a celebrated fashion photographer, which spanned decades. A smorgasbord of the world's most beautiful people paraded through my child-hood living room, much like a *Vanity Fair* afterparty, colourfully broadcasting two messages: be beautiful and be a feminist. You'd think that one would contradict the other, that they'd be mutu-ally exclusive. Or at the very least that there would be a healthy element of scepticism about whether these two seemingly oppos-ing belief systems could co-exist: the successful career-wielding feminist and the girl who subscribes to *Vogue* and now gets her eyebrows microbladed. But somehow, both messages came across as invaluable life lessons. After all, don't forget that I was the girl who had the world's shortest career as a PA, all due to one sensational ensemble.

Much like musicians' children grow to appreciate Mozart's 'Symphony No. 40 in G minor', or a complex Hendrix guitar riff, I grew to appreciate the power of beauty. I have always enjoyed the compliments I've received for a sensational dress I've worn well, or for an ensemble where everything right down to my Chanel Rouge Coco lip gloss sparkled. To clarify, I don't subscribe to the vacuous attitude that we have nothing more to add to the world than a perfect eyebrow arch or an ass you can crack an egg on, although, the Kardashians have built an empire on precisely that. And sure, one might accurately accuse me of having too many pairs of impractical shoes, but you know what? I earned the money to pay for every heel that has ever borne my fluctuating weight, and I will not apologise for that. I've worked hard trying to like what I see in the mirror, although there are certainly days I'd best describe my style as 'I never intended to get out of the car'.

But being beautiful doesn't belong to me; it doesn't belong to any of us. Instead, it is merely on loan. Youth didn't teach me that beauty is fleeting; ageing is responsible for that lesson.

And if anyone under the age of 30 is reading this, as Nora Ephron said, 'Go, right this minute, put on a bikini, and don't take it off until you're 34.'

I gained a whopping collective 103 pounds with both pregnancies – proof to the world that I deprived myself of absolutely nothing. I had 24-hour cravings for Rice Krispies treats, which I'd sometimes consume so quickly I'd burn the roof of my mouth on the hot, sticky marshmallow mixture, incapable of giving it three minutes to cool down. Or I'd pour an entire box of Lucky Charms cereal into a giant bowl and one by one pick out the tiny, magically delicious pink hearts and green clovers. I developed a weird aversion to poultry limbs, so extreme that I once had to leave a restaurant after seeing a duck leg on someone's plate as I walked to my table. And my new extraordinary bloodhound sense of smell would mean I could find sensory offence from the odour of water holding a fresh bouquet of flowers sitting in the next room.

I felt like my body and brain were hijacked and at the wheel was an irate madwoman with a tendency for foods made from marshmallows. I wasn't one of those glowing, sexy pregnant women either. You know the bitches: they smell like an Aveda spa and carry so perfectly with that round, basketball belly neatly in front of them that you can't tell from the back of the yoga class they are pregnant. Nope, I was pregnant in my ass, and I didn't glow, I sweated, like a prize-winning Sumo wrestler eating chillies in a sauna.

Twenty-four hours after giving birth to Samantha, my reaction was 'Linda Blair-esque', according to one of the hospital nurses, when I stepped on the scale. This after a two-and-a-half-day labour, painfully pushing out an eight-and-a-half-pound baby, a shit the size of a Mini Cooper that I left on the table, and whatever else got flushed out.

'Ten pounds?' I screamed in incredulous agony. 'I only lost ten lousy fucking pounds?'

Doing the math, I still had 42 pounds to lose. That was the equivalent weight of a fully formed six-year-old human child. It marked the first in a long line of fits of weeping and pathetic diatribes about how much I hated my body.

Maybe I shouldn't have been so hard on myself and my post-baby body, which I not only didn't recognise but which repulsed me. And perhaps my reaction was no different to a teenager's hysterical meltdown on finding a zit on her otherwise flawless face just before a party. And sure, my issues with my body couldn't be solved with a dab of Clearasil, but this was only a phase in my development. It's a path we travel on to get from one stage in life to another, not the final destination.

Of course, sex took on a completely different 'vibe' to the crazy, spontaneous shagging that had got me pregnant in the first place. I guess this is the part where I over-share with unfiltered honesty about what it's like to have sex after pushing out a baby with a head the circumference of a county-fair-prize-winning melon. I was looking forward to having sex again much like one would look forward to an un-sedated colonoscopy. Six weeks, we were told. Six weeks before you can start having sex again. By that time, I should no longer have needed to be sitting on a bag of frozen peas to reduce the swelling from where I'd been ripped from one tender opening to the other. By then, the many stitches that had reattached my privates' two hemispheres should have been pretty much secure, and with a bit of luck, my cracked, walnut-sized nipples would have scabbed over to contain their bleeding. Of course, I hadn't had three consecutive hours of sleep since I'd accidentally fallen asleep in the bathtub. I regularly smelt of sour milk, vomit and baby shit, something my nose had entirely stopped smelling, for survival purposes. But sure, let's have sex.

I knew I needed to get back on that horse. I like sex. No, I love sex, but this upcoming experience had all the eroticism of a pelvic exam. My ground rules, and you've gotta know there were ground rules, were the following:

Complete blackout darkness.

Missionary position only.

Be generous with the lubricant.

Eyes must never drop below my chin.

And if I say stop, you'll have to be content with a well-meaning handjob.

I lay there afterwards, staring up at the ceiling and thought, *Not only is God not a woman, but he's a nerdy, vengeful, dejected man, who never got laid at university.* The best way to describe it would be to compare it to a chickpea rattling around inside an empty tin can. Where is that written in the pages of *What to Expect When You're Expecting?* I could've benefitted from a little heads-up.

If I could go back in time, I'd give my postpartum self a serious clap upside the head. I'd tell her with unfiltered honesty, 'For fuck's sake, Christina, chill. Look what you've created. Look at those tiny perfect humans you grew inside of you. Be kind to yourself, don't compare yourself to your beauty queen mother, don't compare yourself to anyone. You'll once again proudly rock a bikini, you'll shimmy into your skinny jeans, and you will dare to have sex with the lights on.'

After having a baby it's hard figuring out who you are as a couple, as you desperately navigate through those early years of late-night feedings, walking-dead fatigue, shifted priorities and a non-responsive libido. It's the most significant, earth-moving shift one can have in their life, and young couples everywhere are thrown into the new uncertain world of parenting overnight. But I held on to the belief that what John and I were going through was common. Couples everywhere manage to come out of it stronger, more in love or, more succinctly put, as 'a family'. But that didn't happen to us, and very sadly, that didn't happen to me.

A few months after Samantha was born, I hired a personal trainer. Dominic came to the house twice a week to start me back on the long road of reclaiming my pre-baby body. Dominic, no more than 25, with arms the size of giant sequoias, knew absolutely nothing about training postpartum women, and had to deal with me, a woman who knew very little about her body and its new limitations. My sessions were unwisely scheduled just an hour before Samantha's feeding time. Thus my breasts were like massive, pressure-packed zeppelins, making up a good third of my body weight. With the training regimen of Muhammad Ali, Dominic handed me a skipping rope, took out his stopwatch and said, 'OK, three minutes: go.' I don't know how long I was skipping. I just know that as my enormous zeppelins slammed hard against my chin, something crackled, popped then snapped. I screamed out. My premature attempt to get my body back in shape had thrown out my back.

For about two weeks, I required physical help getting in and out of bed. I'd have to have Samantha brought to me, gingerly laid on top of me like a small sack of flour, feed her lying on my back, then she would have to be lifted off. I refused to take any painkillers as I didn't want my milk tainted with drugs. Nor did I want to abandon the idea of breastfeeding which, at the time, I have to say was not coming easily. I knew that this was super important from everything I had read, at least for the first six months. *Dear God, pleeeease, I have to make it through the first six months. Don't let me fail so immediately as a mother. There will be plenty of opportunities for failure throughout her life.*

It was then that I saw it for the first time – a moment that danced with a warning, like the flame on the head of a match. I was called 'selfish'. John found my bedridden state a personal annoyance and an unnecessary inconvenience. Because I couldn't move on my own after our lovely new nanny Fernanda left for the day, in the evenings the task of bringing Samantha to me fell to John.

'You're being selfish, Ford,' he said, handing me our screaming daughter one night. 'You'd be up and about if you took a few painkillers.'

'How's that selfish?' I asked, honestly.

'It's selfish because all you can do is lie on your back and I have to drop everything just because you refuse to take a few pills or crack a can of formula.'

John left the room as Samantha eagerly latched on. I watched her sweet, small face happily tuck in, reminding me of a nursing kitten, milk surrounding her perfect, tiny mouth. With sadness, I thought, *How can your daddy not put your needs before his own?*

CHAPTER 5

Death by a Thousand Cuts

*'Love doesn't die a natural death. Love has to
be killed, either by neglect or narcissism.'*
Frank Salvato

When two people first fall hopelessly and passionately in love, when they can't keep their hands from ravaging every part of each other's delicious bodies, when they stare deep inside each other's very souls and only see perfection, how are they to know whether they'll make good parents? I compare the decision to have kids to getting a face tattoo: you have to be damn sure it's something you want. And there should be some sort of questionnaire you fill out, a true-or-false test, and perhaps a thousand-word essay, 'What It Means to Be a Parent', before you make the biggest decision of your life, bringing home the world's worst roommate to live with you for the next eighteen years.

I often asked out loud, usually in a crazed, fevered state, struggling, without a single blasted clue what I was doing, 'Where's my owner's manual? My kids have come without an owner's manual!' But the hope or the greater understanding is that new parents figure it out as they go, together. They shift their priorities; they give up that party they were looking forward to when their child spikes a fever; they spend endless hours going from store to store trying to find that sold-out Tickle Me Elmo their child has asked Santa for. A parent's life, in large part, belongs to someone else, the tiny dictators, as I've lovingly come to call them. Becoming a parent is a long-term invest-ment, full of sacrifices, into the most essential, extraordinary, important asset in your life, your children.

John and I agreed on having two or three kids. Jokingly, his reasons were that if you have one child and you lock them in the basement, it's child abuse, but if you have two and lock them in the basement, they're playing. But after that, we pretty much disagreed on everything else. In every single aspect, in every stage of their life, be it baby, toddler, child or repugnant teenager, we disagreed. Maybe it was because John was away so much, and he never got used to the grunt work of child-rearing and was more likely looking for friends, playmates. He wanted the fun, playful side of raising kids, not the part that required discipline, curfews, rules, boundaries, time-outs and consequences. And who can blame him? So John took on more of the qualities of a part-time playmate with our daughters. A fun, crazy Disney dad, which fed my resentment at always tak-ing on the disciplinary role. I was the miserable, nagging voice of unreason, the parent of three instead of two. I regularly felt like screaming, 'I was a girl before I was your mother, and I too was fun once.'

Parenting is difficult, but when you have someone like Peter Pan contradicting your every move, well, that's how the wine industry is kept alive. It allows moms like me to self-medicate in a socially acceptable environment, like the Four Seasons lobby bar, or the bathtub. Some of our most epic fights were consistently grounded in our vastly different parenting ideals, and with that, the activities that accompanied them. Perhaps, as a mom, I just wanted to cover my kids in bubble wrap until they were eighteen. Even now, I still feel a pang of nervousness when my daughter Sam, now 24, grabs her roller-skates and tells me she's heading out for a couple of hours. Maybe I worry too much. But if that's the case, John didn't worry enough, or that's how I saw it.

He would take four-year-old Sam, much to her delight, for rides on the back of his Indian Chief motorcycle. He fashioned a slide from flattened grocery boxes covered in green garbage bags, so that he and the children could race each other down our staircase. As soon as I stopped the race, John led the girls in a collective chant of 'Mommy is mean! Mommy is mean!' Our second-born, Briar, had barely mastered walking when I realised I had the only two little girls, still with all of their baby teeth, who knew Hooters had the best curly fries in the city. Sam, by age thirteen, could blow perfect smoke rings, as taught by her father at a hookah bar he'd regularly take them to. And both girls, Sam fifteen, her sister twelve, upon returning from visiting their dad in LA, were detained by Canadian customs because inside Sam's suitcase they found a 40-ounce bottle of vodka in the shape of an assault rifle (a gift from her dad). This resulted in their NEXUS card being immediately revoked.

John drilled holes and installed climbing holds 30 feet high into a huge old maple tree in our backyard to create a mini rock-climbing wall. But instead of having any safety cords or belays permanently attached, it was a climbing free-for-all most of the time, purely relying on someone standing below, arms wide, calling up, 'I gotcha,' if someone fell. Sam climbed so high one time to show off her skills to a little school friend. From the kitchen I heard her screaming and looked out to see her paralysed in fear clinging to the side of the tree like a tiny kitten, unable to find her way down. She must've been twenty feet in the air as I frantically searched for a ladder.

News of Sam's rock-climbing tree travelled quickly through her school. This resulted in a few parents refusing to let their children come over and play until John removed the easily reached climbing holds. John's reputation as a 'fun dad' even resulted in some parents denying their children playdates or sleepovers if he was going to be left alone without 'adult supervision'. And that hundred-year-old maple, as it happened, bled to death from all those holes he drilled into the trunk, and cost \$2,500 for an arborist to bring it down. But only after a lengthy Agatha Christie-worthy investigation by the City, in which I had to prove that we hadn't deliberately murdered the maple. I could go on. Having John in the house was like having a third child with an American Express Gold Card and a driver's licence, whose frontal lobe, I was convinced, had never adequately developed.

There were last-minute cancellations for playdates or Dad weekends that left me with indelible heartbreaking images of two tiny girls sadly rolling their small Disney princess suitcases back to their rooms. In many ways, John held steadfast to who he'd always been: becoming a parent didn't change him or his lifestyle. Maybe I changed too much.

Was this what was waiting for us at the arrivals gate that day I wore my 'Yes' T-shirt? Tiny dictators, who came with a transport truck packed with needs, wants and demands, clutching in their little human fists two-thirds of my heart and one-third of my brain? Because if we had known all this chaos was to come, I would all but guarantee that John would've taken one look at that T-shirt and boarded the next plane to anywhere the hell outta there, and I would've bought his ticket.

I could write a thousand pages about the highs and the lows of my marriage to John. Perhaps I don't possess the objectivity that makes my account of the relationship unbiased or even worth reading. I can only tell you what I observed, how I felt, and how I reacted. I grew impatient with the sounds of crying, including my own. I was quick to snap and lose my temper.

I was trying to balance the working mother's demands all the time, convinced that everything I was doing was a complete and utter failure.

There was also darkness, a heaviness I was experiencing. Looking back, it was more than being overworked or exhausted. It was darker, scarier. Some days it felt like I was holding back the walls of a dark, lifeless room, closing in on me from all directions. I was screaming for something or someone to flip a switch and stop the encroaching walls from crushing me. A heavy cloud surrounded me, blocking out the sunlight, creating a constant, haunting feeling of dread that I could not shake.

I don't recall postpartum depression being as widely discussed back then as it is today. This was before Scientologist Tom Cruise declared publicly to Brooke Shields that prescription medicine for postpartum depression was unnecessary and that women could simply resolve any imbalance with vitamins. Like Cruise would know what it felt like to push a cantaloupe out from the end of his tiny penis. I'm an absolute believer in whatever drugs are required to get me through the vigorous pain of childbirth. I've often defended my choice to those pregnant purists with their doulas and home-birthing plans by comparing it to voluntarily having a dentist drill deep into your gums without Novocain. If it suits your purpose, sure, you can deliver that fourteen-pound baby in a warm pool of lavender-infused Evian water, accompanied by the looping sounds of gentle whale song to distract from the agony, but not I. John was given one task and one task only when I went into labour. To locate the anaesthesiologist immediately, and, if possible, to order my epidural from the parking lot. I knew my limitations.

But even if postpartum depression had been discussed in any real way, I most certainly would've dismissed it, as I seemed an unlikely candidate. What did I, a Type-A, financially sound

30-something mom, have to be depressed about? It wasn't until my girlfriend Lizzie had to check herself into a hospital after her second child's birth that I started to get it. Lizzie was so profoundly tormented with this 'black dog', as she called it. Suicidal thoughts that she never could have fathomed began to plague her. She was a happy, brilliant, successful executive with big-dick energy. I remember thinking, *Wow, if this can bring down Lizzie, no one is safe*. I'd been naive, or just uninformed, thinking that because I was a strong, accomplished woman, I was immune to that kind of depression. I've only recently learnt to forgive myself for not knowing what I didn't know before I learnt it. Thank you, Maya Angelou. So, as they say, I soldiered on.

I was under no misguiding illusions that John and I were the only young couple on the planet having difficulty adjusting to parenthood. I knew enough to know that I loved him. I loved our children and believed that eventually, we would create a new normal, with date nights, uninterrupted sleep and hot passionate sex. John optimistically told me over and over, 'Ford, we're just stuck in a rut. You and the girls are everything to me.' I held on to those words like they were a life raft.

But as the months passed and I was working hard to run a company, raise a baby or two, looking to find time and energy to shave my other leg, things became vastly different. There was an unkindness to John that took hold. My mother called it cruelty. At first, the body-shaming was presented as a joke, private and casually lobbed digs, small and thin like paper cuts. He'd put his arm around me and squeeze the fleshy folds around my waist: 'Yo, I guess there's now more of you to love.' Or after sex: 'You were jiggling like Jell-O, but don't worry, I like Jell-O.' But then the comments started to escalate from little private digs thinly disguised as humour to all-out humiliating public assaults. He'd accuse me of not having a sense of humour or of being too sensitive. I'd frequently tell him he had no 'off' switch, no filter. His stepmother, Annie, witnessed John's cruelty one night at an awards ceremony. 'Shut the fuck up, John,' she yelled twice, after he colourfully shared with the table how my breasts looked like 'deflated cow udders,' then continued by asking if anyone could recommend a good plastic surgeon so I could 'get them puppies fixed'. I felt humiliated, ashamed, and my usual strong voice was meek and quieted from depression. Just like with his proposals, John was relentless, unstoppable, only this time it was death by a thousand cuts.

It wasn't enough that I was hard on myself – no one is harder on me than me. But you should never have to tell someone you love to treat you nicely. I don't remember how I handled things back then, as no one has ever accused me of not being able to defend myself, but I do recall I didn't like myself much. I had developed a distinctly unfeminist dependence on John's approval, losing complete faith in the power and the beauty of my body. Through John's assaults, I was seeing myself through his lens. So, with the understanding of controlling what I could, and as a feminist raised in a household of beauty, I thought it was time for a good old-fashioned kick-in-the-ass makeover.

CHAPTER 6

The Swan and the Giant

'A woman who cuts her hair is about to change her life.'
Coco Chanel

There may be a better place to solve all the world's problems, to do one's best thinking, than in the bath, but if there is, I've not found it. As I lay soaking in my tub one evening, looking down at my naked body under a thin film of bubbles, I had sudden thought of, *Enough is enough*. It had been about a year and a half since my youngest daughter Briar's birth, but my body still looked like it belonged to someone else – a sort of *Invasion of the Body Snatchers*. I must have been carrying an extra 25 pounds of 'baby weight', although that baby was now a toddler capable of giving me a manicure. Looking down to where my once-ample, bouncing C cups used to dwell, there were two deflated empty sacks of flesh floating in their place. I mean, they were honestly floating on the surface of the water like dead fish.

'They're badges of distinction', one Pollyannaish, doula-loving, let's-give-birth-on-a-trapeze mom friend said to me. She was referring to the wear and tear your body goes through for the privilege of bringing another tiny, beautiful human into this world. One of those moms who believes your children should tell *you* when breastfeeding is over. 'Wear those stretch marks proudly,' she trumpeted, before I told her to fuck off and unfriended her forever. That was a mantra I wasn't prepared to live with, especially coming from a woman who had frozen her placenta and had secretly incorporated it into her family dinners. Something had to be done. I needed to rehab my image.

I don't know if you ever saw an American TV show called *The Swan*? It was an extreme makeover show that took tired and rundown-looking women in their thirties and forties and transformed them like Cinderella's Fairy Godmother did for her. It was so extreme, with nose jobs, breast enhancement, liposuction, tummy tucks and hair extensions, that I'm certain that at the end of the process the contestants' family members would have had a tough time picking them out of a police line-up.

I wanted, no, I needed a change to empower me. I possessed all the glam and self-confidence of a ten-pound sausage stuffed into a five-pound casing. I needed to get back into what I like to call 'killer fighting shape'. To reinvent this mother of two, take back my power, have sex with the lights on. There's nothing like a good old-fashioned makeover to make a girl come to life.

The next three months looked something like this:

* 7:00am: Wake up. Skinny latte. Get Sam to nursery school. Leave Briar with the nanny. Go to work.
* Lunchtime: 90-minute yoga class. Two hard-boiled eggs.
* Snack: Atkins peanut butter bar.
* 6:00pm: Spin class with Abbey (a perky, size 00, high-Ariana-Grande-pony-wearing masochist).
* 7:15pm: Home. Kids, bathtime, books, bedtime.
* 9:30: Eat something high in protein, or if feeling lazy then another Atkins peanut butter bar.
* 10:00pm: Bath.
* 10:30pm: Watch *Chelsea Lately*.
* 12am: Bed.
* Repeat.

There was microdermabrasion for my skin and injectables for the very scary '11' frown crevasse now scored deep between my eyes. I even changed my fragrance, opting for the spicier Poison by Dior. I was committed, focused, and, one might even say, a little obsessed. About three months later, when I was about five pounds away from my self-imposed 'ideal weight', I made an appointment with a plastic surgeon for something in the category I affectionately call 'paint and bodywork'. This was a massive step. I was now going to take care of those dead floating fish. I decided that I'd do this when John was off on a big shoot in Tokyo. I wanted to surprise him, give him a mini-*Swan*-like reveal, restore 'the girls' to their former pre-breastfeeding bodaciousness.

I had one last thing left to sort out, and that was my hair. This was going to be the blonde icing on my freshly baked new-me cake. I strutted into the salon with my dark, dense, coconut-matting-like hair and a tear sheet of Meg Ryan as inspiration. I had two-thirds of my hair lopped off into a sexy, shoulder-length, *When Sally Met Harry* bob, and officially entered my blonde years. So, without the need of a team of experts, I manifested my own mini version of *The Swan*. John would be back in a few days from Tokyo, and I was excitedly ready to surprise him with a Christmas bombshell gift: new boobs, new hair … a new me.

It was late in the day, three weeks before Christmas. I was at the office getting ready to leave when I got a message from John. He had arrived in New York the day before, having wrapped the Tokyo leg of the multi-city campaign he was shooting. He'd be back home in a few days, and I was eager to see him, and for him to see me and my sassy new look.

John had purchased a bunch of items on eBay before he had taken off for Japan, mostly old cameras and lenses, as he had a passion for photography. Not untypically, John had not deemed the sellers' numerous and urgent requests for payment via email something he should've looked after before heading out on his lengthy international shoot. He asked if I would go on his computer in his office and respond to the half a dozen or so angry emails and organise payment.

With a list of the sellers scribbled on a piece of paper, I entered John's office and rolled up a chair in front of his large computer. One by one, I responded with apologies, authorised payment, and moved on to the next. As I got to the end, scrolling down through his inbox, there was an email with the subject 'Giant' that, for reasons I can only describe as instinct, I clicked on.

I started reading.

It began with a casual, business-like tone, discussing what time to meet in the lobby, location scout photos, and the upcoming day's agenda. I quickly ascertained that the correspondence was between John and his PA, whom the Tokyo production company had hired. I'm still not even sure why I felt compelled to read on, past the call times and location recces, but with the time it took to scroll down a page, there it was: my new life, my new reality, decided for me. Intimate utterances now informed me, assaulted me, destroyed me. In just a handful of words, everything had changed. The emails were littered with passion, intent and sexual purpose. The words fired off the page, assaulting me with a blinding, searing light, as my eyes agonisingly adjusted from the darkness I had been living in. Nausea flooded my body as the accumulating weight of the words buckled my knees, splintered my heart and forced the air from my lungs.

In my head, I could hear John's velvet voice, his playful teasing, whispering, purring, as if his breath was tickling the nape of my neck. Word by wretched word painted unimaginable, yet vivid images that ripped my soul apart. And the girl, whose face I could not see and whose voice I did not know, spoke in words I'll never forget, as she playfully called him Giant.

Trembling and struggling to focus, I got to the final email, dated two days before. It was the flight details of a business-class ticket from Tokyo to New York in her name. I sat there breathless, numb with the wretched sickness that can only come from betrayal. My world was now annihilated. Breaking down in front of the evidence, paralysed with grief, a voice inside my head silently screamed with unremitting, cruel honesty, *She is with him now ... She is with him now.*

'Giant' was less than six years after triple-digits marriage proposals and a 'Yes' T-shirt fluttering with anticipation. John knew infidelity was a dealbreaker for me, yet he'd asked me to dig through his emails when he hadn't even loosely buried the evidence. Maybe this was his exit plan. Perhaps this was how he'd planned to leave, with every speck of my being screaming, 'You cheating bastard, it's over.'

The following weeks were agonising, devastating, desperate. Like a wounded lion left bleeding, my howls were relentless and excruciating, as I lay immobilised with grief. As Christmas was so close, we'd wait until after the holidays to tell the girls, I insisted. I would not destroy their holiday with this crushing news. John stayed in the guest room with the plan that in early January, he'd move out. Ironically, any weight I hadn't been able to lose melted away almost instantly. The stress and sorrow of my broken marriage provoked a hunger strike much like I was an imprisoned suffragette. My frail little body was now a wire hanger for limp, baggy clothes.

When I sat down to tell my staff, I can't honestly remember if John was there or not. Their worried faces grouped around the long table where we'd all eat lunch together or celebrate a birthday with inappropriate anatomical cakes. I told them stoically that John and I were splitting up, that he'd continue to work at Imported, and that we'd make best efforts not to let it affect the day to day. Exactly how I was planning on doing that, I had absolutely no idea. My colleagues were my other family, children of a sort that needed reassurance that all would be OK.

John's remorsefulness seemed deep and he gave all the appearances of being sincere. His apologies were frequent, unrelenting and as passionate as all his pursuits. There were days of excruciating, painful conversations, tears, sadness, pleading for forgiveness and begging for 'one more chance'. So much of that time is blurred to me, as if someone spilt a glass of water, ruining a watercolour painting, as one thing bled with another.

'Please,' John said, not holding back the tears, 'please let me make this up to you, Ford, to you and the girls.'

There are volumes that fill libraries, well-researched books of why people cheat. Asking fundamental questions like 'Does monogamy make sense?' or 'Are people meant to be faithful forever?' I have two fundamental beliefs regarding infidelity that I would like to share with you. That's not to say there's nothing more about the subject I could rattle on about. Still, I understand, as a woman, a lover, someone who has been cheated on, and embarrassingly, someone who has cheated, that there are some basic fundamental rules for a monogamous relationship.

My first belief is a simple one. It doesn't contain any groundbreaking, enlightened way of thinking. Simply stated, if you or your partner crosses that obvious line where penetration of any orifice occurs outside your relationship, it is forever done. For me, this was a non-negotiable dealbreaker – a clear cut-and-dry crime possessing no possible forgivable explanation, no matter how genuine the remorse. Wipe the dirt off your hands at the side of the grave and walk away.

The second and more difficult belief I've come to understand about cheating is that rarely is the affair the cause of a relationship's breakdown, but rather a symptom of an already-broken relationship. It took me some time and much therapy to not only understand that philosophy but to feel it in my bones. Sure, there are exceptions, like the guy who is a chronic cheating scumbag who always thinks there's something better around every corner. The guy I'd further define as: 'Show me a beautiful woman and I'll show you a guy who is tired of fucking her.'

So what was I to do when something I'd seemed so sure of, so confident in, started to disintegrate like a loosely packed sandcastle, dissolving with every wave that rolled over it? In the beginning, we spoke in poetry, but that was lost to insults and revilement. He celebrated my body like a maestro, but that was abandoned to motherhood. I had never been so romantically pursued in my life, but it felt like the moment he got what he wanted, he didn't want it anymore. The moment we went from two to three, then to four, almost to the second, it started changing. What possible weight could my words or promises hold for myself in the future, as I recalled with the certainty of a born-again believer 'If I can't make it work with John, I can't make it work with anyone'? Was that it? Done? Had I confused obsession for love? Had he?

I was staring down my unbreakable rule of monogamy. This time there was something more at stake: in my case, two small girls under five. I know that many relationships have survived infidelity, but have they thrived? I have no way of knowing. I've heard so frequently that 'we stayed together for the kids' marriage cliché, but rarely have I seen the upside in that. A few almost tote their miserable, selfless sacrifice as some ultimate gift they gave their children. I'm one of those people who believe staying in a loveless marriage, mirroring for your children nothing more than an unemotional, unaffectionate coexistence, would be the last thing you should want to show your daughters. I also had too many friends who'd been fucked up by living with dysfunctional parents. No, if I was going to fuck up my kids, it would be through me trying to show them what a healthy, loving relationship looked like.

The fate of my marriage came from something my mother asked me. She was neither trying to keep me in my marriage nor pull me out. She simply asked one question that hung thick in the air like a dense fog, clouding all directions until answered. By the light of the Christmas tree, she put her arm around me and asked me to ask myself one thing: 'Did you do everything you could do, and the marriage still failed?' If I answered 'yes', she continued, I could leave my marriage and not be plagued later on with self-doubts of *If only I did this*, or *If only I did that*. If the answer was 'no', then I might go forward in life, always wondering if things might have been different had I only tried harder.

I thought about my role in my marriage, as a wife, a lover. I was trying as objectively as I could to take an honest inventory of my shortcomings, my many failures and my inability to acknowledge what clearly was depression. I loved John. I knew I did, but I was uncertain what that was worth anymore. How could this be the net result of two people in love with each other? I was in so much incredible, crippling pain that it hurt to breathe. I felt like I was standing on top of a burning building all the time, recalling that lit match that John had held as he'd called me selfish for the first time. Should I let the flames engulf me, or was there someone down below, beyond the smoke, waiting for me with a net? I was angry, crushingly sad, but as I said earlier, John's infidelity was not the cause of our marriage breakdown. It was a symptom of something else that was wrong. I sat surrounded by my ingrained beliefs about monogamy, cheating and crossing that unforgivable line. Battling with who I knew myself to be and what I felt I needed to do, trying to decide between walking away and trying harder.

Had I done everything I could, and my marriage still failed? It didn't matter how many times I asked myself that question or what justification I could effortlessly spin around it, the answer was always the same: it was a clear and undeniable 'no'. And no amount of pain, rage, or well-justified anger that I could torpedo towards John would alter that truth. So, doing what was likely one of the hardest things I have ever had to do, unsure if I was being brave or stupid, or if there was even a difference, I dug deep into my fragile soul and gave my marriage an honest, loving effort. I worked to reframe my fundamental thoughts on cheating and forgiveness. I found a psychiatrist who prescribed me 20mg of Celexa and a marriage counsellor we agreed to see regularly. This all with the understanding that we both held some element of responsibility.

When I finally had that conversation with John after nearly two months of his impassioned pleading, there was something about his response that should've been a giant red flag. In his hesitation is where I should have found my answer.

'Oh,' he said flatly. 'I've promised Adam I'd take his apartment, even paid the first month. What should I tell him?'

I looked at John, not understanding that after all his pleading, tears and promises to work it out, this would be the first thing he'd say.

'How about you tell Adam you made a bigger promise to me than you made to him?'

That was my darkest, most bitter of winters. My frostbitten fingers and shattered heart painfully let go of everything I'd thought my life would be. And now, with the anaesthetic of false hope, I waited for spring.

CHAPTER 7

A Mistake Made More Than Once Is a Decision

'There are some things you learn best in calm,
and some in storm.'
Willa Cather, *The Song of the Lark*

A few defining memories make up that final year from one Christmas to the next. We took a family vacation to Saint Lucia, where, having spent a stupid amount of money on sexy new lingerie and bathing suits, I paraded my tiny, lithe body in front of John *à la* Kathleen Turner in *Body Heat*. Her femme fatale character lured William Hurt into such a fever of lust and sexual desire that he smashed her window.

We had a lot of sex, most of which was too rough or animalistic to be described as makeup sex. For me, it was revenge sex in its purest form. Makeup sex could possess elements of forgiveness, gentleness, playfulness, redemption and even romantic overtones. That was not in my general wheelhouse at that time. Revenge sex is primal, punishing fucking, often in a public place like a restaurant bathroom or up against a dimly lit alley wall. If done correctly, it leaves both parties sweaty, without words, wondering, *What the fuck was that?* I needed to remind him of who I was before we had two children. Remind him and remind me. The condoms during sex were an unpleasant reminder that all was not quickly forgotten. Until his STD tests came back negative, the foil wrappers that he'd rip open with his teeth were like tiny inconvenient souvenirs of his time in Japan.

I started suffering from painful anxiety attacks. My throat and chest would constrict in agonising, deepening contractions. I discovered the scary magic of Ativan, a drug as essential to my mental health as my psychiatrist, or my new obsession with exercise. My routine was intense, frequent and punishing, as I pushed through the burn of heavy weights or used my pounding, accelerating heart rate to strangle the screaming voices inside my head. All of this was crucial to curb my urge to leap from the burning building that was my life.

Those early months were filled with couples therapy, weekly scheduled date nights when possible, and a gruelling work schedule. But as the months continued, John found excuses to make fewer appearances at our therapy sessions, citing work conflicts coupled with assurances of 'We're good' or 'You get more out of it than I do, Ford.' Some days I managed pretty well, and I was grateful that I was not drowning my pain in vodka, pills or assault eating. I had seen the ugly results that those choices wreaked on women who looked a lot like me. My fuse was uncharacteristically short. At the office I grew impatient with those who had difficulty finding practical solutions to what I deemed simple problems.

But there's one thing that stands out from that year, much like a natural disaster does in a weather forecast that promised sun. It's said that when a tsunami hits, just before its power-ful waves slam onto the shore, destroying homes and lives, the water retreats, leaving an eery stillness, a false sense of peace so reassuring it lures people further and further into the water, away from the shore. After months of our own false peace, I was standing in the kitchen, in front of John, when the tsunami came crashing in. A force so powerful it effortlessly and without conscience tossed me about and dragged me under.

My period had been a few days late. Rummaging around, I

found an old pregnancy test in the back of the bathroom cabinet. *Why not?* I thought, looking at the box. *Just to be sure.* As the very faint double blue line appeared, I stared in outraged disbelief at the positive result. *No, this must be a false positive,* I said to myself in a reasonably confident manner. This result had to be medically impossible, as I was on the Pill. I grabbed my keys, jumped in the car, and went to the drugstore to buy a new test. *Maybe these tests expire,* I thought. That had to be it. It was the only possible explanation.

A few days later, I was lying alone on the examination table at a Planned Parenthood office, feet in the stirrups. I was unabashedly sobbing, my chest heaving as a gentle older woman with kind eyes and a cold ultrasound wand was explaining my options.

'You're still within a couple of weeks of being able to terminate the pregnancy,' she said. 'If that is indeed what you want to do.'

When I was in high school, I remember thinking that if I was ever so careless as to get pregnant, then sure, I'd have an abortion. I'd even known a few girls who'd had them, and they had seemed to fare just fine – no permanent scarring, no lifelong regrets, as far as my limited scope could tell. My judgement around these girls was for their recklessness, having sex without birth control, or so I imagined. *I'll never be that careless,* I remember thinking. Lying on my back, the thin paper crackling around my ears, I pushed my fists hard into my eyes like a small child. I was married. I was a mother. I loved my children. I was not a sixteen-year-old girl. *No,* I thought as my tears dripped off my cheeks and onto the paper, *this is not that.*

This wrenching unscheduled visit had been precipitated by a brief yet gutting conversation a few days earlier when I'd told John I was pregnant. Standing in the kitchen, I'd heard his key slide into the lock. It was late, the house was quiet, and the girls were asleep. He must've gone to the fridge for a beer because, more than remembering what I said, I remember him standing on the opposite side of the kitchen island with a Heineken in his hand. My exact words are blurred, faded, but how many different ways could I have said, 'John, I'm pregnant'? Like a patient anxiously awaiting the results of a biopsy, I stood there, raw, in front of him. His chocolate-brown eyes that once danced with fire were doused with icy water. His words I remember as if it was this morning; they were brief, surgical, like a swift, deep cut slicing me open. In a moment when he could have chosen compassion or cruelty, he took no time to decide. Giggling with an uncomfortable, nervous laugh, he said with a certain air of annoyance, 'Your body, your choice, Ford.'

He sipped his beer, then added with disdain, 'Although I can't imagine wanting to have another baby with you.' With that, the conversation was over. In the other room, I heard the sound of CNN come on as he sat down to watch television.

I stood alone in the kitchen, clutching the island that had separated us a moment ago. I didn't cry. I was too weak to cry. I had lived so long with the idea of being strong, but I was now brittle, numb, a shadow of my former self. As I gripped the granite countertop I could hear the screams and moans my body was making, like a tin hut being slammed by a storm. It wasn't the sound of it being ripped apart, it was the sound of me desperately attempting to hold it all together, fighting like hell to stay in love. In that moment of shameful surrender, my exhausted, futile attempt to hold on gave way to being torn apart. All of me shattered, splintered and was pulled deep below the cold current as everything was swept away.

I'm genuinely uncertain how I got through that time. So much has been eradicated from my brain, as if a decision was made for me; it was simply too painful, too dangerous to grant those memories existence even one second longer than was absolutely required. The conflicted suffering consumed me in those grief-filled days, magnified every time I hugged my two beautiful daughters, whom I loved unconditionally. The guilt was septic, heavy, shameful, as I painfully came to terms with what I knew was my only option. The most gutting, aching, overwhelming observation, the source of my deepest pain, was recognising the vast chasm of comparison between the pure elated, celebratory joy we'd felt when we'd found out I was pregnant for the first time five years earlier, to where I now lay, alone in a stark, antiseptic examination room, with the feel of cold jelly sliding across my belly.

I can always tell the exact moment I fall in love with someone and, conversely, the exact moment I fall out. The word alone, 'fall', tells us immediately that we have no control. 'Captain Jack' softly serenaded me into love with John one rainy Sunday morning, and the smell of disinfectant as I wiped the gel off my belly propelled me out. Abortions won't let you forget. There was nothing left to try, as my mother had previously suggested. I could walk away, painfully resigned, knowing that I couldn't change the man or the outcome. I had run out of options and now motive. I wasn't sure exactly how I would leave, what door I would walk through, but the night of the office Christmas party, when I saw 'her', by the light of the exit sign, their fingers gently lingering, I knew that John had already blasted his way out.

A few days after that Christmas party, for a second time in our marriage, sexual declarations and desire-fuelled promises ran off the page and pummelled me in the chest. Words drenched in bile, laughing at my naivety, mocking my trust. Love letters to another, like seeds he'd scattered now seeking the light. You would think that he would have become more expert in deleting incriminating evidence the second time. I could only conclude that John wanted to be caught. Why else would he be so careless? I printed out these freshly unearthed emails in the middle of my hectic office. John, standing beside me, anxiously pacing, nervously giggling and nattering on about a new constitution for a country that no longer existed. In what's likely the world's most colossal cliché, he said, 'It's not what it looks like, Ford.' See, that's the thing, it is invariably exactly what it looks like. My marriage was over, and I held the unofficial decree in my hand. I was calm this time, detached, as I watched the pages spit out from the printer. If anyone in the office saw me as I collected those printed pages filled with sexual invitations, they'd simply assume I was gathering up some television scripts or a director's treatment.

My real reaction to the crushing end of our marriage was on its way. It came with my daughters' tiny, pained voices when we told them that Mommy and Daddy would no longer be living together anymore; images as enduring as family portraits, painfully seared into my mind and lying impossibly heavy on my heart. Briar, not yet three, silently clutched her love-worn blanket, as she rocked and comforted her Barbies. Samantha, almost six, sounded like a wounded baby animal, her painful plea, 'You have to try harder ... You have to try harder.'

I was devastated, knowing that this moment would be the only memory of their parents together that my daughters would carry into adulthood. They were too young to remember a single moment of happiness, but old enough to never forget this.

Reassuring them, I wept, 'It's not your fault. Mommy and Daddy love you tremendously, and yes, it's OK to cry.'

It came from the empty spaces in the drawers and closet where his clothes no longer took up space, the toothbrush holder with a single brush, or the large queen-size bed with one side always tucked in. The vacancies were crowded with him. It came in grievous, hurtful industry gossip, as it seemed that everyone in our shallow advertising pond relished the colourful, salacious details that this kind of breakup would provide. It came when John chose a 21-year-old dominatrix, eighteen years his junior, over me. It came when he married her. And it came again when they had two children.

There's a saying, 'An apology without change is just manipulation.' Giving John a second chance was like giving him a second bullet for his gun. It would take me a very long time to stop questioning what I often referred to as 'the lost year'. I couldn't stop wondering if I had gained essential insight to move forward when I took him back after Tokyo. Yet, over the years, I've come to ask my friends going through their breakups what my mother had asked me, eventually concluding that although painful, the year and its insights were not entirely wasted.

There is a lot I've left out about John, memories perhaps distorted with time or tales too long to tell. But as relentless and unyielding as John's pursuits were at the beginning, so would be our divorce. The same intensity I'd had for loving him, I now had for hating him, and I could safely assume that emotion was equally mirrored. Our untangling would span painfully over years, with separation agreements and affidavits he'd deliberately disregard, arrears in child support he had no intention of paying, and restraining orders when things became dark and scary. I don't know what signs I'd missed, or had blissfully ignored at the beginning. John had mastered the art of lying long before he'd met me, blending a perfect smile with a morsel of truth. Or, as John's ex-business partner once told me, 'John lies when he says, "Good morning".' Like Austen's George Wickham, with his handsome face and charming manners, 'he simpers, and smirks, and makes love to us all.'

John had a phrase he used with unusual frequency, right from the early days in our relationship, even before the darkness overtook us.

'One day, Ford, I'm going to open the cloak, and then you'll see what's underneath.'

To me, this immediately conjured Dickens's Ebenezer Scrooge as he meets the Ghost of Christmas Yet to Come. In the dark shadow of that holiday, the spirit opens his cloak to reveal two emaciated children named Ignorance and Want. When pressed for an explanation, John would smile and playfully dismiss it. My relationship with John began with the romantic promise of an Austen novel, but maybe it was more like Dickens, an apparition foreshadowing the future. Perhaps John knew exactly who he was and what he wanted, with his handsome face and his disarming charm, and I, I suppose, was both ignorant of the truth and wanting for love. Maybe he foretold our ending with his metaphoric cloak, opening it wide to show me what was hidden underneath, who he was. If that is true, then I suppose no one could ever say I wasn't warned.

The Book of

Blurry Men and Skinny Bitches

CHAPTER 1

How Stella Got Her Groove Back

'Either give me more wine or leave me alone.'
Rumi

I'm going to guess that the majority of divorces involve varying degrees of 'Hell on earth' suffering, and although my divorce from Brandon was painful, it was nothing compared to my elephant of a clusterfuck split from John. We were stitched together by two small children, heaps of expenses and a painful mistrust. But there was another element that pushed this split into a new, unprecedented level of agony: we still worked together.

For some reason, and please don't ask me why as I don't think I have a justifiable answer, we decided that my company would continue to represent John as a director. If I had to hazard a guess, I'd say that neither one of us was ready to let go of the one part of our relationship that had always worked well. I was somehow able to disconnect our work life from our personal life, at least for a time. The Warner Bros cartoon characters, Ralph and Sam, come to mind – the wolf and the sheepdog who had two totally different relationships in and out of work, one cordial and the other – well, they were looking to kill each other. I can't answer to how well I did as president of Imported Artists while working alongside the man who had effectively stomped on my heart with hobnail boots. Most of my work life was a frenzied blur of client pitches, pre-production meetings, shoots and temperamental directors doing their best to ignore approved budgets. But outside the office was a lot less blurry: I was a complete disaster.

'This is 40?' I cried. I mean, there were days when I seriously asked myself, *Why am I out of bed? Where did it go so off the rails?* I'd usually try and look for answers in my more alert, introspective moments, usually sometime between 3am and 5am. It had all unravelled. Like a much-loved hand-knitted jumper, I watched row after row of my life come apart, lying useless, a long, matted, twisted pile of yarn on the floor. I was unrecognisable to myself, a collection of cuts and bruises that had slowly drained my self-esteem. I was divorced not once, but twice. Twice! How I hated the sound of that. I didn't know if I had been picking the wrong men, or if there was something wrong with me. After all, I was the common denominator. I'd believed I was venturing forward with some super-practical hard-knock wisdom – avoid alcoholics and don't get married until I'm 100 per cent damn sure – yet here I was, single again, with two little girls, carrying with me a whole campervan full of new lessons.

Around that time, on the strong advice from just about everyone who loved me, I started seeing a new therapist, Nancy Pope. Nancy was thrust upon me by Lizzie and Marie, who – not unlike an episode of *Intervention* – had formed a barricade of two formidable 40-year-old women locked arm in arm with a well-rehearsed speech: 'Honey, you know we love you, but you're fucked up.' I started seeing Nancy weekly, and quickly felt at ease unloading intimate tales of my tragedy to a mild-mannered woman who looked a lot like Billie Jean King. Nancy had short, spiky jet-black hair (which looked like it could've been the last holdover from a much earlier goth phase), a calm manner, and a wardrobe that seemed best paired with Birkenstocks and woolly socks, no matter the season. Nancy rarely showed emotion, which I guess is what you're looking for in a therapist. She was the yin to my frequent 'someone might have to die for this' yang. I can't recall her laughing at my regular, vain attempts to get her to crack a smile behind her heavy-framed black eyeglasses. I tried not to take her lack of response as a personal affront, as even in the depths of despair I did think I was fucking hilarious.

Some days all she would have to say was, 'So, Christina …?' and like a horse bolting out of the gate, I'd ramble, rant and rage for an hour. This would be followed up by Nancy saying, 'Well, I think we need to stop here for today.' Glancing at my watch, I'd think, *Did I just speak nonstop for an hour? Am I paying her $200 to listen to me rant?* I mean, I could've done that at home with our new dog, Hunter (a surprisingly good listener). But it was worth it just to unload, as some days even with yoga, wine and girlfriends, I still wanted to slap somebody.

Nancy suggested I 'give myself permission', a phrase she liked to use, and take a break, a mini-vacation. Permission from a therapist is like getting a slip from the principal allowing you to skip school, and it was essential for me at that time in my life. I felt the tremendous relentless, punishing guilt that only a recently separated, single working mom can experience. My friend Maya suggested Canyon Ranch Spa as a perfect escape. Maya was a new friend I had made through the business, and possessed the qualities of a mama bear protecting her cubs, and I was grateful for her. At the same time, I felt she hadn't built up enough equity in the 'friendship bank' for her to witness, from an inner-circle vantage point, the complete garbage-fire that was my life. But regardless of whether Maya had earned her place in the front row of my breakdown, there she was, booking tickets for a much-needed vacation, and for that alone, I was immensely grateful.

Just the thought of a five-night escape to Canyon Ranch, a fabulous spa and wellness centre in Arizona, was lifting my heavy spirits. It was the perfect combination of hiking the beautiful Sabino Canyon, yoga, exercise classes and spa treatments. Hell, perhaps I'd even learn to meditate this time. And at the end of every day, all efforts would be duly rewarded with a chilled bottle of Chablis. It sounded perfect.

Perfect until I learnt that the ranch did not serve alcohol.

'Wait, WHAT?'

I knew their acai berry wheatgrass shots weren't going to cut it. These were times of great distress, and wine had become a welcome companion, like a hot-water bottle on a cold night. However, I did jubilantly praise someone at the ranch named Darlene when she told me over the phone that we could ask our driver on the way in to pick up alcohol for us, as long as we were 'discreet'.

I mentioned that Maya moved quickly into my inner friendship circle. She had not earned her way into that personal sanctum like Marie and Lizzie. So maybe, looking back, I should not have blindly trusted her. I mean, there are various reasons friendships end, right? Some friends just fade away for no real reason you can think of. I might find myself years later saying, 'I wonder what happened to Jeannie ...' Like she was a lost toy I had stopped playing with and hadn't seen in years. Some friends you simply grow weary of, discovering they're best enjoyed in micro-doses or require friendship sabbaticals from time to time. A few girlfriend breakups could result from something more jarring or dramatic. Perhaps one of you broke the girl code. In my younger years, this could've meant someone had slept with someone they shouldn't have (most likely someone's ex-boyfriend, or worse, their current one). That's usually hard to bounce back from and has been less commonplace as I've got older. Maybe because by the time we hit 40, we've already started to weed out the friends we don't require or who no longer serve us. The group becomes smaller, tighter, more loyal. We're not interested in surrounding ourselves with a stadium full of friends like we did in our twenties. Our tolerance for drama significantly lessens, much like when a round of tequila shots changes from being a generous gesture to a pain in the ass for everyone.

But what happened with Maya wasn't a breakup. It was abandonment.

Three days before our trip to Arizona, Canyon Ranch called me. They were looking for my flight details, to arrange a driver to pick me up from the airport. As I gave them my details, I mentioned that Maya would be on the same flight. There was a pause.

'Honey, I'm afraid your friend has cancelled her reservation.'

I deeply inhaled, 'Excuse me?' I said with shock and total confusion. 'Are you sure she's cancelled? We booked this together …'

'Yes,' the woman said, 'positive. I spoke to her myself two days ago.'

Two days ago? She'd cancelled this trip two days ago and hadn't told me? I wasn't sure if I was about to explode into a white rage or instantly dissolve into a quivering puddle on the floor. I mean, I was just barely holding my life together and it felt like it had the strength and durability of a house of cards in a hurricane.

'I'm sorry,' the woman said, sensing my confusion and shock. 'You might want to talk to your friend. But she has definitely cancelled her reservation.'

I put down the phone. I felt like I was drugged, disorientated. This didn't make any sense. If Maya had been having second thoughts, she'd have told me. It was Thursday, and we were leaving Sunday. I immediately called her, hoping this was all some sort of mix-up. I got her assistant, who said Maya was unavailable and asked if she could give her a message.

'Yes,' I said. 'Please have her call Christina right away. It's urgent.'

I hung up and immediately emailed her.

Hey Maya, I just got off the phone with Canyon Ranch, and they've told me you cancelled your trip. I know this can't be right. Please call me ASAP. Freaking out here. xo

I texted her. A whole day passed, and then another. I tried again and again. Not a single word. Nothing.

By Saturday afternoon, I still hadn't heard from Maya. I knew she was alive. She wasn't lying in a ditch somewhere with a massive bloody head injury, the only acceptable excuse. Here I was, only three months out from learning my cheating husband had left me for a 21-year-old dominatrix, and the entire advertising community were revelling in the intimate details. I was riding the crest of crushing depression, and it was becoming painfully clear that my new friend Maya had not only pulled out of the healing, therapeutic girls trip my therapist had given me permission to go on, but had ghosted me.

Saturday at 4:10pm, and less than 24 hours before my flight, Maya's name flashed on my phone. I picked up after one ring.

'What the fuck is going on?' I screamed into the phone.

'Hey, Ford, listen, I'm sorry,' she said, like she was apologetically talking to a waiter about returning an overcooked piece of meat. 'I changed my mind. Work's too insane, and I didn't want to upset you, so I was afraid to tell you.'

'You didn't want to upset me? ... Upset me?' I said, trying to catch my breath. 'In what part of this scenario, Maya, did you think you wouldn't upset me? I'm a fucking wreck, barely hanging on, and you know that. Why? Because you've got a front-row seat to the clusterfuck that is my life.

Now barely able to speak, I took a painful breath which I slowly and fragilely exhaled. I squeaked out, 'How could you do this? Three days, Maya! You cancelled your trip, didn't tell me, and then did not return my countless messages … for three fucking days?'

Maya was silent. I was in so much insufferable pain that my body started trembling.

'I'm really sorry, Ford, I am' she said meekly.

She knew no magical words could explain this, fix it, so that even the tiniest bit of it made sense. I got off the phone and collapsed on my bed. *I'm not going to get through this,* I thought. *Any of this.* Maya and I did not speak again for years.

As my plane touched down at Tucson International Airport, I only had one question running through my mind: what was I doing here all alone? I had just spent four hours on a plane, yet aside from brief interruptions from the unusually large man beside me sputtering awake from his sleep apnea, I remembered almost none of it. I stepped into the back of the waiting SUV with 'Canyon Ranch' stencilled on the doors. My driver introduced himself as Ronny. He was an older man, in his late sixties, with dark leathery skin, aviator sunglasses, and a sleepy Southwestern accent.

'Welcome to Arizona,' he said in a neighbourly manner. 'Is this your first time at the ranch?'

'Yes,' I said, staring out the window, too exhausted to meet his gaze in the rear-view mirror, 'first time.'

'Well, you're in for a special treat.'

Ronny went on cheerfully, sharing all the fabulous adventures awaiting me as I stared silently out the window. Outside were vast stretches of marmalade-coloured sandy fields and tumbleweed often drifted by, something I'd thought only happened in old Westerns. We passed an aviation graveyard scattered with thousands of rusted, skeleton-like remains of old aircraft that continued for miles, sticking up like tombstones against the vast, blue Arizona sky. Looking back from the window, I jumped into the first welcome break in Ronny's bubbly conversation.

'Hey, Ronny.' My eyes caught his in the rear-view mirror. 'Is there a place we can stop to get alcohol?'

'Yes, ma'am,' he said, and I felt his polite judgement. 'Just a couple miles down the road.'

'Perfect, Ronny. Thank you.'

The rest of the trip was silent. I guess Ronny had run out of things to tell me that he thought might genuinely interest me.

The SUV pulled into the palm-tree-lined driveway of Canyon Ranch. The buildings were all adobe ranch-style houses, painted in burnt sienna, with terracotta roof tiles. Rising 30 feet high, straight up from the dusty, parched earth like ancient monuments, were the saguaro cactuses. Closer to the ground and lining the coral cobbled paths, were barrel cactuses, desert sage and marigolds. The enormous skies were a shade of bright tropical blue so intense that it almost hurt your eyes to look at them. Something about the quality of light is different in the desert. It is crisp, clean, unfiltered, and everything the sun touches looks like it's been kissed by flames. I had never been to the desert before. The real desert: blocks of neon-lit casinos and endless all-you-can-eat restaurants in Vegas don't count. It was like what you would see on a travel brochure for a *Thelma and Louise*-themed adventure. Yet here I was, Thelma without Louise – or was I Louise? Whichever one of them didn't get with Brad Pitt, that was me.

I was greeted by the friendly, exceptionally tanned staff, all welcoming me with an upbeat 'Howdy.' As advised, I had pre-booked some of the activities and treatments. Tammy at the front desk took me through my upcoming itinerary. A 90-minute goat-butter massage that evening, a level-four hike at 5:45am the next day, a one-hour physical assessment at 2pm, dinner at 6:30pm, followed by something called Abhyanga: a massage performed by two synchronised masseuses using warm sesame oil. This, I thought, would be the closest I'd ever come to a threesome.

Aside from the very early start for the hike, which wasn't so bad considering I'd gained three hours from the travel, all in all, it wasn't a bad way to start this trip. Despite that, I had to keep trying to tame my mind by circling back to all the good things I had in my life. How fortunate I was to be in such a wonderful place. How lucky I was to have the means to afford it. But I was in a losing battle with the terrorists who had taken up residency in my head. There was a mind-numbing angry internal diatribe between myself and the ghosts of both John and Maya. It would take more than a four-handed massage to quiet those thought-crimes; the sacrifice of a small animal and a sage smudge might have been more helpful.

I arrived at one of the ranch's six gyms at 2pm the next day for a one-on-one trainer session and a physical evaluation. There, standing with a clipboard, was a guy the likes of whom up until that moment I'd only seen on the covers of *Men's Health* or Mills & Boon romance novels. Never in real life, not so close that I could inhale the light scent of his Irish Spring soap. I reckoned he was in his early thirties, although it was hard to tell until my eyes came back into focus. His Christ-length, dark hair was wavy and tousled, taking on a sexy just-rolled-out-of-bed kinda look. His chest muscles strained against his tight Canyon Ranch T-shirt, making me think I should stand back to avoid getting seriously injured, since it seemed like his shirt might give way at any moment.

'You must be Christina,' he smiled. 'I'm Noah.'

With gleeful sincerity, I smiled and said, 'So nice to meet you, Noah.'

Perusing my profile on his clipboard, he began with a series of 'How many times a week?' questions.

'So, Christina, how many days a week do you exercise?'

'Six,' I lied. At that point, it was more like two.

'How many days a week do you consume alcohol?'

'Three,' I really lied, thinking I was probably the only guest who had arrived with a case of wine.

'How many units of alcohol do you consume in a week?'

OK, this was going nowhere. He might as well stop right there, because short of my name, this would be as creative as a Danielle Steel novel. He then put down his clipboard and started putting me through my paces. Cardio sprints on the treadmill, thick, heavy ropes frantically whipped back and forth, then back to the treadmill for another sprint. This went on for a while. We then moved on to the exercises I actively avoid and truly detest, upper body. Noah's strong hands lifted me by my newly unearthed bony hips and told me to hold on to the bar.

'OK,' he said, 'let's see how many chin-ups you can do.'

'You're not playing to my strengths,' I said, dangling from the bar.

He playfully ignored my pleas. 'I saw you with those heavy ropes,' he said, smiling.

When I told him I wasn't capable of more than one pull-up, once again his hands wrapped around my hips as he assisted me, bringing my chin up and over the bar.

'One,' I said, gasping. 'I'm pretty satisfied with that.' He laughed. We were getting along brilliantly.

I didn't see Noah again for a couple of days, although rest assured, I did look. I was going out of my way, walking through the wide, bright corridors that housed the gyms and the yoga studio between classes. For what purpose, I wasn't entirely sure. I just knew I'd like to see him again. One of the corridor's walls was lined with twenty or so photographs of the fitness team, all smiling with their names and specialisations below. Under Noah's smiling photo, it said: 'Personal Trainer, Yoga, Group Activity Leader'. I thought Noah looked more handsome in person, more relaxed and tousled than in his corporate-looking staff portrait.

When I walked into a yoga class on day three, I was more than pleased to see Noah sitting peacefully at the front of the room in the lotus position, his long hair piled into a man-bun. I smiled, thinking he reminded me of Gaston from *Beauty and the Beast*, then inwardly rolled my eyes, thinking how completely pathetic I was: with two small children my immediate point of comparison for a handsome man was a Disney character. There was something more artsy and zen about Noah in the yoga studio than there had been in the gym. He looked sexier, more relaxed in an 'I grow my own organic soybeans' kinda way. I took a mat, positioned it near the back, and sat down. He acknowledged me with a gentle smile.

It was somewhere towards the end of the yoga class, in a stretching posture, when I was lying face-down, eyes closed as instructed, that Noah walked around the bodies to adjust us. He quietly whispered in my ear, 'Is it all right if I touch you?'

Like, how was that not a trick question?

'Yes,' I said with equal softness, without opening my eyes.

With that, Noah lowered himself face-down and lay on my back. This caused me to let out such a surprising, thunderous moan that I was confident it would disturb the Zumba class going on down the hall. It was electric, the energy of his body running through mine. *Will he be doing this with all the other women in*

the class? I thought. I don't remember if he did, and I certainly
don't recall hearing any uncontrolled moaning from the others.
I just know that, hands down, it was the most incredible yoga
class in the history of the practice.

My last night at Canyon Ranch had come. I had a very early
flight the following day, and aside from those two times, I had
not seen Noah. I had pushed myself very hard that week, diligently trying to distract myself from my problems. The intense
early-morning hikes in the Arizona canyons were truly breathtaking, and, dare I say, almost spiritual. I sampled a variety of
classes in the afternoons, from African drumming to Zumba.
All the while, everywhere, I kept an eye out for Noah. I was
heading for an early dinner, and I thought I would finish off
the visit just as I'd started, with a Canyon Ranch signature goat-
butter massage following my meal. There, outside the gym
where we'd first met, was Noah. He was sitting on a bench,
chatting with a few other guests after an intense game of something called murderball.

'Hey, Christina,' he smiled.

'Hi,' I smiled back.

'Where are you off to?' he asked.

I told him of my early dinner plans, the goat-butter massage
and my early flight in the morning.

'Hey,' I tried to say ever-so casually, 'are you allowed to join
guests for dinner? Is there a policy against it?'

Looking back, maybe I was trying to make the first move. But
more than anything else, I had been lonely that week, and I had
enjoyed our playful banter. Noah looked at me and smiled, the
kind of smile that Tom Cruise successfully pulls off in most of
his films when there's some unresolved sexual tension between
him and his leading lady.

'Sadly,' he said, 'it's against ranch rules.'

'Too bad,' I smiled.

As I lay in the treatment room, goat butter liberally slath-ered onto my pleasantly sore muscles, cocooned in some sort of heated plastic bladder-like hammock, I thought of Noah. My thoughts had all the trappings of a well-produced soft porno. I imagined Noah knocking on my door and me answering it wearing nothing but an old Van Halen T-shirt. Don't ask me why Van Halen. I hate the band, I don't have the T-shirt, but that's just what popped up.

'Oh,' I'd say coyly, 'I wasn't expecting company.'

He'd ask breathlessly, 'May I come in?' And without waiting for an answer, he'd boldly enter my room.

'Christina,' he'd say, with a voice borrowed from Barry White. 'Since that first day I held you by your bony hips, I can't stop thinking of you.'

'Same,' I'd feverishly spew.

Then he'd slam the door shut with his foot, and with the skill of Marilyn Chambers and the energy of the Duracell Bunny, I'd spend my last few hours at Canyon Ranch having my lithe, deeply moisturised body tossed around like a sexual rag doll. It was nice in there, in my inner world, and for that hour, not once did John or Maya dare enter.

When I got back to my room, my red message light was blinking. I pressed 'play'.

'Hi, Christina, it's Noah. I was wondering, if you aren't too tired after your massage, if you'd like to come over for some tea? Just thought it would be nice, and I so enjoyed meeting you. Oh, I don't normally do this ... you know ... call guests.' He left his number and said he'd be up for a bit.

I listened to that message three more times. The first was for pure verification. I needed proof that I had not imagined it. The second was for tone and any possible innuendo that I could read into every syllable. And three, because it made my whole body and heart burst with excitement. Had I just manifested an alternative beginning to a potential fantasy that had been playing in my head for the last hour? Could tea be a euphemism for something else? Was I really that powerful? Damn straight. To all of it.

The clear moonless night made the sky look as if it were littered with a billion twinkling lights. I thought of Osho's quote, 'A certain darkness is needed to see the stars.' *Maybe it's some sort of metaphor for my life,* I thought. The temperature had dropped to single digits, and the only thing I could see clearly was my breath swirling in front of me. Noah lived on the outskirts of the ranch property, within its gates, about a ten-minute walk from my room. Nervously, I walked up to his ranch-style home and knocked on the door. Noah opened it and smiled. His hair was wet and shaggy; clearly he had just stepped out of the shower. He was wearing loose-fitting grey sweatpants and a white T-shirt that hung flawlessly on his chest. He was absolutely perfect.

'Come in,' he said. 'Welcome.'

The house was warm and furnished in a Southwestern ranch style, with natural-hide sofas and chairs. Geometric Aztec-print rugs covered the red tile floor, and there was a massive antler chandelier over a large rustic harvest table. The house smelt of incense, which reminded me of the yoga studio, and there was a fire crackling and popping in the large flagstone fireplace.

'Have a seat,' he said, gesturing to the animal-hide sofa. 'Tea?'

Surely this is a job for wine, not tea, I thought.

'Do you have any wine?' I casually asked. I hoped my urgency for wine wasn't noticed in the nonchalant delivery of my question.

'Oh, no, sorry,' he said. 'I don't drink alcohol. So I guess I'm not properly set up for entertaining.'

'Not a problem,' I lied. *How am I going to get through this without a glass of something to relax me?* 'Tea sounds great.'

He brought the tea and placed it on a round cowhide otto-man set on top of a cowhide rug.

'A lot of cow,' I said, looking around. 'Clearly not the home of a vegan.'

He smiled. 'It belongs to my cousin; he has a few proper-ties here on the ranch.' Noah went on to tell me he was from Rhode Island, from a Jewish family with money. He had bucked the parental expectations of being a doctor or a lawyer, becom-ing what Lizzie would call a trust-fund radical artist. Noah had spent time in India practising yoga, as all hip yogis tend to do. He told me he'd been working at the ranch for about six months and was leaving to go back to India in about a month.

'Have you been to India?' he asked. 'It will change your life.'

'Never been,' I said, 'but it's on my list.' I was lying again. I'd never wanted to go to India. I imagined my stomach would rebel instantly. This was from a girl who'd barely survived Acapulco Princess hotel.

Noah turned to me and smiled. 'Do you smoke?'

He motioned his bright, Paul Newman-blue eyes to the bag of pot stashed in an armadillo-shaped clay bowl. *Praise be,* I thought. If there was no alcohol, then weed was the next best thing. Noah rolled a joint, lit it, and passed it to me. I inhaled deeply, maybe too deeply.

'Aaaaahhhh,' I moaned as I exhaled. Smooth.

It was about then that I started coughing, I mean yakking, like a teenager smoking her first cigarette. He got me a glass of water as I continued to cough. Then he put his hand on my back and playfully laughed, 'You gonna live?'

I nodded my head yes, not being able to get the words out. Noah smiled. I think he found it either endearing or amusing. Either way, he stubbed out the joint and moved in to kiss me.

Now, I will not go all *Fifty Shades* here, writing the intimate sexual details of my encounter with this near-perfect man, but here's what I will say. After my girls were born, I was made to feel so unattractive by my children's father that I had a hard time believing that anyone could ever find me attractive, let alone beautiful. So regaining a sense of self-confidence had come slowly. But now, here I was, in the strong arms of one of the most handsome men I had ever seen close up, and he made me feel beautiful and sexy and desired.

Noah celebrated my body with the skills and strength of a world-class ballet dancer. The effortless way he lifted me up and held me there as my super-moisturised legs wrapped around his waist. The energy that ran between us was erotic and intense. I surrendered myself entirely as I 'gave myself permission' to feel sexy, worthy and desirable. Our fatigued bodies collapsed in a sweaty, perfect mess, limbs still intertwined, catching our breath. Noah's strong body made me feel small and feminine. *This,* I thought, *this is the most incredible, healing therapeutic fuck that there has ever been. And I'm not just talking in my life but in the history of fucking mankind.*

I knew I was leaving in a few hours, so I thought I should get up and go back to my room.

'You're not going?' Noah asked, looking genuinely hurt, as he drew me closer to that Photoshopped body of his.

'I have to check out in about four hours,' I said. 'My flight is at 7am.'

'Stay, beautiful,' he said. 'Sleep here. I'll make sure you're back in time.'

I guess this is what I'd call a no-brainer decision. With his gentle, light breath on the nape of my neck, the salty taste of his skin still teasing my tongue, he wrapped his warm naked body around me and held me as I slowly closed my eyes.

I listened to the eery, haunting sound of the coyotes somewhere off in the distant canyons as I drifted in and out of a light slumber. I wondered how many times, if ever, Noah had done this. But as soon as the question entered my mind, I realised I didn't care. This night I had manifested was perfect. It gave me what I'd so badly needed: to feel beautiful. I knew this was the evening that changed me, empowered me, brought me back to life. It wouldn't fix everything, but it was one terrific, massive leap forward, teaching me that sometimes, a one-night stand can be more effective than years of therapy.

I've returned to Canyon Ranch many times. Upon arriving, I immediately walk by the gym corridor and stop in front of the wall with the smiling photographs. Looking, always looking, to see if Noah is there. He never is. But even now, years later, when I think back to that beautiful starry night, the coyotes howling, and the grace, strength and passion of Noah making love to me, I will affectionately and forever refer to it simply as the night Stella got her groove back.

CHAPTER 2

Let My People Go Drinking

'There is nothing I would not do for those who
are really my friends. I have no notion of loving
people by halves, it is not my nature.'
Jane Austen, *Northanger Abbey*

I want to talk for a moment about soulmates. Yup, that annoy-ing word that gets overused by couples in love all around the English-speaking world. Generally, I loathe the word. It's right up there with 'moist', 'panties' and that horrible 'C' word Brits use with incredible regularity that rhymes with 'hunt'. Seriously, look at me, I can't even write it down, yet I have no trouble speaking in exacting detail about my post-baby vagina (or should I say post-baby 'hunt'?).

Lovers often use the word 'soulmate' when discussing a partner they are penetrating, or the other way around, and good on them. But I have a few conditions if you're going to start dropping that word with the British frequency of 'hunt'. First, there needs to be some sort of timeline estab-lished. Just like after a couple of dates you don't yet use the word 'boyfriend' or 'girlfriend', it's something that takes time, something you graduate towards, grow into. It's not dissimilar to the term 'life-partner': how can you even think of describ-ing your relationship this way if it's had a shorter lifespan than a season of *The Bachelor*? I'm open to debating the length of time, but I have to say I think it has to be at least twenty years, and if I'm honest, I would throw an additional five years on top of that, just to be sure. I don't want to hear someone using the word 'soulmate' in February only to switch to 'mother fucking cocksucker' come October. Look at me, that one I have trouble writing.

That said, I want to speak of my soulmationships. Connections of heart and mind, mutual respect, and an unbreakable kindred spirit that I have definitely experienced, and they would be, without question, with my girlfriends.

I've been described once or twice in my human existence as a 'big personality', which, for the record, I take as a compliment, although I'm very aware it's not always intended as such. I'm actually a little shy and somewhat reserved outside my own handpicked colourful village of misfits. Rarely am I keen to strike up a conversation with a stranger, even if I'm sitting beside one on a twelve-hour flight, with a finished book, broken headphones, and nothing else to do but play with the air valve above my seat. I'm not a bitch or a snob but rather tend to sequester myself inside my own little bubble. However, in a safe space with either proper introductions or common purpose, I spring to life, much like a hen party when someone starts playing 'Dancing Queen'. Then the question that's generally asked is if anyone knows where my volume dial might be.

Since elementary school, I've sought out friends with 'bigger' personalities than mine. Emily Goldenblatt, aged eight, was the first who possessed those bigger-than-life traits. Emily was a brawny girl with a booming, raspy voice and a deep laugh that rattled like wind through a barn. She wore her pigtails high like horns on a bull and had a crooked fringe which gave the clear impression that she cut her own hair. She was a little crazy, which equally intrigued and terrified me. She called me Teenybopper, a version of Tina, which I was called in those days. Emily threatened to beat into next Sunday anyone who called me Teenybopper outside of herself. I interpreted that as devotion, although I don't recall her ever actually fighting anyone in the schoolyard over it. I liked that she protected me, although truth be told, I think it was because of my friendship with Emily that I needed protection. She had a way of finding fun in places I'd never have thought to look, and if she feared anything, one would rarely see a hint of it on her dirty, steely-eyed little face. Emily Goldenblatt was a loyal friend.

I continued to pick friends or be drawn to people who appeared big, fearless and possessed the skills, if required, to break me out of a Turkish prison. Friends more outrageous, more flirtatious, than me, so that by association, I'd be perceived to share those qualities. Friends who were there for you in the bad times, and would commemorate big events by adding liquor to ice in the good times. Those kinds of friends.

In every stage of our lives, friends are essential. I can say with complete certainty that I don't know what kind of massive rock I'd be living under or what padded cell would be containing me if it weren't for my friends. They've cried with me, held my hair back after one too many Jägermeisters, stopped me from drunk dialling my ex at 1am, and made me laugh so hard that I peed, just a little.

But never are friends more important than when you're going through a crisis, be it illness, death, a break-up, a disastrous perm, or any of life's unscheduled cruel crap. That's when friends take on a superhero existence. I first met my dear friend Lizzie in high school, where on occasion our social circles would overlap, most often at the parties the Snell brothers would regularly throw. She's two years younger than me, which she'd tell you today without being asked. Lizzie graduated to super-friend after discovering me naked in bed with her brother one morning. It's funny what bonds us in life. Lizzie married Mike, a middle-school teacher whom I adored. She's a beautiful powerhouse and still the one I'd most blindly trust to get that organ transplant cooler box into the surgeon's hands. Then there is Marie, sweet Marie, whom I describe as the ultimate prize I got from surviving Jackson Tilney. To this day, Marie has the most contagious, perfect laugh I've ever heard.

When I think of Lizzie and Marie, I honestly feel so bloody honoured that they both have found something in me that's made them hang around for all these years. These fabulous babes, my queens. These skinny bitches and I have gone through absolutely everything – a plethora of boys (and a few girls), a host of careers, bad choices, good choices, death, births and an innumerable number of firsts (and lasts). They're my proverbial port in a storm, a safe harbour of female wisdom, dispensers of sage advice and the occasional 1 mg hit of Ativan.

After John and I split, Lizzie and Marie were rock star goddesses getting me through that horrible, shitty time. Those first three months, I can't recall a single day when they did not show up unannounced, call or check in, just to make sure I was still breathing. They are perfect human beings. But both were contently married, enjoying their 'couple lives'. I didn't consciously know it, but I required single-mom friends. Not to replace Lizzie and Marie, but to add to my support group, people who were adrift in the same uncharted waters of singledom without a life raft.

There are some people you meet by chance. Your paths intersect over a moment in time; they randomly float into your personal space, and you think, *Yup, they're my kinda crazy.* Some you meet through shared interests or commonalities. Like the classic friendship-making moment when, having just overheard your conversation, someone smiles and says, 'I hate that bitch too.' But sometimes, someone comes into your life at such a serendipitous point that it could only be described as a gift from the universe, and Ally and Sloane were two of those gifts.

I met the two moms at our kids' small, progressive, artsy elementary school. It was a 'kumbaya' alternative school, for Birkenstock-loving, turquoise-wearing artists and psychotherapist parents, who seemed to make up the fabric of our year. The three of us did stand out as different, if only in our choice of footwear. But our most noticeable difference became apparent with the illustrious distinction of being the only moms in that tiny school getting a divorce – all in the same year, affirming our status as a trio.

Ally was a spectacular ginger-haired beauty, with translucent skin and distracting blue eyes, and a dusting of freckles on her cheeks. Our social worlds rarely overlapped much beyond school fundraising committees, field trips, bake sales and the occasional mothers' luncheon the school was known to host. Traditionally I loathed attending such luncheons. First, I worked for a living, so I didn't have a ton of time, but more importantly, I didn't want to go. But I'd heard a rumour that Ally and her husband Colin had split, so for the sole purpose of finding out if that was true, I decided to attend.

Ally arrived late, forcing me to bide my time discussing where one might source organically grown cotton T-shirts to be sold at the school's upcoming gala fundraiser. I'm not sure how much time passed after she arrived, but I'm pretty sure I pounced on her the moment she walked through the door.

'Ally,' I said bluntly, 'I don't know if you've heard. John and I have recently split up. I heard a rumour you and Colin are no longer together. So, if it's not too personal a question, is there any truth to that?'

Ally's face lit up, in a way that made me think she might've not understood my question.

'Indeed we have,' she beamed. 'And from this moment forward, Christina, you and I are going to be best friends.'

A week later, Ally invited me to join her and Sloane for dinner at Sotto Voce, an upscale Italian restaurant in the heart of Little Italy. During dinner, Ally and I unloaded the details of love, betrayal and the sordid tragedies that accompanied our broken marriages. Sloane, still married, sat there wide-eyed and captivated as Ally and I expressed the genuine love we'd once had for our husbands. Of course, you as the reader know the ending of my marriage to John, but Ally's husband, Colin, well, let's just say there was a wee relationship overlap with his office temp, whom Ally took to calling Twinkie, a moniker used to describe something that tastes good out of the package but quickly goes stale once unwrapped.

'I've never loved Danny like that,' Sloane said about her husband. 'Not like you guys are describing … Still don't.' Not that we were campaigning – at all – but, somewhere between the beef carpaccio and the free limoncello shots the owner of the restaurant was lubricating us with, Sloane said, 'You girls have convinced me. I'm going to break up with Danny, and we'll all be single together.'

The funny thing about Sloane and her marriage to Danny was that he was actually one of the nice guys, and Sloane herself would tell you that. He wasn't a narcissist, like many we knew; he wasn't cheating on her like some. In fact, Danny really loved her, or did his best, taking into account his emotional limitations as a forensic accountant. It was just that Danny was exceptionally dull, the human equivalent of everyday china. If he were a colour, for sure he'd be beige. Sloane was anything but beige. She was a florescent rainbow-coloured unicorn. Sloane had liked Danny a lot, which she'd thought counted for something, and had thought he'd make a great dad, which he certainly did. So when he'd proposed, her thought process was, *Sure, why the hell not?*

As our night dialled up, we found ourselves drunk dancing at a bar across the street. To this day I can't think of anyone but Sloane when I hear The Animals 'We Gotta Get Out of This Place'. What Helen Reddy's 'I Am Woman' did for a generation of women, The Animals did for Sloane. It instantly became her anthem, her call-to-action theme song. Two weeks later, Danny found himself in a tired rental flat with 1970s decor, where many a husband transitioning out of their marriage lands. That poor beige forensic accountant did not have a clue what the hell had happened.

Thus my single-mom squad was born. Ally and Sloane quickly became the backbone to all things that, for me, defined friendship. We were more than friends: we were a tiny wine-drinking gang. They were my marvellous new mentors of misbehaving, and not dissimilar to Emily Goldenblatt, they found fun where I dared not look. My girlfriends are my soul-mates. They've earned that distinction. As we've watched men come and go, they're still here, ready with a box of Kleenex, a bottle of chilled Chablis, and an alibi that would stand up in court. More important than the platitudes offered in abundance was the knowledge that we were all in this together, an incredible joyride, a fabulous lifelong adventure, and as for me, well, I was just happy as shit to be driving the getaway car.

CHAPTER 3

My Year of Living Dangerously

*'Friendship is certainly the finest balm for
the pangs of disappointed love.'*
Jane Austen, *Northanger Abbey*

It was a year of growth and regrowth that first year I was single ... My own year of living dangerously, as I affectionately called it. I was ushering in two completely new and opposite stages of my life, single parenting and single eligibility, and I have to say they represented two totally contrasting realms of the human experience.

I had come to a major pivot point in my life, almost like I had optimistically boarded a train going in one direction and had found myself unexpectedly booted off in the middle of nowhere, and was now on a Greyhound bus heading to God knows where. I was going through a divorce from a man I'd once loved madly. I'd go from mourning the death of our marriage with the collective grief of a small town after a disaster, to lying in bed in the middle of the night with my least favourite memories, imagining different painful ways that he might die.

Emotionally, I was as volatile as a one-man sailboat in the middle of the ocean, at the mercy of the rain, wind, sun and tides, hoping, really hoping, that if I could just weather the storm, eventually I'd get to land.

At 40, I had calculated, by what means I can't be sure, that I only had ten good years left, convinced that after that I'd be a mothball-scented dried-up old fossil, playing Pinochle every

Saturday afternoon surrounded by a houseful of cats. I was smack dab in the middle of *This won't last forever*, and *Oh, dear God, is this all there is?*

Parenting had scared me. I'm betting that there had been teen moms out there more prepared for motherhood than I had been. But parenting on my own? Well, that was a whole new world of fear. I questioned daily if I was doing a good job, especially in those early days after the split. I was so heartbroken, sad and deeply damaged. How can you do your best for your kids when you're just barely hanging on yourself? Can you be an emotional, sorrowful basket case and still be a good mom? Or do you have to wait 25 years until the kids are fully baked, off the payroll and have successfully avoided any serious jail time to be sure?

I knew I wasn't a bad mom, but as a single working mom, I was plagued with the kind of guilt that assaults you with the power of a nuclear blast. I mean, I never missed a doctor's appointment, a dance recital, a sport's meet, or a parent/teacher interview and always contributed to bake sales, even if that meant icing cupcakes at midnight. But my daughter Briar will tell you, even now, that I wasn't there for a single school pizza lunch like the stay-at-home moms, and rarely was I there to pick her up after school. I know these are small things, but if she's reminding me of this fifteen years later, it means they had an impact.

I think nature certainly gives us a hand. Decades on from having my own tiny newborns, if I hear the cry of a very young baby, my breasts automatically tingle like phantom milk is letting down and it's my biological responsibility to feed the babies of the world. But I'll tell you now, there were times when I felt like running from the house screeching like a banshee, or when you'd find me whimpering for an indeterminate amount of time in a lukewarm tub, seriously questioning what the hell I was doing, pleading, 'Somebody ... anybody ... please save me ... Save them.'

My father said this about raising children, right after my sister Jennifer showed up hammered at my parents' wedding anniversary: 'Christina, the first 30 years of parenting are the hardest.' And if I'm honest, Alan's parenting yardstick continued to stretch upwards as we got older.

One of the things that stopped me from ramming my head through a wall that first year was that Ally, Sloane and I rented an old rustic cottage in Muskoka, a picturesque lake district a few hours north of Toronto. The cottage had a musky smell of cedar and smoke, and I was convinced it was on a superhighway for black bears, as evident from the strewn garbage and the watermelon-sized craps we'd find around the property. This was where my two new worlds collided: single mom and single eligibility. Some days I was a warrior, some days a broken mess. Most days, a little of both. Two dramatically different coming-of-age stories, where I learnt that not only does it take a village to raise a child, but also it takes a village to mend a broken heart.

On those summer cottage weekends we had our kids, we'd share big, family-style meals, bake cookies, toast marshmallows and barbecue hotdogs. We enjoyed waterskiing, swimming off the dock and gunwale-bobbing in the canoe. Firm in the belief that no one could be unhappy holding an ice cream cone, we'd pile in the boat and head to Port Sandfield Marina for a rocky road or a rainbow sherbet cone. On rainy days the kids filled their time with arts-and-crafts projects, jigsaw puzzles, and endless games of Snakes and Ladders and Candy Land. On sunny days we had to chase every child and hold them down long enough to apply a thick layer of sunscreen.

In the evenings, as the kids gathered to watch *SpongeBob* or the latest Mary-Kate and Ashley adventure, we ladies would head to the dock. With a bottle of chilled Whispering Angel rosé in hand, we'd sip, chat, share, question, answer, reflect, ponder, cry and laugh as we'd watch the sun go down and the bugs come out. We were chauffeurs, sherpas, chefs, nurses and washerwomen, were all unofficial mothers to our collective spawn, and, as Sloane used to joke, we were one quilting bee and freshly churned dish of butter removed from the Amish. I had always understood the importance of friendship, but that summer, those incredible single moms, a tiny circle of keepers, became my family.

On the flip side ... when our kids were with their respective dads, it went from a Montessori-like day-camp dressed up with all the responsibility and importance of *University Challenge*, to the hedonistic, pleasure-seeking escapism of *Love Island*. It was the kind of adolescent rebellion one might imagine if spring break came pimped out with Jimmy Choos, a sensational wine list and an American Express Gold Card. Something interesting can happen to women once they are let out of the cage of marriage. In our case, it could be best compared to ending a lengthy prison sentence, except when your time is done, they don't just let you out of jail, they send you to Hawaii. We saw a steady stream of emotionally unavailable hockey players, stockbrokers and second-tier celebrities who spent many an afternoon playing drinking games like Caps or Beer Pong on our dock. Parties went all night, as evidenced by the littering of bodies scattered throughout the property by morning. There were frequent drunken calls of 'Yeehaw!' as naked male party-goers hurled themselves off the two-storey boathouse, cannonballing into the dark, cold lake at 4am. The same large harvest table where we'd gather to have meals with our kids, filled with fresh veggie platters and hot dogs sliced up into tiny non-chokeable bits, would also be used for body shots, and on at least one occasion, Sloane doing a striptease to Rod Stewart's 'Da Ya Think I'm Sexy?'

That summer, you could safely say, made up for a few key milestones I missed in my youth. I'd never had a kick-ass 'let's howl at the moon' rebellious period in my life that one could frame as coming of age. I didn't go to university, a time when friends were doing Jägerbombs in togas, kissing girls on dares, and having tons of casual sex. I'd met Brandon when I was 21, and after that, I was fully in the stream of adulthood. And here's a confession I just shockingly unearthed about myself: I've never had a first kiss without at least two glasses of something fermented coming before it. Not back then, not ever. But you'll be happy to know I'm working on it.

Having recently adopted the catchphrase 'I'll be damned if I'm not going to at least try to fuck my way through this,' Ally crafted a bucket list she called 'Summer Goals', or as it was quickly renamed, her 'Fuck-It List', an adult take on 'What I Did on My Summer Vacation'.

Her list included:

* Have a threesome
* Have sex with a much younger man
* Take a lesbian lover.

I have to give kudos to Ally, who previously had only slept with four men. That summer, that girl ticked all those boxes, and, if I recall correctly, she got her hat-trick all in one night.

I knew I wasn't ready to shackle my heart and life to another man, so the men and the cocktail-fuelled choices I made ensured there was no real danger of that. I had one lover that summer. He was young, delicious and blissfully uncomplicated. His name was Daniel. He was fourteen years my junior and loved the comparison to Ashton Kutcher and Demi Moore that followed us. And I'm just going to say it: he was a large plate of crack cocaine for my ego. He was the guy I'd openly pray I'd run into John with, a sexy, gorgeous man-child declaration of 'Look at me – I'm over your ass.' Daniel was safe, and I needed safe. I think we all did, and that was what that summer was for. No lasting commitment, no fear of falling in love, and no broken hearts, as mine was still under repair.

Now, if these women merely represented a continuous hot-mess, tequila-slamming, drunk-dancing, day-drinking, oyster-sucking singledom lifestyle, my time with them would've been brief, seasonal, like Freshers Week. But there was a wonderful, healthy element to my new friendships, as well as the unbridled aspect, and we needed every last bit of it. As it is, years later, although scattered across the planet, these two fabulous babes have remained solid rocks in my foundation of super-friends. So sure, there were some morally deficient judgement calls, some lost hours under the umbrella of 'next time you'll know better'. We were embarking on the massive undertaking of rediscovering ourselves, shedding one of the many skins of break-up melancholy while trying to find ourselves and lose ourselves simultaneously; struggling to restore a balance that had toppled the scales so far in the other direction that certain things didn't make sense anymore. Because if any of you have been in a brutal, unhappy marriage or relationship, especially if there are kids involved, you know that you get lost, undeniably and utterly lost.

Eventually, for most, the spring break of singledom does come to an end. The abstaining from restraining, the burst of hedonistic adolescent rebellion, is never supposed to last too long. As the saying almost goes, 'A reason, a season, not a life-time.' It's a temporary Band-Aid fix of casual sex, body piercings and weekend trips to South Beach. A colourful parade of blurred man-flesh distractions whose names will still be Hockey Thighs,

Yoga Dude or simply That Guy From Carlos 'N' Charlie's years from now. But like any good rave, eventually, the house lights come on, and you need to pack up your yurt and go home.

That summer was like a poem, a brief stanza to look back on and occasionally recite. Perhaps its purpose was a little like jump-starting a car whose battery had died over a long, harsh winter, or like those pads that send an electric jolt to restart your heart as the doctors yell, 'Clear!' And maybe I'm repeating myself, but I think this bears repeating: we were rediscovering who we were, or weren't, before we were someone's wife ... before someone started calling us Mommy ... before we spoke of separation agreements, parenting plans and alternating years for Christmas.

If you ask me, everyone needs a period in their life to look back on like this. Sure, most of us experience this breaking free a little earlier than 40, but don't discount it as not every bit as valuable, every bit as much a coming of age. It showed me that there was life after John, and although what that would look like was still unclear, I was alive: divorce hadn't killed me. I had some fantastic stories and some golden-nugget souvenirs of life. Some secrets I'll keep, and some, if I'm lucky, I'll get to share with my future grandkids, decades away, glorious proof that once, long ago, Granny was cool.

Divorce is hard, and parenting, single or otherwise, is harder ... and it's forever. So it's essential that, just a phone call away, my 'sister-wives' are there for advice, reassurance, or a much-needed reminder that, no, I don't need a CAT scan and I'm not out of my ever-loving mind in this uncertain world we call life. And although I couldn't see land yet, and was still at the mercy of unpredictable weather, their presence reminded me that I was not alone.

I was now in a bigger boat.

CHAPTER 4

The Man Menu

'Let's mask our shame in online dating by constantly disparaging the bar scene. A place where back in the olden days we would meet people and let alcohol and poor judgement decide our future.'

Unknown

I have a sassy single girlfriend, a self-proclaimed serial dater. 'No one has been on more first dates than me,' she declared, with all the pride of someone who holds the world record in something a tad more impressive than the most Tinder matches. She compared the delights and disasters of dating to picking up a hitchhiker. With a Dark and Stormy in hand, and a tutorial-like tone, as if she had a PhD in the subject, she began.

'Christina, it's like this. You meet a guy. He's cute, exciting, and seems to be travelling in your general direction. So he gets in your car. He could be a serial killer, an Oxford business professor, or both, you just don't know. But regardless, there you are anyway, embarking on a road trip with this stranger. The journey could be very short, minutes even, ending with an immediate ejection of him from your car. This is likely prompted by some offensive one-liner, like, "Hey, saucy thang, do you like to be urinated on?" or perhaps it could go on for years. But eventually, the car ride is over. He gets out. Maybe you barely slow down the car and yell, "Tuck and roll, dickhead!" as you toss his sorry ass out to the kerb. And then you go on your way … picking up the next handsome hitchhiker you see along life's highway.'

This all made perfect sense to me. I've never been a serial dater. I've tended to fall from one monogamous relationship to another. Many of my relationships have been a result of friends morphing into lovers. One day you could be actively debating current affairs, or tactically problem-solving a client's latest insane demands, then *BAM!* The next thing you know, you're lying in bed together as you draw tiny circles with your forefinger through your new lover's chest hair.

Dating is a world that I only truly immersed myself in after my divorce to John, as even in high school I wouldn't say that I played the field. Here are some hints to indicate just how long it had been since I was actively dating: Margaret Thatcher was prime minister, Air Supply was 'All Out of Love' on the FM dial, and I had to rewind the tape on my answering machine once I got home to hear who'd called. We were now in a time when the act of dating took on all the appearance of an uncomfortable series of Diane Sawyer-like job interviews. Only, unlike a job interview, the lucky candidate, if 'hired,' would see me naked.

The dating skills I'd been working with all came from circa 1980s television, including a *Charlie's Angels'* hair flip to signal interest, which I have to say worked exceptionally well for me in 1981. Or here's another provocative pointer, this time from Amanda Woodward from *Melrose Place*. I'd flirtatiously take my forefinger and seductively trace the rim of my cocktail glass while gently biting my lower lip – you know ... for intrigue. Oh, the shame. Therefore, we can safely conclude that my dating experience was as relevant and useful as a rotary phone in today's world of swiping left or right while browsing a menu of men on an iPhone.

In our twenties, we try men on like dresses on final clearance sale. If this one doesn't fit or look right, let's add another to our heaving basket. And why not? We are figuring it out, exploring and developing our unsophisticated palette, trying to find our style. In our thirties, the dating swamp gets drained, with a lot of us coupled up and settled down. I was having kids and doing adult things like making a living, contributing to a retirement savings plan, and wondering if perhaps the grass might be greener somewhere else.

As I re-entered the world of dating in my forties, I was hauling along a hell of a lot more baggage than when Thatcher was sworn in. My baggage held kids, exes, battle scars, internal bruises, sagging skin and a few vacillating self-esteem issues. All this is to say is that although the caveman-like desire to be thrown over some handsome man's shoulder and carried into his cave was strong, a hell of a lot had changed.

But there's a reward for reaching your forties having survived the previous decades, and that's called experience. I've found that a certain weeding out process has been internally programmed in me, pretty much automatically. Experience has gifted me (hopefully) insight into what I want or don't want when it comes to looking for men. With minimal thought and effort, I now know if the guy sitting across the table from me on a first date has any staying potential, usually before he even shakes my hand and says, 'You must be Christina.' Short of wearing a brown burlap Obi-Wan Kenobi robe, I can take on the power and certainty of a Jedi Master: *These are not the men I'm looking for.* That's what age has gifted me, an ability to separate the sheep from the goats.

There's something else I do, and it's a real time-saving question we girls need to ask ourselves, a question I'm pretty confident I've not seen chewed over in any Austen novel: 'Do I want to see him naked?' This is an immediate leveller. It efficiently separates boyfriend material from those destined to be nothing more than a good friend, leaving some men never entirely understanding why the two of you never hooked up. He could have all the qualities you want in a guy, be 'perfect on paper'; sharing the same love for old Cary Grant movies, and coming from a family of sisters, so have a deep respect for women. Yet something is missing; there's no spark, no chemistry. You look at him, still genuinely laughing from the joke he's told, and for reasons you're unable to put your finger on, you just don't want to see him naked. So sure, you could see this guy for a second date or a third, but I'm just saying that sometime in the not-so-distant future you'll be suggesting to him out loud, with conviction, 'You should really meet my friend Charlotte, I think you guys would hit it off.'

I was actively resisting online dating, much like getting a flu jab or a suspicious mole looked at, but somehow I knew it was just a matter of time before I caved. I'm sure there are those out there who could talk in more depth and delicious detail about the cyber-dating world. I've not logged endless woman-hours sifting through thousands and thousands of profile photos of men with no last names. But my experience has taught me you don't have to log 10,000 hours to get the swing or swipe of it. It's not brain surgery, or *MasterChef*.

Zealously, my super-annoying coupled-up girlfriends (the ones who spew the word 'soulmate') want nothing more than to feverishly spread the Gospel According to Tinder. With a complete disregard for any of my objections, supported by an enthusiastic determination usually reserved for pyramid schemes and cult recruiting, they commandeered my phone. Fuelled by an impressive quantity of Don Julio, they collectively discussed the answers on the dating profile questionnaire they were joyously filling out on my behalf.

'Do you think Christina would use the word "fun-loving" to describe herself?'

'What do you think is the one item she could not live without?'

'Cell phone,' they all answered in unison.

Phone returned, and presto, my new online dating profile was live, and I'd officially crossed (or, rather, been shoved) over the threshold into a new alternate dating paradigm. What did I have to lose? So, with the right balance of intrigue and trepidation, I entered the world of the Man Menu. Let's discuss. Much like Uber Eats, catalogued men magically appear on your screen. And just like the food ordering service, it's advised not to be doing this if you're starving. In a moment of surrender, I thought, *OK, this will make my dating life easy-peasy, as my good friend Nicole likes to say. I can pick up men from the comfort of my home, wearing nothing but my White Company cashmere onesie and an aqua-ocean detoxifying face mask. Just look at the pages and pages of potential Mr Darcys searching for love.* I opened a bottle of wine and poured myself a large glass of Chardonnay, adding an ice cube, thinking I could be here a while. I plopped down on my sofa and excitedly started to dig into my Man Menu.

In my mind, here's how I imagined The Guy: a Tom Cruise smile, piercing Bradley Cooper eyes and a Hemsworth-insane ripped body (either Hemsworth would do). The kind of eye candy that evokes pure, animal chemistry and pheromones that, once released, surge through your body like electricity freshly squeezed from a hydro station. However, after a few minutes of surfing and swiping left and left again, a thought surfaced. *Did the dating site not receive my questionnaire that my girlfriends filled out on my behalf while hijacking my phone?* Of course, my immediate second thought was, *Just how did they answer those questions?* The questions that ask what you're looking for in a partner, as well as describing yourself in moderate detail. Simple things such as age range, height requirements, ethnic and/or religious preference. Do you have children, want children? Are you a dog person or a cat person? Smoker or non-smoker? On a scale of one to ten, how important is it that your partner has all his teeth? OK, maybe I made that last one up, but after looking at some of the guys, I respectfully suggest that that might need to be dropped into the company's feedback box. I felt like I had entered that bar in *Star Wars*.

Puzzled, I stared down at my phone screen. Could this really be what the app's algorithm had in mind for me? Were these my carefully screened, data-supported potential soul-mates? Another thought entered my brain like a detonated bomb bringing down an apartment block. *Oh, dear God, am I not hotter than this?* I could feel my aqua-ocean detoxifying face mask hardening. This was not going to be as much fun as I'd thought.

For me, there are a few basic non-starters, non-negotiables, an unwavering list of no-gos, ain't-never-gonna-happen. My first requirement is that any potential man be a non-smoker. Occasional weed is fine – hell, it might even be preferred – but I cannot be with anyone who smokes cigarettes or cigars. Another essential is that he looks after himself. He doesn't have to look like he's leapt off the cover of *Men's Health*, but someone who gives a shit about what he looks like. I may not possess the ability to ski better than the average seven year old, or throw a ball that doesn't land in a small Charlie Brown-like arc mere feet from where it started, but I'm active and fit. And sure, there was that frozen shoulder sports injury when I found myself trapped inside my sweaty Lululemon sports bra after spin class, but still, I'd appreciate a guy who, you know, keeps it all together. That's why they have the questionnaire, right? To offer you a filtered collection of potential partners, carefully and meticulously selected based on your answers. So excuse me if I politely ask,

What the fuck is the guy with the Santa bod and a Cohiba hanging from his mouth,
reeking of inappropriate, doing in my filtered selection of men?

As I browsed the Man Menu, I was gobsmacked and confused. Aside from the app's total disregard for the fact that I
prefer my men looking like they hold a job or have not been held
up for years in some isolated cabin in Appalachia, I couldn't get
over the lack of effort or thought that was sometimes put into
that oh-so-important profile photo. You know, the ones you'd
assume would be carefully thought out and crafted, specifically
selected to impress and to lure a like-minded, lifelong mate.
After all, this is their one chance to make a first impression, an
impression you only have a fraction of a second to capture. Even
though my friends had mostly crafted my profile, don't think
for one second that I hadn't had some sort of input. Even if it
was just me yelling across the table, 'Use the photo of me from
the Dior exhibit ... the one with me in the white dress ... No,
not that one ... the halterneck ... Oh just give me the phone,
I'll find it myself.'

This is the modern-day version of Tarzan beating out his
mating call on his chest; it's a carefully crafted résumé for a
lifetime of love. These apps use a highly advanced algorithm
that, if required, should be able to track missing children and
match potential organ donors. So how is it possible, as I search
for Mr Darcy, that I'm finding Tony Soprano, with not a hint
of Prince Charming, or even his less desirable second cousin,
Prince Adequate?

I quickly put a system into place for immediate rejection,
no second-guessing. I straight away gave a swift swipe to the left
if any profile photos included the following:

❋ Posing with a cigarette or cigar
❋ Posing with a gun (more an American thing)

* Posing with a pint (more a British thing)
* Posing with his children
* Posing with another woman
* A faceless torso
* A bodyless face
* Posturing in front of a car, motorcycle or speedboat
* A bathroom selfie

Let's discuss this last one in more detail. I mean, seriously, just how much effort is he putting into this, and likely all aspects of his life, if he only has the marginal energy to snap a photo of himself in his bathroom mirror, somewhere between brushing his teeth and his morning crap? The whole experience was making me nostalgic for cocktail-fuelled bad man choices in smoky bars.

But wait … I'm not done. I need to add more 'immediate rejection' conditions:

* Any man I suspect is hiding small critters in his facial hair
* A body type that forces me to ask: *When was the last time this dude ate a salad?*
* Any photo with even the vaguest similarity to a mug shot or surveillance footage
* A man euphorically holding up a fish (more of a Canadian thing)

I looked at these men, and I seriously asked myself, *Who are the 'lids' to these girlfriend-seeking 'pots'?* Maybe I'd inadvertently pissed off one of my friends with one too many 'soulmate' disses, and this was penance. Perhaps I was being punked.

I regrouped about a week later with my friends, the ones guilty of this punishable crime, and we went through the trials and tribulations of being single and online dating in much detail. It was agreed that not all the men showed zero potential. It was further agreed, of course not immediately by me, that I might not be giving this online dating a real chance. So, urged to keep an open mind, I re-examined those men who had a classically warm smile, a kind, friendly face, and for me, my ultimate weakness, those in a tuxedo. And there, among the rubble of fallen men, something sparkled. Armed with cautiously optimistic curiosity and a recently adopted attitude of *What the hell*, I swiped right on Reid with no last name.

CHAPTER 5

My One and Only Online Boyfriend

'Well, I must endure the presence of a few caterpillars
if I wish to become acquainted with the butterflies.'
Antoine de Saint-Exupéry, *The Little Prince*

Here's the thing about me, I'm usually one who embraces new ideas, especially when it comes to technology. I've been having lengthy conversations with Alexa for years; my Apple Watch tells me when to stand up, reminds me to breathe, and informs me how many steps I've walked; Google Maps shows me how to get there; Calm lulls me to sleep; Siri answers my questions, and Find My iPhone can inform me that it is stuck between two sofa cushions. Therefore, with all my techie enthusiasm, I'm not sure why this whole online dating thing intimidated me.

I'm not a suspicious person by nature, but for some reason, cyber-dating set off a few of my sensors, making me a wee bit overly cautious. Maybe because I like the idea of meeting someone the old-fashioned way. There's something about a good old face-to-face that allows chemistry and instinct to play a part in the decision-making process. So instead of immediately giving Reid my number, as I didn't want to go to the trouble of changing it, you know, in case he turned out to be a serial killer (not to mention the fact I've not successfully memorised a new telephone number since 2004), we embraced the lost art of letter-writing ... well, email-writing. There's something romantic about receiving a letter in this world where texts and little yellow-faced emojis have replaced emotions or feelings. Reid would write lengthy, humorous emails that I found myself eagerly anticipating. When I finally agreed to meet him, it should surprise no one that it was only after thoroughly creeping him online with the skills of an FBI special agent.

We agreed to meet at 6pm in the lobby bar of the Four Seasons. I picked that place because my sister Victoria's husband, Anthony, was head of security at the hotel. I even gave Anthony a heads-up I was there on my first online date, insisting he come into the bar and, with a deep, intimidating voice and eyes communicating *I could make your death look like an accident*, say, 'So ... who do we have here?' Reid needed to know I'd brought back-up.

Reid was not a serial killer, as you might've already guessed. He was a single dad with part-time custody of his three-year-old son, and lived in a suburb outside of Toronto. He owned a wholesale bathroom fixture company and was a part-time musician. Not going to lie to you, it was the musician part I found a little sexier than the faucets. Reid was hot. Like, Jon Bon Jovi hot. He had shaggy, tousled shoulder-length auburn hair, striking green eyes and a cheeky, sexy smile. To emphasise his musical credentials, he sported a soul-patch tuft under his lower lip, which his bandmates called his 'flavour savour', a name I later discovered was a reference to oral sex.

With all the cliché of an *SNL* 1970s parody, Reid's Foreigner cover band played regular gigs at a gritty downtown venue called The Phoenix. Proving no man is ever less sexy when playing the guitar, the women surrounding the band were a fascinating glimpse of something akin to a nature show observing an animal species' mating habits. In fierce, feline, rhythmic motion, like a perimenopausal mosh pit, the females of the species desperately try to get the attention of a band member, any band member, for the sole purpose of immediate copulation. And on at least one occasion, I saw the lead singer, Rick, use bandmate Jerry's van, the guy responsible for carrying the amps, for precisely that purpose. Let's face it, musicians are sexual kryptonite. Do you think for a second if gnarly-looking Keith Richards had been an accountant or a pipefitter he'd even have got to hold supermodel Patti Hansen's door open? No! He got his wife Patti because he was a musician, not to mention a Rolling Stone and top of the musician royalty rock heap. Ronnie Wood, also a Rolling Stone, left his wife for a girl 41 years his junior. That, my friends, doesn't happen if you're an orthodontist. So, for all the reasons stated above, I wouldn't have sex with Reid, even with a condom, until he presented accredited documentation showing his negative test results for HIV and every known STD out there. A girl can never be too careful.

Reid had a smouldering, sexy, come-hither quality, which I have to say worked exceptionally well for me. But I knew I wasn't destined to end up with him. I also knew that I was in no danger of falling in love with him, I just didn't feel it. I was 'in like' for sure and 'lust' most definitely, but not love. I was simply enjoying myself. I even made my rock-goddess debut, joining the band on stage at the very prestigious Pickering Ribfest, a coveted gig, to be sure. Channelling my inner Stevie Nicks, I rhythmically freestyled to 'Hot Blooded' on a cowbell, proving that popular saying true: everyone can benefit from a little more cowbell. All in all, it was pure, uncomplicated fun.

From start to finish, my relationship with Reid lasted seven months, with its colossal, chaotic climax coming during a disastrous short holiday to Barbados, which I took with Reid, while he attended a bathroom-fixture convention. Yup, it's a thing.

Here's a little backstory to give this event some much-needed context. A few years before I met Reid, his marriage had abruptly ended after he'd caught his wife in bed with his best friend. As many of these stories start, he came home early, to see his wife and best friend naked, intertwined, deep in the act. The way Reid told the story, he stood there silently watching, pretty much paralysed with shock, waiting for a notable break in their activity to make his presence known. But most worrisome, whenever Reid spoke of either of them, his face would change. His skin would deepen in colour, his eyes grew Clint Eastwood fierce, and an intense, sharp bite came into his tone. I quickly learnt not to ask too many questions, to avoid the risk of losing Reid to his very raw, nostalgic pain, which could easily hijack a night.

I can't say for sure what Reid's temperament was like before his devastating discovery of betrayal. Maybe he was always jealous and thus insecure, incapable of really trusting, on a continuous hunt for the slightest blush of a lie. Or maybe it was the discovery of his best friend and his wife that gave birth to this emotional demon. I just know that Reid, with his collective life experiences, was the most jealous human being I'd ever encountered.

With two nights left on our Barbados trip, we were enjoying dinner at a lovely island restaurant. Reid enthusiastically talked about taking our relationship to the next level, moving in together, a conversation he delayed until the coconut gelato had arrived. He wasn't looking for that immediately, he assured me, but he was looking for a plan, a commitment, something the two of us could work towards, look forward to. Reid and his son moving in with me was not in my plan, nor could I see myself warming to the idea. I was quite happy to hang out, have sex and clang the occasional cowbell, but I didn't feel the need to engage in a deep or lengthy conversation about plans for our future, a future I honestly knew would never last as long as Reid's romanticised account. My *laissez-faire*, non-committal mantra of 'Let's just enjoy the ride' was something that left Reid uneasy. I mean, I wasn't pulling the emergency exit hatch and jettisoning, I just had little desire to talk about a plan that genuinely didn't have my name attached.

As a result, Reid seemed a tad raw and somewhat deflated when we returned to the Sandals resort. He suggested that we have a nightcap at their poolside bar. It was a hot and sticky Caribbean night, and the bar was crowded, loud, with a faint aroma of coconut-scented suntan oil. Reid went to get us drinks while I waited for him on the busy patio. When he returned a few minutes later, he found me talking to a tall, sweet guy from Georgia named Kenny Klassen, who, as I'd immediately discovered, was on his honeymoon.

'Kenny got married yesterday, and he's here on his honeymoon,' I told Reid.

Kenny jumped in with nervous, fevered excitement, in his broad Southern accent, 'But y'all will never guess what happened … My ex-girlfriend is here … right now … in this bar. Like, I'm thinking, *Shit, my wife* – still getting used to that word – *my wife is going to freak*.'

'Where's your wife now?' I asked Kenny, genuinely curious.

'She's inside talking to some new friends we met today on the Lovers' Sunset Cruise. I saw Clementine, that's my ex, who I don't think saw me, and excused myself and ran out here. Now I'm talking to you lovely couple.'

'Wow, Kenny,' I teased, 'sounds like you've got your hands full.'

He laughed. Reid did not. I could tell by Reid's body language that Kenny's presence was unwanted and was annoying him. Kenny rattled on as he kept nervously looking over his shoulder to see if his wife and/or Clementine were looking for him.

'Well, Ken,' I smiled, 'you'd better go find your wife, give her a little heads-up. Your marriage is certainly off to an interesting start.'

Kenny laughed as he put his arms round Reid and me, squeezing us both in tight, then kissed me on top of the head.

'Y'all are the sweetest couple, and yup … it's an interesting night for sure.' Kenny paused for a second, his face suddenly serious. 'Hey, you don't think Clementine's a stalker and followed me here, do you?'

'God, I hope not,' I said, thinking the same thing.

Reid shrugged Kenny's arm off his shoulder and said, 'You better go and deal with this.'

Seeming concerned he had over-shared, Kenny apologised sweetly for taking up so much of our time. He offered to buy us drinks, which Reid quickly and curtly turned down. Kenny thanked us again and disappeared into the thick, hot, coconut-smelling crowd.

Sipping my Tanqueray and tonic, I glanced at Reid. His face was intense, his body stiff and his blue eyes once again reminded me of Dirty Harry.

'What the fuck were you doing with him?' he started.

At that moment, I was honestly confused about what he meant. I asked, innocently enough, 'Are you talking about our Southern friend on his honeymoon?'

Reid raised his voice. 'You were flirting with him, his hands were all over you, and you let him kiss you.'

'What?' I said in complete shock. 'I wasn't flirting, I was being nice, and he didn't kiss me. What the hell are you talking about?'

'Didn't kiss you? Of course he kissed you, right here, in front of me, he kissed you!'

I paused for a moment to recall the last five to seven minutes. 'Are you talking about the kiss on the top of my head?' I asked.

Reid was in a rage, something I had seen glimpses of but nothing like this before. 'Of course I am,' he screamed. 'You allowed him to touch you, kiss you. You encouraged it.' Then Reid said something no man should ever, ever say to a woman, especially after suggesting they move in together. 'You're a lying whore.'

This immediately quietened the boisterous drinkers around us. I was shaken. I had never been called that before, and in no way was it acceptable.

'What did you just call me?' I said, totally enraged. 'You're jealous of that man on his honeymoon? The one with his ex-girlfriend here, as if you don't think he has enough on his plate, you think he was hitting on me?' I was furious. 'Reid, aside from the platonic kiss on the top of my head, much like my father used to give me, he had his arm around you too. Did you do something to encourage that?' I asked.

Reid's eyes shot into me. There was fiery rage inside him, making me take a step back.

'Jesus, Reid, seriously? This guy, his story, our brief interaction has set you off on this jealous rant?'

Reid interrupted me, now moving back and forth in a quick, pacing motion.

'You're fucking naive, Christina. I've seen this kinda thing before,' he yelled. 'Before you know it, he'll be inviting you back to his room to have sex with him and his wife, and he'll be using words like nig—'

'Oh, sweet Mother of God,' I interrupted. 'You've projected all of this onto him, created fictitious dialogue, and why? Because he's from the South, therefore he's a racist swinger?'

Reid glared at me, his red, angry face inches away from mine, and like a poisonous, vexed snake, he hissed, spat in my face, then turned and left. I stood in fright and embarrassment, the hot spit sliding down my cheek. A few people around me reacted.

'Hey, he can't do that to you,' said a burly drunk man in a tank top that read 'I'm Only Here for the Beer'. He made a move as if he was going to go after him.

'No, please don't,' I said, as someone handed me a damp cocktail napkin that read 'Love Is All You Need: Sandals'. I wiped the spit from my cheek.

'You need to report him,' he suggested.

There had now formed a small group of sunburnt enforcers; buff bodyguards in tank tops, board shorts and mullets surrounding me.

'Is he your boyfriend?' another asked.

'Yes,' I quietly answered.

'You can't go back to your room. That guy is violent.'

As I stood there, dazed, in the middle of this motley vigilante mob, I knew that the guy was right. I couldn't go back to the room.

I went to the front desk and emotionally explained the situation, hoping there might be a spare room, but I guess between people peddling faucets, honeymooners and their exes there wasn't a single empty room. So, I lay quietly by the pool most of the night, hoping with each passing hour, that Reid had fallen into a deep sleep, instead of anxiously sitting on the edge of the bed waiting for me to return.

Gazing at the sun peeking up from the horizon, I watched as night made way for the next day. Thoughts of Jackson washed over me as I lay in the stillness, staring up at the tropical sky. This wasn't going to change, just like it never had with Jackson.

The considerable difference was that this time I knew that. I didn't love Reid, and that in and of itself was freeing. For it was in large part my love for Jackson that had held me hostage, caged. I had been determined with the deepest desire to fix, or even keep alive, that deeply damaged human being. My absence of love for Reid saddled me with no such obligation. Nor did I have the slightest desire to prolong this obvious ending. *Who are these men I'm attracting into my orbit?* I thought defeatedly, staring into the brightening sky. Was I deliberately looking to ruin my life? I had more questions than answers, but what I did know was that Reid and his demons had no place in my world.

Returning to the room, I found Reid asleep, a couple of empty miniature bottles of Jack Daniel's on the bedside table. He was up with his alarm a short time after I had climbed into bed. The sounds of the shower, the opening and closing of drawers, the dragging of a chair to sit on and tie his shoes were all magnified, as I kept my eyes tightly shut.

He had one last day of the convention, and we were scheduled to fly out the following afternoon. I'd checked if I could get on a flight later that day, leave, not even tell him, but I wasn't successful. Flights were full, and I was stuck. That night I told him we were done. I wanted nothing more to do with him. Reid had calmed down, even apologising for his outburst, but kept insisting I look at my role of enticing Kenny into being so 'forward', for 'granting him permission to touch me'.

It was a silent ride to the airport, and when we checked in, I asked to be seated away from Reid. It was a full charter flight and they couldn't move me, so all I managed to do was torment him. There was some light attempt on his part to get into it again: my role, his jealousy, even a vain attempt to justify it all. I said nothing. I mean, what do you say to the person who spits in your face and calls you a whore? The answer is absolutely nothing.

Once we landed, I lost him at the airport. The last time I ever saw Reid, I was slouched down, hiding in the back of an airport limousine as it pulled away from the arrivals level, Reid angrily searching for me on the empty pavement.

I caught up with the girls on the phone when I got home, then a few days later in person, as this story required face-to-face girlfriend time and wine in its retelling. Of course, there was chatter about getting me back online, like I had fallen off some proverbial horse, to return me to surfing the world of catalogued men. But for now, I thought, this, my first online relationship, was about all the excitement this girl could handle. I contemplated with great longing becoming a lesbian, or at least bisexual. *Girls have got to be less complicated than this,* I thought. Plus, you know what they say about being bisexual: it doubles your chances of getting lucky. If only gender preference were a choice, I swear to you right now I'd be happily paddling around in a much prettier pond.

Damn my heterosexual tendencies.

The Book of

Edward

CHAPTER 1

The Man in the Park

*'It takes all the running you can do, to keep in the
same place. If you want to get somewhere else,
you must run at least twice as fast as that!'*
Lewis Carroll, *Alice In Wonderland*

You tell me. What would you call a stage in your life when
you've mentally kicked off your shoes and unhooked your
bra? Have therapists come up with a term for this phase when
you'd sooner plop yourself down on the sofa and watch gar-
dening shows all night, every night, than go out to one – and I
mean just *one* – more crowded, noisy bar? By this point in my
life, the days of me queuing for anything were long gone. To
that, I'd say, HA! Or I'd even give it a double HA-HA! I was
officially now that person you see leaving the concert during
the encore to get a head start on the crowds. It wasn't that I'd
given up on life, crawling under some massive boulder, never
to be seen again, but instead, I'd reframe it as a bit of an emotional surrender. I was giving in to the unsexy label of 'single
working mom'. Or maybe I should just call it what it was, my
middle-fucking-forties.

It was five years since my split from John and dating was not
high on my list of 'events worth attending', not since Reid. Not
that he'd left me jaded or cynical when it came to the world of
men, but I was relishing JOMO, the joy of missing out. I was
neither passionately for nor against the idea of having a serious
romantic relationship. But the way I saw it, I was already in a

fully committed relationship. I was deeply and platonically in love with my girlfriends, who were the threads of my sanity. Besides, I had two essential, all-encompassing life tasks: raising my children without totally fucking them up and running my company. And even if I'd wanted to get involved in something more profound, I don't know where the time would have magically appeared from. And if, say, an extra day had shown up every calendar week, I'd undoubtedly have spent it with friends and family (OK, maybe not all my family) or receiving eight-hour foot massages, blissfully disabling me from forming words. It wouldn't be in the lingering embrace of some guy who, given time, would be asking me to make him a sandwich.

I wasn't lonely. Exhausted, yes, overworked, for sure, but never lonely. My loneliest times had come in a ballroom surrounded by a thousand people in tuxedos and floor-length gowns as I'd watched John flirt with a pretty girl. Or sitting in a packed school auditorium, resonating with parental applause, as Briar disappointedly gazed out from the stage to the empty seat beside me. My source of loneliness was never in my solitude; it had been when I was deep inside my marriage, surrounded by a crowd of people. So no, loneliness wouldn't be an emotion I'd use to describe being single.

The same wasn't necessarily true for some of my girlfriends, who always seemed to be casting around for new messiahs. One friend described being single in a world of couples as 'being disabled', often feeling like she was excluded from dinner parties or social events — that she was not enough on her own, that without a partner or date, her presence would be distracting, incomplete to those 'whole' couples around her. As a result, she was on more of an active 'seek and capture' mission on those evenings when we'd hit the bars or clubs, or she'd do a deep dive into dating websites or high-priced professional matchmakers with fancy downtown offices. Then there was Sloane, the opposite of that. She'd openly and frequently declare, 'Why would I want to marry again? I already have children to look after and don't need one more.' Sloane talked about sex like it was a team sport. She was sexually fearless, even during moments when I think fear could've served her well. She had a playful belief that men were there for one purpose: to provide her with the crucial skills her vibrator, Thor, lacked (and to talk as little as possible). I think I fell somewhere in the middle, never needing to define myself as someone's wife nor declaring with any absolutes that I would never remarry. I guess that's why the Man in the Park caught me totally off guard.

I have a bit of a superpower, not that it would warrant me my own comic book. I have an uncanny recall of what I've worn during every significant moment of my life, as though I have a series of photographs I carry with me. That particular evening in May, I was wearing a faded pair of Chip & Pepper jeans and a T-shirt that read 'You Have More Power Than You Are Using', when our small neighbourhood park officially came out of hibernation. I can't say for sure who the T-shirt was speaking to, me or the Man in the Park I would meet that day, but regardless, it was the message I was broadcasting.

There were a few things about him that made him stand out immediately, aside from the BlackBerry attached to his ear and that he was the only man in a sea of moms and nannies. To start with, he looked like he'd just stepped out of the pages of *Town and Country* magazine, wearing a fine tweed suit with matching waistcoat and shiny dark-chocolate brogues. His tie was loosened slightly, giving me the impression that this was as casual as he got. He looked significantly older than me and the other moms, with his full head of neatly trimmed silver hair and manicured nails. His skin was tanned and gently weathered, suggesting he wasn't one to spend his leisure time indoors. He was trying desperately to manage his angry nine-year-old daughter, who was tugging at his trouser leg, while dealing with some business matter on the phone. It was the first day of the softball season, and she was having an emotional temper tantrum. My daughter Briar, who was also signed up for the team, against her eight-year-old will, was sitting on third base building little dirt piles along the baseline. She was blissfully oblivious to her surroundings, and was therefore surprised when the man's daughter started yelling at her.

'Hey, girl! Girl on third base, stand up and play. Daddy, get off your phone. This girl is sitting on the base, and she won't get up. Daddy, do something! Dad … DAD!!!!'

With a voice that had all the markers of British aristocracy, the Man in the Park calmly apologised to the person on the other end of the phone and said he'd call them back, and then turned his attention to the serious outfielder problem at hand, the third baseman.

'Who does that little girl on third base belong to?' he asked the moms and nannies.

At this point I looked up from my phone and realised all the commotion was around my daughter.

'She belongs to me,' I said. 'Briar, dear, you need to stand up. You're playing softball.'

Briar slowly and begrudgingly stood up, drawing a little circle around her small dirt piles with her pink *Powerpuff Girls* running shoe, as if to protect them.

'I guess your daughter hasn't played much softball before,' he said to me in his cut-glass British accent, sounding very much like a BBC Radio 4 announcer.

I smiled and said, 'Not the one on the field,' then nodded towards where my other daughter, Sam, an eleven year old whose entire body was covered in a thick layer of playground dirt and magic marker, was readying herself to bat. 'This is more Sam's thing.'

Sam reminded me of Pig-Pen, the dust-clouded character from the Charlie Brown comics. Her deep olive skin and dark-chocolate eyes, which she'd got from her dad, and her 'filthy and fine with that' attitude made me wonder just what I had in common with this little Mediterranean-looking child of the mud. I recalled my mother's words shortly after I'd spent 52 gruelling hours forcing that child from my body. She looked down at her dark, hairy newborn granddaughter and said, 'Christina, you're going to need a DNA test to prove you're the real mother.'

The coach signalled to the outfield to move in, hoping for an easy out since a girl was at bat. Just then, Sam cracked the bat on the first pitch and sent the ball flying over every outfielder's head. I jumped to my feet and cheered as Sam casually rounded the bases, with the kids on the field scrambling to try and retrieve her well-hit ball.

'Great hit, Sam!' I yelled.

Sam smugly smiled as she landed hard on the home plate, kicking up a small cloud of dust, clearly making a point.

'I guess they won't be calling in the outfielders next time I come to bat, Mom.'

'Not a chance they'll make that mistake twice, Sam,' I said.

'What total losers,' she said, victoriously kicking the home plate, loud enough for all to hear.

And there it was ... evidence she was actually mine.

The man's daughter had stared in silent awe at Sam's home run.

'I'm Edward Crawford-Clarke,' he said, smiling, 'and that ... that is my daughter, Quintana, Quinn for short.' So the spring season began. Every rainless Tuesday evening at 6:30pm, Edward, the neighbourhood moms and I would gather on the park bench and watch our children round bases, catch and throw, win and lose, as we engaged in friendly banter, sharing tidbits about our lives. I learnt that Edward worked as a compliance officer for a large global pharmaceuticals company. He had been transferred to Canada from his company's head office in London over twelve years ago, and had met Karina, his second wife, shortly after he'd moved to Toronto. He was an old Etonian and a Cambridge lad, thus explaining his Queen's English and impeccable tweedy fashion sense. I thought he couldn't have been more British if he had been draped in the Union Jack, wearing wellies, and holding a cup of PG Tips.

I also learnt from the moms who were friends with his wife, Karina, that she was battling a rare form of brain cancer.

'She has four to six months,' one mom told me.

'That poor little girl,' another said. 'I heard they've brought in special grief counsellors to deal with their daughter.'

I learnt that Edward and Karina had recently consented to a clinical trial that included radical brain surgery, experimental drugs and radiation. I remember thinking that Edward's calm demeanour gave no hint at all of what he and his family were fighting. Perhaps it was his English breeding, that stiff upper lip and 'keep calm and carry on' attitude. If he ever spoke of it, it was as though he were describing a secondary plot point from a Movie of the Week. *Maybe that's just what you need to do in a crisis,* I thought. *Emotionally detach yourself, so it allows you to get out of bed in the morning and function without wanting to drive your car straight off a bridge.* After softball ended and throughout the summer, I didn't see Edward or his daughter. If he did cross my mind or his name came up in conversation, I'd speak of him casually, referring to him merely as the Man in the Park.

When autumn's flag football started, I saw Edward again in the park, looking very much the same as the previous spring, BlackBerry holster and all. I was giving my dog, Hunter, a much required quick walk, and if it hadn't been for the events of the previous night, I most likely would not have had the dire need to stop and speak to him. The evening before, I'd arrived home later than usual, ten-ish, I think, having just returned from a client dinner. My nanny, Fernanda, was waiting up for me in her flannel nightie. She was upset. You'd think I'd remember what had made Fernanda so troubled, almost in tears as she talked about my daughter, but the event that immediately followed has permanently erased any memory of that conversation.

Standing in the kitchen, I was listening to Fernanda emotionally discuss Briar's bad behaviour, when she suddenly stopped mid-sentence. There was a slight confusion on her face, like she was struggling to remember someone's name, or trying to recall something that was just on the tip of her tongue. Silently straining, she started mouthing the words, reminding me of a struggling fish out of water, its mouth gasping for life.

'Fernanda?' I asked, concerned. 'Are you OK?'

Fernanda's eyes flickered and rolled back into her head. I rushed towards her as she collapsed in my arms, the light scent of a Downy dryer sheet surrounding her. She had had a brain aneurysm.

When I saw Edward the following evening in the park, I was running on fumes. Fernanda had survived the night, barely, but was in a coma and in a critical condition. I was on the desperate hunt for a temporary nanny, and was praying that Fernanda, who meant so much to me and my girls, would recover. My conversation with Edward was brief, factual, like a journalist reporting from a crime scene.

'If you know of anyone?' I said. 'I need someone immediately.'

'Of course,' he said empathetically. 'I'll see what I can do.'

I thanked him and left.

On my way back home, something unexpected happened. I was flooded with a deep swell of emotion, the kind that sideswipes you, like when some bittersweet, nostalgia-inducing song starts playing. It wasn't just Fernanda's situation that had caused me to feel this way, it was Edward, it was the Man in the Park. Walking away from him, I was overcome with an unsettling feeling at leaving his side. I mean, I hardly knew him, not really, which made this all the more confusing. Something had shaken loose in me, and I felt rolling over me a palpable melancholy, a longing, as Hunter led me down my street. I recognised an emotion I hadn't felt in a long time: without his doing anything, the Man in the Park had made me feel lonely. As if something was missing from my life, something significant, which had been painfully pulled away from me the moment I'd walked away from him. In a moment of absolute clarity, I stood motionless on the pavement and knew this almost-stranger would be one of the most significant loves of my life.

Two and a half seasons would pass before I'd see Edward and his daughter again. I hadn't thought much about him, and had mostly dismissed that fleeting moment of enlightened loneliness as nothing more than emotional and physical exhaustion. It had never completely left me, like a faint shadow on a cloudy day, but it was Edward's daughter Quinn who ultimately drew me in like a powerful magnet, drew us all in.

Quinn was sadly gazing down at her trainers, her short, dark, messy hair covering most of her freckled face. She was kicking the wood chips from the outer edge of the playground when I saw her. My daughters on swings, their gleeful shouts of 'Higher, Mommy!' or 'Give me an underdog!' left her long-ingly watching us. There was something about her little face that haunted me as she stood there alone, on the outside looking in. I hadn't heard anything about her mother's health. I didn't even know if she was still alive, as there was very little overlap between my world and theirs that went beyond the park. Calling out to her, I said, 'Hey, Quinn, come before someone grabs this empty swing.' At that tiniest of invitations, and with the enthusiasm of a puppy, she came bounding into our lives.

Weekends often came to include Quinn, and on warm summer days I'd find her in our pool with Briar. Sometimes the two would record dance routines to *High School Musical* in clothes and shoes they'd pulled from my closet. They ran a short-lived dog-washing business (I believe Hunter was the only customer). Elaborate forts with giant footprints filled the basement – lovingly constructed from every single sofa cushion, blanket and unclaimed sheet the girls could find. This was where I'd find them in the morning, peacefully sleeping, grateful the whole thing hadn't collapsed on them in the middle of the night. When it was nearly time to go, Quinn's instructions to me were always the same: 'Christina, when my dad comes to pick me up, offer him a beer. He'll always say "yes" to a beer, and that way I can stay longer.' She was right. He always did.

With Edward's wife still deep within the clinical trial, the five of us became a little makeshift family, venturing beyond my pool on hot days to places where you'd find nothing but outwardly happy families. As the seasons passed, my friendship with Edward blossomed, and took me and my lifelong-disdain for winter outside the city's dirty snow and treacherous sidewalks, and introduced me to the peaceful, rolling snow-covered ski hills of the rural countryside. It was there, in my mid-forties, staring death in the eyes, that I strapped on my first pair of skis. I'll be honest, this injury-likely sport didn't come easily to me. As my kids were racing down the slopes, and in Sam's case sometimes backwards, just to show off, I was surrounded by four- and five-year-olds on the bunny hill. I'd hear the gleeful, exuberant calls from Sam to her friends as she exited the clubhouse: 'Hey everyone, you gotta check out my mom! She's over with the toddlers trying to learn to ski. It's hysterical.'

Some evenings after Edward had put his daughter to bed, he'd join me at the farmhouse I had rented to drink a full-bodied red by the fire. As the embers burned to an orange glow and with the wine deliciously masking the day's ski lesson humiliation, Edward and I would talk effortlessly for hours. It was the best winter I'd ever had.

Through that winter, Edward's wife, Karina, made a bit of a miraculous rebound in the clinical trial she was by then well into. She was nowhere close to being healed, but doctors were remarkably hopeful for the first time. Edward was even able to bring Karina to my annual family Christmas party, a tradition I'd started after the Yuletide spirit was sucked from me, much like by a Death Eater from *Harry Potter*, after my split with John. There is nothing worse than a nasty divorce to kill the Christmas spirit, and since John's two affairs had nicely coincided with two consecutive Christmases, for me, the holiday had had all the joy of a root canal. However, these Christmas parties quickly became a new source of seasonal happiness for me in what was generally a bleak, unhappy time. I'd hire a wonderful Santa, who'd announce his arrival by rapping on the frosty windows to a house full of excited kids. The happy little squeals – 'Look! Santa is here!' – would temporarily bring the joy back into that holiday for me, as Santa entered our warm house that smelt of gingerbread, mulled wine and Douglas fir.

My mother would arrive smelling of Chanel No. 5 and sparkling like New Year's Eve at The Ritz. My father, close behind, carrying Elena's signature caviar pie and various other Christmas treats. Led by Santa, we'd sing carols, and all take turns sitting on Santa's lap, children of all ages posing for photos. The twelve years I threw this party guaranteed at least one annual family photo. My parents, sisters, nieces, nephews and whoever else might've made up the fabric of our family that year were all happy to nostalgically reflect and re-enact earlier days, when Santa was proof that magic was real.

As I lived through them, I didn't fully understand those times as significant, more than knowing they were getting me through the brutal heartbreak I'd come to associate with the Christmas season. But as I think back, those parties just might be the sweetest memories I have with my family. How I wish during those times that someone from the future had gently tapped me on my shoulder and said, 'Christina, look around, this is what you will miss the most.'

Regardless of the season, Edward always seemed present for his daughter, and I physically ached for my girls to have that kind of male role model in their lives, a father figure who showed up and was unconditionally there for them, no matter what. *Is this how a modern-day Prince Charming dresses?* I wondered. *Wearing a Harris Tweed suit, sounding like a member of the British royal family, wearing a BlackBerry like some sort of fashion accessory?* I had never previously dated a man who needed to wear a suit to work. In fact, it was something I was proud of, in a reverse snobbery kind of way. Proud that the wardrobe of my people was overpriced ripped jeans, vintage concert T-shirts, and leather biker jackets that had never come close to riding a motorcycle. Had I been fishing in the wrong pond this whole time? A shallow creative swamp filled with temperamental, self-important directors and

emotionally stunted ad men who'd often mistake the importance of their latest Bud Light campaign with curing cancer.
Shouldn't I stop looking for love in the same place I had lost
it? Edward was the furthest thing I could imagine from that
pond, and his allure was growing by the day.

As winter gave way to spring, some described Karina's
commitment to life as nothing short of a medical miracle.
Conversations with doctors were no longer hopeless, or even
sombre: no more 'These were not the results we were hoping
for,' and no further advice to 'get her affairs in order'. Karina's
frail body grew sturdier, and on some warm evenings she even
ventured outside to sit and watch her daughter play softball in
the park. Her sparse, wispy hair did nothing to hide the giant
scar that wrapped around her head like a long, thick centipede.
At the crack of the bat or as she ran the bases, Karina's daughter
was visibly irked by her mother's faint cheers, and she'd run and
hug me instead.

'Quinn,' I'd whisper uncomfortably, struggling to untan-
gle her little arms from around my waist, 'go hug your mom.
She's excited about your home run.' But Quinn would take
off running in the other direction, or worse, hug me tighter
and declare openly to Karina, and all those watching, that she
wanted nothing to do with her sick, broken mother, as there
was someone better suited to the job of loving her, of being a
mom … and that was me.

As I enjoyed the upside of a well-hit ball or the pure pleasure of a little hand happily finding its way into mine, Karina
endured it silently. I felt I was the source of tremendous happiness and incredible pain at the same time. Karina was frail,
scarred, maimed, not dead but not quite alive, and there was
me, a healthy version of her former self, who'd precipitously
stepped into her role, possibly stealing from her what must've

been her primary motivation for living: the love of her daughter. I felt both heroic and evil. I had effectively given Quinn the mother she so desperately needed, but wasn't Karina now without a daughter, at least in an emotional sense? An act of genuine love should come without motive, so maybe that's what I was struggling with the most. I'd positioned myself into that family as Karina's successor, prematurely sliding my chair around their family table. And didn't that mean I was shamefully waiting for some poor woman to die so I could take her place?

Despite my vacillating emotions, Edward happily reassured me that he was grateful for my presence in his and his daughter's lives.

'Karina's not up to the task,' he'd say, almost with promise, as if his affection and his need for me tied me to him, drawing me further and deeper into his world. How I hated myself for not hating myself more.

But I could almost smell the change that was coming, like the metamorphosis of the seasons. Edward's eyes conveyed an unspoken promise, foreshadowing the secrets we would keep. We had not so much as held hands, but I could feel the thunderous rattling of the few barriers that stood between us. Edward carried a massive steamer trunk full of tragic bits and pieces: illness, a damaged daughter, all painted with a thick coat of Protestant guilt. *This isn't something I would choose,* I told myself. I believed this had been chosen for me, perhaps serving as my justification. I could not fix Karina, but I believed I could fix, heal and love this man and his daughter like I was a messiah, and they were my new religion. And Edward could give my children the type of dad they so desperately needed. They needed me, my children needed him, and now I believed I knew what the words on my T-shirt were telling me: I had more power than I was using.

CHAPTER 2

A Family Affair

*'I had to touch you with my hands, I had to taste you
with my tongue; one can't love and do nothing.'*
Graham Greene, *The End of the Affair*

I t just happened ... I didn't mean to fall in love with him.

Isn't that what we all say at the beginning of an affair? As
if by somehow declaring that overused, clichéd excuse to the
world, or maybe just to yourself, it exonerates you from your
actions or choices, leaving you in the wake of decisions that
somehow you weren't responsible for making, stuck between
'what if', and 'fuck it'.

The word 'affair' gives birth to a sensation I'd best describe
as paradoxical, an agony and an ecstasy, a crazy-making 'I
have to see you NOW before I kill myself' passion paired with
a healthy balancing dose of self-loathing and guilt. My body's
response was also a dead giveaway, often creating an intense
swelling in my chest making it hard to breathe. The butterflies
in my stomach were now replaced by tiny jackhammers pounding away at my insides, and my heartbeat rattled my eardrums
as if I had just run up three flights of stairs. An instant surge
of blindness hit me when Edward entered a room, plunging all
others around him into darkness. If I hadn't known better, I'd
have thought I was having a stroke.

I knew I was locked in, addicted. I was in the thick of it, this
heroin-like, supernova love-drug holding me in place. It's the
kind of addiction so intense that there needs to be something

catastrophic to blow you out of each other's orbit. Something that intense rarely fizzles away. Sex was a delicious forbidden fruit, as told by foggy car windows on a cold night. It was quickly devoured in parks, parking lots and movie theatres. I was alive, awoken from a long, cold hibernation with an intense starvation, a hunger I could only describe as ravenous. I ask you, how do you quit something so incredibly intense?

There are many reasons one might have an affair. It's even socially acceptable in certain cultures, an understood fact, much like that cappuccinos are not to be sipped after noon. The French immediately come to mind. But that European philosophy tends not to translate too well to English-speaking Anglo-Saxon countries that have feasted on the lofty expectations that movies and books have given us about love and marriage … once again, I blame Disney.

When I asked him straight out if he had ever had an affair before, he told me he had, but immediately assured me that 'this' was different. He told me about her, the woman who came before me, who'd had an amazing golf swing, had drunk martinis with a twist at business lunches and had reported directly to him. I thanked him for his transparency, although I have to say I took that news with an uncomfortable silence. I understood their affair had lived in corporate hotel rooms with staggered arrival times, surrounded by glass office towers, views they never saw, and tiny packaged soaps they both would smell of later. Theirs had not been in the shadows of giant forts made of pillows, blankets and gingerbread-scented air. Theirs had held no promises, no talk of leaving, divorcing, blending. Theirs had been uncomplicated hotel sex, scheduled between a quarterly accounts presentation and Karina's chemotherapy. Not all affairs are meant to break up a marriage.

I was in love with a married man, one with a sick wife who

was committed to living regardless of any diagnosis. In my more optimistic moments, I leant into Edward's assurances that his marriage had been on life support years before Karina had got sick, that I was not the cause of its inevitable ending, but rather the shiny new beginning for him and Quinn. My darker moments always circled back to my strong beliefs about affairs and cheating. Wasn't I doing to Karina what Dom 1 had done to me? I was now realising that perhaps John had assured her with equally compelling reasons.

'Patience,' Edward would say. 'I love you, my daughter loves you, my future is with you.'

I'm not the other woman, I'd tell myself and him. But if that were true, why were we hiding? That in itself told me I was doing something wrong.

My affair, as I choose to call it now, but didn't back then, started long before our first kiss, before that first knowing glance that foreshadowed intent. Who knows, maybe it started with a crack of the bat. It existed for two years before Edward would move out of his and Karina's bed and into the nanny suite of their house on Dawlish Avenue. It would be two years before we'd walk holding hands on a busy downtown street, or I'd be introduced as something other than 'a good friend'. I was hiding in plain sight.

We broke up several times during that period I called purgatory, constantly circling back to the same impossible, punishing impasse. I was exhausted, tired of chasing a moment I wasn't sure was ever coming; not certain what Edward was waiting for, but certain he was waiting. My guilt, without mercy, chastised me, as the voices inside my head gave me more reasons to leave than to stay. There were inane, looping dialogues and exhausting rationalisations where the prayer became the argument. It's going too fast … It's not going fast enough … Give it time …

I've given it time … We need to be careful … I'm tired of being careful … I can't live like this anymore … Neither can I. These would lead to weeks of radio silence, mourning the possibility of something so close, so real, something I could almost but never quite touch, like the vanishing tail of a beautiful dream. Excruciating, silent suffering immediately shattering like a thin sheet of ice beneath my feet after a simple text from Edward: 'It's me.'

But it wasn't just the two of us who climbed into bed. That's not a fair account of how it unfolded. That's not what happens when you come with young children, pre-programmed like some bonus DVD content you never planned on watching. It was all of us, five in a bed, six if I include Karina; a family affair one might call it, and I have to say it was crowded, with little people not accustomed to sharing. Before Edward and I had the customary privilege of becoming a couple, before going on a date, we were a family. We were a family with Karina still actively holding on to the titles of mom and wife, and with that came a host of complications and a banquet of consequences.

Edward rewired me. He showed me my girls needed a better father, and he did this by just showing up. He had me longing for the structure of a family I hadn't been searching for, confident in my belief that I was enough for my daughters, until I wasn't. I didn't know this was missing in me until I met Edward, and after that, it was all I could see, the hole he'd unintentionally created in my little world. Yet I was encouraged to remain confident, trusting that love and time would heal the wounded and that the glorious end would more than justify the adulterous means.

I think it was Dr Phil, or maybe Oprah, who, when talking about affairs, said, 'Two years … If they don't leave after two years, they ain't going.' I guess Edward had seen that episode.

'This is it,' we both excitedly agreed, looking around an old cottage on Georgian Bay. This would be our middle ground. This would not be his, or hers, or mine … this would be ours. It had been about three years since Edward and I had been officially 'out', five years that we'd been together, and roughly seven years from when we'd met. Karina had beat cancer, although the aggressive treatment targeting her brain had left her frequently confused, and she required a full-time caregiver. I always made a special effort when I saw her at family events. She'd often blush when I complimented her on something like a colourful scarf she had draped around her neck. She was always friendly, although she could never remember my name.

Buying a summer cottage together instead of throwing our collective spawn into a full-time living arrangement in the city, an arrangement that could not guarantee survivors, was something both Edward and I agreed on. The kids were like chalk and cheese, as my dad would say, and I don't think you could find three more completely different children if you spent an entire lifetime looking. Quinn and I got along well when it was just the two of us, but she didn't like sharing me with my girls, or her dad, for that matter. In public, to her friends, to her teachers, to the ladies who did our nails, she'd introduce me as her mother, and like that little girl with the octopus arms in the park, she was often affectionate and so in need of a healthy, traditional mom. Edward was at his happiest when I was engaging with Quinn, often spontaneously offering me a gentle hug and a soft 'I love you' after any drama-free day.

'You happy?' I'd frequently ask Edward.

'Happier,' he'd respond.

Never once was the answer to that question, 'Yes, I'm happy.' I took that on like a personal challenge.

I worked hard to bring joy and normalcy into his family – like I was pulling open dusty curtains and bringing fresh-cut flowers into a stale, dim room – but it was something he rarely, if ever, did with mine. Edward seemed unable to engage with my girls, especially if Quinn was around, and my girls felt in part ignored by him. If I am honest, I short-changed my kids with my relentless quest to heal the Crawford-Clarkes, to keep the peace or make concessions in their favour. I shrunk myself, and with that my children, and if I were granted just one do-over in my life, that would be what I would change. As mothers tend to do, I carry that guilt with me, a long laundry list I call 'If I Could Go Back in Time', a regret-filled apology about the difficulty and guilt of parenting. Perhaps if Edward had stepped into the role of stepdad, the imbalance wouldn't have been so extreme. It's a bloody difficult role, stepparenting, made more complicated when one parent tries too much, perhaps to the detriment of her children, and the other parent, also to the detriment of his child, is too paralysed to try at all.

The days when Quinn and Briar would build forts and record dance routines together were long gone. Now teenagers, which in and of itself can be a wholly repugnant time, both girls had a quiet, but growing, disdain for each other. It's not like they were fighting, at least not with each other. It was a quiet, eery discord one might see in a movie just before the shark attacks the blissfully unaware swimmer and drags her beneath the surface. Or when the woman alone at night hears the sound of breaking glass outside her window. You know something's coming, you know it's not good, you just don't know when.

When Edward was with his daughter, there was a tension that our part-time summer living arrangement brought into blinding focus. She'd throw tantrums if she didn't get her way, or start raging arguments. His positive mood could instantly vanish, triggered by something as simple as an aggressive eye-roll or a well-stomped little foot pointed in his direction. His cocktail of emotions vacillated between love, dislike, obligation, loyalty and annoyance, all drenched in a supersonic level of parental guilt with kryptonite-like properties. The guilt would manifest in Edward in one of two ways: either in an earth-rattling rage or in quiet, heaving sobs as he held his head heavy in his hands. I'd temporarily lose the man I loved to these raw emotions, and both came with the same declaration: that he'd failed as a father.

'Teenagers are supposed to be vile,' I playfully reminded him. 'It's to ensure we kick them out of the nest.'

I had never seen someone work so hard to be the father he wanted to be yet be so beaten down. This led me to anxiously attempt to keep everything as calm as humanly possible on my end, walking on eggshells, doing the best I could to make everyone's life a little bit nicer, making each room more beautiful than it needed to be. I didn't want to find my girls in the centre of his storm, and for the most part, they never were. In what was likely one of my worst parenting moments, and they are abundant, one weekend I paid my children to behave. 'Be extra helpful,' I told them. 'Clear the table without being asked.' This was me projecting my own fears onto my daughters. This was my anxiety growing inside of me like weeds overtaking a garden.

That Christmas, Edward presented me with an engagement ring. I say 'presented', as technically he never popped the question that usually goes along with a diamond engagement ring. Nor could I remember him formally sliding the ring onto my finger, as tradition might dictate. My father would've described the proposal as 'implied', as Edward handed me a small velvet box, and I happily said 'yes' to a question that was never asked. Edward did ask one question that night, confirming the ring's intention. Moments after it had found its way onto my finger, clearing his throat as if he were signalling the start of a meeting, he asked, 'So, how are you with a prenup, Christina?' Something was unsettling in his voice, it was that of an accountant or a lawyer, not a man in love. Maybe it was his uncanny ability to instantly transform a romantic celebration into a business transaction that bothered me. I can't explain exactly what it was. I was happy, but something stuck with me that night I got engaged, like a small warning.

Thoughts swirled around in my head. First, make no mistake, I was happy with his proposal, implied or otherwise, and no one could ever mistake Edward for being romantic. He would tell you that. Sure, he was technically still married to Karina, but I had resigned myself long ago to the fact that the complexities of our relationship would never make it traditional. I believed or still wanted to believe in a happy ever after ... for all of us. Edward was a good man, and sure, he wasn't perfect, but God knows neither was I. I just didn't know at the time that the most he could give my children was the least they deserved.

I smiled, shifting my focus from the brilliant ring sparkling on my finger to his question, his only question, and answered, 'I'm fine with it, Edward,' and I meant it. I had no issue signing a prenup. In fact, with assets of my own, it would be preferred. But how the timing of his question sucked the oxygen from the room. I can't tell you how, but I knew at that moment that I'd never marry Edward.

I think Oscar Wilde summarised the situation perfectly: 'There are only two tragedies in life. One is not getting what one wants, and the other is getting it.'

CHAPTER 3

My New 'F' Word

'Time may be a great healer, but it's a lousy beautician.'
Anonymous

OK, I need to go all tangential here for a moment. Permit me to take a small side-step, a wee digression from my narrative search for men, and discuss something huge, mind-bending, a powder keg of hormonal emotion … turning 50.

On the morning of my 50th birthday, I woke with the kind of panic that was usually reserved for watching my phone sink into the toilet. I had my first hot flush. I hadn't even got out of bed, and there it was. Starting at my feet, it rolled up my body like a steamroller you see on the streets levelling hot asphalt and molten tar. My body was fiery, tingling as it started producing what could only be described as a tsunami of sweat. *Fuck, seriously?* I thought. *This couldn't have waited a week, until I had somewhat come to grips with the idea that I'm officially middle-aged?* Wasn't it enough that I'd just turned 50, that I had half a century of questionable men, decades of yo-yo dieting, and a smorgasbord of poorly thought out choices under my belt, all tinted with too much Chardonnay? I'm calling this Mother Nature bitch out. I'm sorry, but I can't imagine she's actually a mother or even a sista. She must be one of those mean bitches laughing away from her place on high, as she metes out her unique brand of punishment to reward those women who have made it this far. Rewards like random new facial whiskers that you can't even call hairs because they are so thick and wiry they could hold beads, or flop sweats, or a metabolism rate that has slammed itself into reverse. Do you know what men get when they turn 50? A new sports car.

If the hot flush were not gift enough, staring into my bathroom mirror, blurry-eyed and seriously depressed that I had now added the term 'flop sweat' to my vocabulary, I gasped. *What the hell?* There, in my right eyebrow, was a white hair standing out like a grain of rice in a bowl of poppy seeds. *You've got to be kidding me.* Fumbling around, I found my tweezers, put on my reading glasses, and began to deal with the task at hand: 'You, my ugly white friend, have got to go.'

In hindsight, maybe I should've waited until after my coffee, when focusing would not have been such a monumental challenge. I went in with all the skill of a toddler with a scalpel and proceeded to pluck every hair around that one white one, forming a little bald circle the size of a pencil eraser, and yet, still standing to attention, was that white eyebrow hair.

Staring back in the mirror was not only the ageing face of a 50-year-old, newly menopausal (the English language's most unsexy word) woman, but I was now missing a circle-shaped chunk of my right eyebrow. Already, 50 and I weren't getting along. I stumbled to the kitchen for my latte. I forgot to put the coffee pod in my Nespresso maker and instead made a combination of frothy milk and beige hot water. Does Nespresso not get that if I haven't had my coffee, operating the coffee machine is a daunting task? I started again, then took my big-ass mug and sat in my backyard. It was May, and the air was sweet from the lilac tree in my garden.

'I am 50,' I said out loud to my latte. 'The big five-oh.'

I took a sip of my hot coffee and let out an audible sigh. This was not where I'd thought I'd be. How had the sum of my choices brought me here? I was too self-absorbed in what I was calling my new 'F' word (fifty) at that moment to be grateful for all that I had. I knew I was luckier than most. I was sitting in this lovely garden behind my beautiful house. I was healthy, and so were my children, and in most scenarios, that should have been enough. But that day, it was my 50th birthday, and I was determined, at least in part, to wallow in a little self-loathing.

I'd adequately warned my friends and family with the absolute promise of death to anyone who dared utter that decade's name. Yet my phone rang, and my mother broke into a mixed octave rendition of 'Happy Birthday', throwing '50th' into every line.

> 'Happy 50th birthday to you,
> Happy 50th birthday to you,
> Happy 50th birthday, dear Christina,
> Happy 50th birthday to you!'

Elena had not heeded my genuine birthday warning. However, I knew that I had grown far too fond of her to contemplate going through with my birthday threat.

'Thanks, Mamma,' I said, reminding her she was now old enough to have a child who was 50. At 76, she wasn't interested in hearing my complaints about 50. I get it. I had the same thoughts when a younger colleague was whipped up about turning 30, weeping openly in the office, crying, 'I'm so old, I'm so old, no one will ever want to have sex with me again.'

That evening there would be a room full of my friends and family waiting at a small restaurant called Le Petit Castor – or as we affectionately translated it, The Little Beaver, due to its immense popularity with the ladies. It was supposed to be a surprise party, but after I had announced to my dear friend Lizzie a few weeks earlier, after finding my first grey pubic hair, that life was more than surprising enough, it had been decided that I had

had enough surprises. Edward had outsourced the planning of this soirée to Lizzie, knowing his limitations on any gathering that didn't have a formal agenda and a PowerPoint presentation.

That afternoon would be busy with 'paint and bodywork': waxing, a facial, and colour and highlights with Mateo, my gay Bulgarian hairdresser. Why I hadn't left my white eyebrow hair to the professionals I'd be seeing later that day can only be chalked up as my first senior moment. I've often said that you know you've spent a lot of money on your hair when you're invited to your hairdresser's wedding. And you know you've spent an absurd, stupid, obscene amount of money on your hair if you're part of his wedding party. That was *moi*. I honestly believe my weekly hair appointments are my only fundamental princess-like trait. I equate blow-drying my hair with pumping gas. If I can have someone else do it for me, it's worth every blessed nickel.

With these weekly trips, Mateo and I had become good friends, and I often confided and gossiped with him. He had been through my breakup with John, and I'd been through his breakup with Andre. I was there to listen to all the delicious details of his first date with Jean-Marc, now his husband. Girls, especially city girls, need their gay BFFs, and mine were Mateo and Jean-Marc, as essential to a perfect day as cheesecake and good wine. They were unfiltered, honest-as-shit fashion police whom I could rely on totally to give it to me straight, even if they weren't.

'Hell, no, Christina, you're NOT going out with us tonight looking like Laura Fucking Ingalls.' I sheepishly surveyed my pleated ankle-length skirt and Shetland jumper. 'Go find some leather pants, for God's sake,' Jean-Marc barked, pointing his arm and flicking his wrist in the general direction of my bedroom.

'And a corset, darlin'... the black one,' Mateo was quick to add.

It was Jean-Marc who'd shown me the more refined touches of giving the perfect blowjob, with the aid of a wine bottle. Who better than a gay man, right? 'Watch and learn,' he demonstrated. 'They don't call this a job for nothing.' He caressed the bottom of the wine bottle. ('These are the balls, Christina. Don't forget to cradle the balls') and wrapped his other hand around the neck of the bottle, and with precision timing his lips moved up and down on its glass shaft. I could not look away. Jean-Marc then brought his lips off the bottle with an audible smack, wiped the corners of his mouth as if to signify another satisfied customer, and handed the bottle to me. 'This, my darling,' he said, his eyes twinkling, 'this is going to be your superpower.' Mateo and Jean-Marc's contribution to my life was invaluable.

Now that I was officially too old for TikTok but too young for a shower chair, I decided that 50 needed to come with some new rules. It wasn't enough that the ads popping up on my Facebook page had seemingly changed overnight, as even my social media platforms were warning me to brace myself. Once plagued with annoying pop-up ads for private schools, nanny services and Club Med singles vacations, I was now assaulted with ads for non-surgical facelifts, funeral planning and Silver Singles, a dating app for geriatrics. Fifty was slamming me from all directions, and if I couldn't stop it, which clearly I could not, I decided new rules about life, love and men were now in order.

Let's begin with the words and/or phrases that meant I would immediately and guiltlessly eliminate any man, old or new, from my life if he said it more than once:

Okey-dokey

My bad

Wifey

Big boy pants

Captain Obvious

Trouser snake

Bro (unless, of course, he's your brother)

No offence (which usually was attached to a sentence
   that was indeed offensive)

As I'm on a roll, here's an abridged list of my new, 50-plus intolerances;

* People eating candies in cellophane wrappers in the theatre
* Gluten-free, dairy-free, lactose-free, vegan dinner guests
* People driving too slow in the fast lane
* A long-lasting red light at an empty intersection
* Room-temperature drinking water
* Scented Kleenex

Oh, and let me add, I was no longer available for things that made me feel like shit.

Moving along, let's discuss sex and honesty as told by a woman now on the other side of the mountain. I'm no longer afraid to say, 'You've got the wrong spot' or 'I appreciate your efforts, babe, but it's just not going to happen that way.' My younger self could rarely summon the required courage or gentle verbal instruction to lead the guys into getting it right. Thus, sex took on more of a non-verbal horizontal dance lesson. A little heel-toe, ball-change, *dos-à-dos*, box step and, with any luck, we were flossing. I think I probably confused a generation of young men into thinking they were Patrick Swayze when the truth was, they didn't know how to dance, dirty or otherwise.

As a woman, I recognise there is a little more to my orgasm than my male counterpart, who could easily get himself off rubbing up against a table leg. But what favours are we doing for mankind if we aren't saying, 'Hold up a sec, buddy, that's not where you think it is.' I mean, honestly, how are we expecting them to bake a soufflé if they've never been taught the proper way to separate eggs? Sure, you will get something if you mix all the ingredients and bake it in the oven. It might taste just fine, but don't confuse that baked, eggy mixture with a soufflé if it doesn't rise.

Another thing, I would no longer be faking my orgasms, not a single one. Nor would I go to the excruciating effort to time my orgasm with my partner's. Life's too short. I now have no qualms communicating with a gentle tap to the top of his head, 'I appreciate your efforts, but I think we're done here.' Oh, and here's something no woman over 50 ever wants to hear: 'Don't worry, baby, I can go all night.' If this takes longer than an episode of *Friends*, I will likely lose interest. Sure, vacation sex, special-occasion sex, or sex that first year of a new relationship are all exceptions ... but as a general rule, this is not Netflix bingeing.

I could also say out loud, with absolutely no sense of guilt or obligation, I would not be having morning sex. Nope. Nada. Not going to happen, even on vacation. My younger self for sure had endured morning sex, more times than my sleepy head could count. But my older, more fabulous, honest self is here to tell you it always was under an unspoken obligation, much like attending a company bowling party. I'll go, but I will tell you right now, I'm not going to have a good time. I know very few women who wake up from an eight-hour sleep and the first thing that pops into that cloudy, un-caffeinated brain of theirs before they pee or even brush their teeth is, 'I know what I could use right now, a penis penetrating me.'

Sex, as I've got older, has only got better, more freeing, and, dare I say, even more adventurous. I can't speak for my married compadres, those miraculous women who've been willingly married and having sex with the same guy who's been leaving the used teabag in the sink and the toilet seat up for decades, but kudos to you, girlfriend, especially if the two of you have continued to up your sexual game through the years. Once I'd moved beyond the mind-fuck of turning 50, I discovered some redefining truths and personal revelations that came with that age that I can only describe as surprisingly liberating. It gave me a clear understanding of what I wanted and didn't want from a lover, coupled with a brazen, blinding honesty to tell them. So, I say this to you twenty-somethings reading this: women over 50 are having great sex.

When I arrived later that night at The Little Beaver, I was happy being ushered into my new decade surrounded by people I just wanted to hug the life out of. I was 50, no getting around it. And Lizzie did a brilliant job, right down to the briefing she gave the crowd just before I walked in.

'Everyone, Christina is two minutes away. And I just want to say, whatever you do, do not, under any circumstances, mention her over-plucked eyebrow. She's had a long day.'

CHAPTER 4

A Broad in London

*'If adventures will not befall a young lady in her
own village, she must seek them abroad.'*
Jane Austen, *Northanger Abbey*

Have you ever thought about all the experiences in your life that were born from a single question? Questions are pivot points, and how we respond can have the absolute power to change our world. For, as I have come to learn, it's not about the questions asked, but rather what is done with the answers. In my life, two questions stand out that I believe reshaped me more than all the others, and they came from two very different men.

The first came in the voice of Don McLean, a formidable advertising legend who owned the Partners Film Company, at one point one of the largest commercial production companies in the world. As a huge competitor to McWaters, where I was working at the time, Don, over the years, had unsuccessfully tried to hire me. Over lunch, four years after we'd first met, he asked me, 'So what do I have to do to get you to leave McWaters, Christina?' Answering totally off the cuff, not giving any real credence to this life-changing question, I said, 'Well, Don, you can start me up in my own company.' He grinned victoriously, shook my hand and said, 'Done.' And that was it. In less time than it took to pay the bill, and with complete financial backing from the Partners Film Company, Imported Artists Film Company was born. My company spanned over an impressive quarter-century, shot thousands of television commercials and won hundreds of awards. Countless people, most I can't remember but some I'll never forget, walked through its doors, cut their teeth and launched their careers. It was one single question that changed the lives of so many, and of course, none more than mine.

The second question that transformed my world occurred some time after Edward's prenup query, also known as our engagement. He asked, 'How are you with driving on the left side of the road?' This was an absolute game-changer. Edward had been formally offered a senior C-suite position back in his company's head office in London, England.

Having worked as long as I had in television production – a 30-year career – boredom had seeped in. I stand before you as an excellent example of 'If you stop learning, you get bored, and if you get bored, you get lazy.' I was ready for something different, a new life, new adventures with Edward. *I can do this,* I remember chanting to myself. I had a competitor ready to buy my company, Briar was sixteen and was pushing to live with her dad in Los Angeles, and Sam was on her way to university, also in LA. I hadn't a clue what this move would look like, and to be honest, I was scared shitless. I was changing almost everything for this man. But I thought this opportunity might never come again, and hadn't we fought too many battles for us not to end up, dare I say, happily ever after?

Packing up my entire life came with a mountain of things to do. I facilitated the handoff of my company, ensuring my staff and directors were comfortable and settled with its new management. My girls made their way to California, confident in their newfound ability to separate white clothes from darks, with the added knowledge that the dishwasher didn't just empty itself. And sadly, Hunter died unexpectedly from cancer weeks before the move. He was ten. This might sound trite, but if you ever go through a tough breakup (or have teenagers), if you can, get a dog. Hunter's unconditional love and blinding loyalty saved me in a way that only dog owners will understand.

We landed at Heathrow after a sleepless overnight flight. Well, sleepless for me; Edward could fall into a coma the moment the house lights dimmed and the overture to *Les Misérables* began. The early-morning September sun warmly greeted us. I was about to see my new London home for the first time. Edward had found the house in Chelsea during a business trip to London in July. It was not the ideal situation, him picking out our new home without me there to gently guide him. In fact, one could describe it as potentially perilous, but we did our best with photos, floor plans and FaceTime.

Meandering through the neighbourhood's tree-lined cobblestone streets, Edward pointed out the various landmarks rolling by the limousine window. I was excited and nervous, like on the first day of a thrilling new job. The car rolled to a stop in front of a lovely cream-coloured three-storey townhouse with a contrasting shiny black-lacquered door. Edward turned the key. 'Welcome home,' he smiled.

The long, narrow corridor was a soft shade of pale grey, with contrasting white chair rails adding a beautiful, elegant texture to the bare walls. The floors were dark hardwood, and I could smell the lingering scent of a fresh coat of paint in the air. The reception room glowed, with the morning sunlight blasting through the large windows. At the back of the house, a sitting area opening onto a quaint, tiny courtyard, somewhat rare for London, Edward was quick to tell me: outdoor space. The neighbours' houses seemed to invade the tiny garden like ivy, as sounds of a crying baby, a couple having a conversation in German, and a woman on the phone making a hairdresser's appointment surrounded me.

'They're so close,' I said to Edward. 'Our neighbours, it's like they're in the backyard with us.'

'This is generous for London,' Edward reminded me again.

I knew it'd take some getting used to, some self-conditioning would be needed to ignore my new Central London voices, rattles and sounds.

'What do you think?' he asked, smiling.

'You've done good, Edward. I absolutely love it.'

Over the next few months, I got to work making the house a home. My furniture arrived, I displayed books by colour and size, arranged glass decanters, vases and candlesticks, and planted flowers in the window boxes. I created a large family photo wall of black-and-white prints and hung them symmetrically in the front hall. Every one of our children had an equal number of photos, as I knew each of them at some point would count them. I painted old filing cabinets and bookshelves with Annie Sloan chalk paint in Paris Grey, Old White and Duck Egg Blue.

'What are you going to do when you run out of things to paint?' Edward teased.

'Run out?' I asked. 'There's always something that could benefit from a good coat of chalk paint.'

Edward was away more than he was around in those early months, and even with the house now filled with my stuff, every time I returned home, I was acutely aware of the hollow sound behind that black lacquered door, with no children, no Hunter, no Edward. The contrast from the gentle cacophony that was my home mere months ago to my new London life was deafening. In Toronto I was usually surrounded by chaos; I regularly housed teenagers (most not even mine), numerous house guests, boyfriends, girlfriends, family members and Hunter, and he was usually the loudest thing in the neighbourhood.

Now outside my window, I'd hear the blasts of horns, detailed conversations in various languages, and the squeaking of breaks on buses. The chaos was now the busy city beyond the walls of my house, and the inside rattled with silence.

There was no morning alarm screaming at me to get my ass out of bed, no late-night phone calls when the girls needed a ride home, no meetings or conference calls, no dinner with friends, nowhere I needed to be and no one noticing I wasn't there. Absolutely everything in my life had changed, almost overnight, and my whole world was unrecognisable. In all the ways I had defined myself, be it boss, mother, friend, daughter, sister, Hunter's human, all of it was now significantly altered or gone for good.

Officially out of things to chalk-paint, I had a massive brain-seizure realisation, I had no real idea of who I was. None! This, I believe, is what's called a midlife crisis. I only knew two people when I moved to London: Elspeth, an old Imported Artists client, and my cousin Catherine, living in Limehouse. That was it. Exactly two! The C-suite spouse role requiring polite smiles and sensible hemline dresses while nibbling canapés at business functions wouldn't hold my interest for long. Nor could my major decision of the day be deciding if the salmon was fresh enough to serve as carpaccio or should I just go with the veal. I was lonely inside the soft grey walls of my new Chelsea home. I felt like I'd walked into someone else's story. I needed a life.

So I started writing a blog, something (for reasons totally unclear to me, with no evidence whatsoever to support my belief) I thought I might have an aptitude for. I saw the blog as a jacked-up letter home, striking just the right balance of fabulous photos woven together with incredible details of my new British playground ... You know, just enough to make everyone hate me, just a little. I basked in comments like 'So jealous, you lucky bitch' or 'Stop flaunting your cosmopolitan life under our noses – there are people out here having to work for a living.' So, inspired by true-life events (me almost walking straight into a bus), my first blog, an essential 'How to Cross the Street Without Dying', was written, and my life as a blogger was born: *A Broad in London, A North American's Guide to Thriving, Surviving and Living in London*. I now had something interesting to do, a legitimate excuse to get out of bed, explore London, and this was nothing short of inspiring. There's something rich, historic, quaint, shocking or bloody brilliant greeting you around every corner. Some days I'd leave the house in the morning and walk the city until dark. Or I'd hop on one of London's famous double-decker buses, sit at the front window on the upper deck and randomly, without a specific destination, venture out to try and unearth London's secrets. In London, I discovered you don't always need a destination, because the city itself is the journey and the destination.

I also knew I needed to make new friends. With no disrespect to cousin Catherine from Limehouse or Elspeth from Saatchi, I needed a bigger, more varied squad, whom I wouldn't quickly exhaust. Making new friends was not without its challenges, at least for me. I mentioned I was never outwardly social, and now I was an unemployed empty-nester, in a new country a zillion miles away from anyone who knows I like an ice-cube in my Chardonnay. I now had to put myself out there in a way I'd never had to before. I had to find myself a new UK tribe, my London Girl Squad, and hopefully at least one spectacular trash-talking gay BFF. I needed to start dating for friends.

I started with a Facebook post: 'Wanted: London friends. Must have previous experience. Please provide reliable references.' OK, the wording might have differed a tad, but the idea was identical. I was advertising for friends. Friends of friends, people you might know or have kinda heard of, distant relatives, old work buddies, school chums, people you've fallen out with, I didn't care. I was up for meeting anyone. Even if all I got out of the 'date' was a recommendation for a good blow-dry salon or which dry-cleaners to avoid, I was game.

I quickly discovered an escalating social stratum for dating for friends in London. Did that surprise me? No! The Brits have a class system for everything, even breakfast meats. My London girlfriend courtship usually started simply with a morning time slot, a tea or coffee at Aubaine, or perhaps the Foodhall at Selfridges. If that went well, it got kicked up a notch to lunch at The Ivy or perhaps The Bluebird Café. And, if I made it to that all-important third date, the one that might spell out I'd found 'the one', I'd find myself blissfully strolling the floors of the Tate Modern discussing who would win *The Great British Bake Off*. And that's how it's done. I was finding my peeps, discovering my new home. I was reinventing.

When Edward was in town, on weekends, we'd occasionally jump in a Zipcar and venture outside of London, exploring picturesque towns whose names ended in 'shire' or 'ham'. Charmed by small seaside villages whose names made absolutely no sense phonetically, I could imagine women in bustles and parasols casually strolling the boardwalk like an episode of *Masterpiece Theatre*.

Although we had lived together part-time in the summer months in Georgian Bay, London was the first time Edward and I had lived together full-time. So there were numerous little moments where he'd learn about my idiosyncrasies, and I'd learn about his. After years of being single and comfortably settled, learning to live with someone else in my fifties came with adjustments, for both of us. For instance, I could only take about 30 minutes of aggressive CNN before I'd have to fight the urge to break my own neck. Edward would happily play CNN 24 hours a day, frequently using it to lull himself to sleep, mistaking it for a Calm sleep story. I was obsessed with shows like *Downtown Abbey* and *The Crown*, thinking everything I could possibly need to know about British history could be deliciously fed to me through episodic period dramas while I sipped wine in my living room. Edward mistook this as me having an interest in the History Channel and Second World War documentaries. And don't even get me started on Formula 1, the monotonous, annoying sound of looping cars that always netted the same result, Lewis Hamilton finishing first.

'How's this interesting?' I'd ask, genuinely.

In turn he'd jeer, 'You know Matthew Crawley isn't real, right?' as I was actively mourning Matthew's fictional death, cursing Julian Fellowes's traitorous name.

I was puzzled by his extensive stockpile of partly used solid antiperspirants. Or his ever-increasing arsenal of a bazillion disposable razors, as he'd almost always use an electric shaver. He didn't tolerate my occasional colourful outburst whenever I was randomly kicked off the WiFi and unable to reconnect, or how I'd free up bathroom drawer space by combining half-empty bottles of TUMS or Cold-FX, regardless of the varying expiry dates. Yup, there was an adjustment period, certain things we had to get used to, habits, routines and learning to make compromises. But regardless of the day, or what was playing on TV, I'd greet him every evening, standing at the bottom of the kitchen stairs, blocking his entrance until he kissed me hello.

Our collective three years abroad held some extraordinary adventures, and I'd accompany Edward on some of his business trips. For the first time in my life, I travelled to places like Sydney, Singapore, Hong Kong, Kuala Lumpur, Dubai and

Tokyo. I'd always loved travelling, but this opened me up to new cultures and experiences beyond what I had ever experienced. As work held Edward hostage in office towers for much of the time, travelling became my most loyal companion and a most outstanding teacher. I'd work my way through the labyrinth of the Tokyo subway or negotiate at the Ladies' Market in Hong Kong for a knock-off Gucci handbag. I sat alone in magical splendour watching Puccini's *Tosca* in the Sydney Opera House, and even used my translation app to carry on a delightful conversation with my Chinese cab driver, well beyond telling him where I needed to go.

Once Edward was freed of work, we'd go dune surfing in the red sandhills of Dubai, pay our respects at the feet of the Giant Buddha in Sichuan, or explore the Batu Caves in KL, with its thousands of pickpocketing monkey residents. In every country, we passionately made love, happily checking off new cities on our 'International Fuck-It List'. Somewhere during this time, and I honestly don't remember when or how, we created our alter egos, Nigel and Veronica, a childless couple of international mystery. Something magical happened to Edward when Veronica would say, 'Nigel ... Darling,' in an indeterminable accent. He'd come alive, become cheeky, flirtatious and daring. Nigel and Veronica, not Edward and Christina, had sex on the giant Ferris wheel in Hong Kong. Nigel and Veronica were broadcast on the BBC turning their backs on the Queen at her Garden Party in order to get a selfie with Her Majesty in the background. Nigel was fun. Nigel didn't have children, but Edward did.

With the highs came some crushing lows. My mother was diagnosed with Non-Hodgkin lymphoma, and as a result, my sisters and I had to place my father in a long-term care facility, very much against his will. This was excruciating. Alan had

Parkinson's and relied too much on my mother for every little thing. I told my dad, 'It's only for a little while, just until Elena gets better,' and I so wanted to believe it, but Elena never got better, and he never left. I watched him slowly shrink away, frail, quiet, angry, sad and small, so very small. My father's tone was that of a soft-spoken hostage negotiator, trying to secure his release every time I visited him. I didn't recognise the frail man with a voice so faint I had to strain to hear it. The man who'd taught me how to summon Wonder Woman now needed help getting up from a chair. I believed he knew that power was still inside him, and that was what made him angry. He just couldn't speak loud enough to summon her.

The nursing home sent my dad to the hospital as a precaution one January afternoon because he had a slight fever and was refusing to eat. In my last conversation with my father, he angrily said, 'Christina, get me the hell out of here.'

'Pappa,' I said, 'you need to eat something.'

'I'm not eating because the food is shit,' he said.

So, crossing the road to the McDonald's, I got him a Big Mac and fries, and he happily devoured them. I'm guessing that was his last meal. He died alone a few hours later, leaving me shocked, sad and guilty for resenting that frail, faint shadow of a man who had replaced my father. All of this resulted in numerous emotional, challenging trips back and forth between London and Toronto.

About a year and a half into our London stay, the bloom had faded on Edward's work. He'd often come home frustrated and pissed off with whatever asshole had done whatever stupid thing to whichever other asshole, and he now measured his days to retirement in cups of coffee. But on the top of Edward's list of challenges always, always sat Quinn. I can't imagine how difficult it must be having a sick wife, a challenging daughter and a big serious job that, if you got it wrong, could result in billions of lost dollars, or even land you in jail. But it was more than that. It was the heavy guilt he dragged behind him like a massive boulder. Even though Quinn had taken a gap year, working as an au pair in Paris, and was attempting to navigate her own life, her chronic, relentless mantra of 'You've abandoned me' pierced Edward deeply. His frequent trips to see her left him drained, erratic, entombed in an icy, grey cloud that could make him roar like thunder or silence him into long melancholic periods of brooding. I suggested he talk to a doctor as he showed classic signs of depression, but this wasn't an idea Edward would entertain, supported by his WASPy beliefs that one should never air dirty laundry in public, even to a therapist.

As I colourfully carved out my new life with day trips, museums, new friends, inspiring lectures and a variety of classes that expanded my mind, I wasn't only stepping into my new city, I was dancing and leaping into my new world, and I could feel Edward's resentment building. His life continued to drain him, and mine was joyously filling me up. Life was slowly being squeezed out of him, and with that, out of us. I'd never describe Edward as an overtly happy man, perhaps for all the reasons I just listed above. He's never been that guy who would tell a joke or laugh hard at one. I believe his heavy guilt almost robbed him of a fundamental belief that he deserved to be happy. It's hard to love someone who doesn't believe themselves worthy of being loved. That's why travelling was magical, for as long as he was exploring, distracted, whipping down the side of a mountain or cantering on a colt, listening to Veronica's whispers of 'Good evening, Nigel,' he was different. He was alive. It was his escape – an escape from his life that clung to him like an illness.

There's a saying that a parent is only as happy as their unhappiest child, and rarely did I see Quinn genuinely happy. Perhaps

I was part of the problem, by trying to be part of the solution and fix something I hadn't broken. This would eventually manifest into a great lesson for me, much like underestimating how a tiny pea-size amount of snow can become a village-crushing avalanche. Listening to his FaceTime conversations with his daughter, I'd say, 'Don't let her manipulate you, Edward. Don't let her speak to you like that.'

There was a palpable fear that stuck to Edward's skin if things didn't go Quinn's way. Fear that she'd stop talking to him, disown him, or stop eating. I believed so much of Edward's parenting decisions were born from that fear, or guilt about what might happen. This exhausted him, drained him, leading him to frequently surrender to whatever she demanded at the time.

I'm sure the two of us had fights or issues that didn't revolve around Quinn (either directly or indirectly), or me combining two bottles of TUMS, but honestly, nothing else springs to mind. As I'd watch Edward pivot or reluctantly change his mind, he'd punish himself. He was angry, exhausted and at times humiliated, but now someone was watching. I had become an inconvenient witness to his crimes and moments of weakness. I'd speak as if my words were trying to break down walls, illuminate dark, unexplored dusty rooms that we might one day occupy. My ignorance and arrogance, thinking, *If I just show up and try, really try, the light will chase away the shadows.* Perhaps breaking down walls did let in some light, but it failed miserably at keeping out the rain.

The choices I've made in my life regarding men – and the reasons why I've made them – are interesting. Maybe the further away I stand, the more clearly I can understand them. With Brandon as an example, I thought I needed to get married. I mean, everyone around me was doing it, so like a twenty-something game of musical chairs, the music stopped and I thought, *I better quickly grab a seat.* But with Edward, I fell in love with appropriate. It wasn't for what we had in common, which was little. Edward was the older, sophisticated 180-degree pendulum swing from John, a relationship overcorrection as I optimistically went from Peter Pan to *Mary Poppins*'s Mr Banks. I didn't pick Edward for me. I picked him because he stood out in a sea of moms and nannies. I picked him because he always managed to show up. I picked him because my daughters' needs were indistinguishable from my own. I picked him for what I believed my girls required and deserved.

I picked him because he wasn't John.

CHAPTER 5

Burning Man

'Angry people are not always wise.'
Jane Austen, *Pride and Prejudice*

This was either going to be the best, most brilliant thing I'd ever done, or my friends would be gathering to hold a candlelight vigil in my honour. *I've taken more time deciding between the Cabernet and the Pinot Noir,* I thought, as panic, fear and reality starting setting in, with no signs of abandoning me anytime soon.

A few days earlier, Edward and I had fought. Actually, it was more than a fight. It was a total come-to-Jesus, 'what do you think you're doing?' moment. An out-of-the-blue shocker which had angered me to such a level that I'd taken the 'fight or flight' literally. I'd boarded a plane, crossed eight time zones, and driven ten hours into the arid Nevada desert, just to get away and to punish him. This is not my usual reaction to a fight, but this fight was something more. It was the first moment I had stared at the man I loved and not recognised him.

Sam was nearing the end of a week-long stay in London and was heading to Burning Man in a few days. We had spent a fun day combing vintage shops on Brick Lane, sourcing her *Mad Max*-inspired wardrobe. That evening, the two of us sat on my bed with my laptop, looking to book a workout class for the following day.

'I'm going to bed,' Edward announced rather abruptly as he entered the bedroom.

'OK,' I said. 'Give us a sec. We're almost done.'

With an urgency I couldn't understand, Edward ignored me and started undressing ... in front of both of us. As he unbuckled his belt and ceremoniously whipped it out of the belt loops and threw it across the room, the look on his face was hard to describe. He stared at me with the contempt he might have for an adversary he was hell-bent on punishing. Unzipping his trousers, he let them fall to the ground, along with his boxers. Then, picking them up with his foot, he flung them across the room. Edward stood naked from the waist down, smugly smiling, dangling, hands on his hips. It felt like some sort of 'fuck you', but for what, I had no idea. Mortified, I yelled, 'Sam, don't turn around,' as Edward just stood there, scowling, as though his extreme reaction was just, even heroic. Sam froze in confusion, her eyes fixed to the laptop as Edward casually slid into bed.

Biting his words, he said, 'I told you, I'm going to bed.'

Sam was thrilled I'd agreed to join her at Burning Man. I wasn't under any illusions: I knew that it was partly because my presence would provide her with a serious upgrade in her accommodation. It took her from a shared tent with her friend Matt to the more comfortable surroundings I'd be paying for: an RV with air conditioning, a refrigerator and running water. This upgrade wasn't lost on Sam's other friend, Ethan, either. Hearing that there would now be a comfortable Winnebago instead of a pup tent, he decided to join us on this adventure, which took us deep into the desert in Nevada, to a temporary city called Black Rock City, home of Burning Man.

Considering this trip would likely involve a banquet of experiences not typically shared by mothers and their barely adult daughters, I was honoured that Sam had allowed her mom to take a front-row seat to what would be a week of radical self-expression. We arrived at Burning Man at 4am, in the middle of a sand storm, with the final five miles taking five hours to drive. The white sand surrounded the RV like clotted cream, thick and opaque, at times not allowing us to see beyond the windshield. Matt was driving, and although it was agreed we'd all take turns, I could barely keep my eyes open. I had been awake for over 24 hours. The sand made its way inside the RV through the air vents, giving me the feeling we were travelling through a gritty, white fog. Unaware I had nodded off, I awoke as Sam gently shook me.

'You should put this on, Mom,' she said, handing me a blue surgical mask to stop the fine sand from getting into my nose and mouth. Out of nowhere came a knock on the door, so loud it shocked me into complete consciousness. Into the RV walked two friendly guys, bandanas tied across their faces, Red Baron-type goggles protecting their eyes, and every inch of them covered with a solid dusting of white Nevada sand. They looked like old Western desert bandits holding up a stagecoach, but, instead of rifles, in their hands were two stadium-strength flashlights. As one guy checked our tickets, the other shone his flashlight, rummaging around for anyone we might be stowing away. The powerful beams panned through the vehicle's dusty interior, creating shafts of light, reminding me of the search scene in *E.T.* He handed us a booklet with a list of scheduled activities for the week and the rules.

Rules …? What possible rules could Burning Man have? I mean, they have a place called the Sanctuary, where a Peruvian sound bath accompanies your acid trip. Or the Orgy Dome, where consenting adults are handed a condom and can partake of any act, fetish or bondage activity they like. Rules …? What possible rules could there be?

'Almost there now,' one of the guys said to Matt. 'Just keep straight. The storm looks like it's passing.'

For the first time in hours, up ahead we could see red taillights – hundreds and hundreds of them – finally giving us a sense of direction. I guess this is what happens when 80,000 people descend deep into the desert during a sandstorm, driving towards a city that weeks ago did not exist and which will be burned to the ground in a week. There's going to be traffic.

The men left our RV and we slowly crawled in a limitless line of caravans, minivans and SUVs, following the trail of taillights. Matt peered through the clouded, dirty windshield and smiled. 'Hey, guys … I think we're here.'

Almost on cue, we heard the loud reverberation of a giant gong from just outside. There was another knock, this time on the driver's-side window. Matt lowered the window; the fine white sand was still suspended in the air. A friendly, energetic man peered in.

'Welcome home,' he gleefully said. 'Please come out and announce your arrival.'

Once out of the car, four or so greeters gave us sandy hugs, lasting, in this girl's opinion, a tad too long. Everyone and everything outside was beige, sandy and entirely coated by a significant layer of grit. I felt like I'd been dropped into a life-size sandcastle, without the relief of an ocean.

'Please,' they said, 'embrace the Playa. Roll in the sand.'

Wait. What? Did someone say, 'Roll in the sand?'

I was already sneezing sand, thanks to the thick air inside the RV. I'd been genuinely hoping to stay clean for a little longer than the sand-covered stranger's suggestion would support. As I replayed this surprising and unreasonable ask in my head, Sam enthusiastically dropped to the ground and started rolling in the sand like a happy dog on the beach.

She stood up, grabbed the giant mallet one of the greeters held out to her and yelled, 'Sam is here!' *GONG!!!*

Matt and Ethan immediately followed her example.

'Matt is here!' *GONG!!!*

'Ethan is here!' *GONG!!!*

Shit, I thought, still holding on to the idea of staying clean. I guess the transparent look on my face conveyed my lack of genuine enthusiasm to roll on the desert floor, as one of the greeters tactfully asked, 'Are you a virgin Burner?'

'How can you tell?' I asked, sarcastically.

'It's just a little warm Nevada sand,' the greeter said.

'Come on, Mom, your turn,' Sam cheered.

'Ya, Mom,' the greeter added.

I thought, *Isn't this why I'm here, instead of in my sand-free house in Chelsea with a man so unhappy he's forgotten how to smile?* I dropped to the ground. The sand was remarkably warm for 4am, not that I had a point of reference. I spread my arms and legs out like a small child making snow angels. Standing up, I took the mallet in my sand-covered hands, swung back, and channelling Wonder Woman, hit the gong.

'CHRISTINA IS HERE … AGAINST ALL ODDS!' I yelled.

Sam cheered in exuberance as the four of us came in for a group hug.

'Let the Burn begin!' I yelled. 'Welcome home.'

The sun was breaking over the vast horizon as we pulled the RV into a camping spot that would be ours for the next seven days. The four of us stood arm in arm in silent awe, watching the sun's brilliant rays roll towards us like a stupendous, majestic wave. Vibrant colours of tangerine, magenta and lavender, more dazzling than anything I'd ever seen before, painted the sky. The sunrise was not just in the east, but rather all around us, as if we were suspended in a celestial symphony of light and colour. I kissed Samantha on the top of her sandy head. 'Thank you,' I said, smiling with loving gratitude.

Sam smiled back. 'I love you, Mommy.'

This is a view everyone should see once before they die.

A few hours later, I awoke to Ethan at our small stove, making a vegan omelette with something called 'cashew cheese'. Sam and Matt were outside decorating the bikes we'd picked up at Walmart earlier. Stepping outside, the surreal, unfamiliar surroundings greeted me like a guest on an unchartered planet.

Try to imagine a giant sundial radiating outwards for miles, and in the centre, a temporary utopia, the Playa. Within the Playa stood kinetic art sculptures, some as large as two-storey houses. A pagoda-like temple welcomed all, and a looming wooden effigy of a man reached high into the sky, as if he was looking down on all he had created. Almost all would be set alight in celebration on Saturday night, something I was excited to see.

The ethos of the place is radical inclusion. There is no money or stores, no commerce of any kind, no 'I Survived Burning Man' T-shirts. All we could buy was coffee or ice. Everyone brings in all that is needed for a week in the desert, and a few things that aren't, to share, gift or give away: all food, water, drinks, drugs, booze, everything. And nothing gets left behind when everyone leaves, not so much as a cigarette butt, bottle cap, condom wrapper or roach clip. The experienced Burners will correct you if you call it a festival. 'It's not a festival,' they told me, 'it's an event.' The difference is that at a festival you walk around taking in the spectacle. At Burning Man you *are* the spectacle.

Matt had already been out on his bike, returning with two bags of ice that were nicely chilling our cooler full of beer and wine. Although it was still early morning, I could feel the heat pressing against my skin. *It's going to be a hot one,* I thought. The days can climb to over 100 degrees, but it can drop into the 30s in the evenings. That is quite the wardrobe range when one has had mere hours to decide what to pack.

Pulling out my new bike, I joined the others and went about creatively decorating it. Bikes would be our primary mode of transportation for the week. Each was its own little art project, decorated with colourful spray paint, LED lights, horns, reflective stickers, tape and bells. This was not only to tell them apart among the thousands and thousands of other bikes, but to help keep us visible at night – the brighter and more illuminated the better.

A short time later, spray paint not quite dry, we biked out to explore this strange new world. It blew my mind. I could not get over its incredible enormity, this pop-up *Mad Max* city and its 80,000 disciples. It continued for miles and well beyond what my eye could see, or my brain could take in. Any thoughts of Edward were instantly blasted away by my new playground in the desert.

Thousands of campers, RVs and tents of various shapes and sizes surrounded me, making the neighbourhood look like a steroid-pumped shanty town. Dome-like tents and constructions that looked like they could have been stolen from *Cirque du Soleil*, with Persian rugs and generator-run lights, were pressed against tepees giving off a far more *Last of the Mohicans* vibe, and nestled between them all were tiny tents reminiscent of Boy Scouts on a camping trip. Even in this radically inclusive utopian village, there was visible economic diversity among the camps.

Around us, people were giving away homemade pancakes, back massages, shots of B12, hair-washing, miso soup, beaded necklaces, amulets, and both permanent and temporary tattoos. Two naked women were wielding leather paddles, imploring bystanders to pull their pants down for a well-deserved spanking. I watched in bewilderment as a few volunteered. We passed a roadside garment rack filled with used clothing, with a sign that read 'Take what you need, leave what you don't!' Everything was gratis.

The people, at least the ones who weren't completely naked, I'd best describe as possessing a fashion sense that borrowed equally from *Mad Max* and *The Flintstones*. A lithe supermodel, dressed in nothing but a pink rabbit-fur vest and a tiny pair of sparkly leather booty shorts, chatted earnestly with four middle-aged men sitting on the roof of a painted bus, with a sign that read 'Really Bad Advice, Free'. In the evenings, as the temperature dipped, fur became the must-have fashion item. People donned coats, jackets, hats, mufflers, vests, bras, shorts and jockstraps, all creatively crafted from raccoon, mink, rabbit, fox and sheepskin. I could just feel the internal conflict of the well-represented vegetarians. It was a post-apocalyptic, unworldly city, and its residents were radical survivors who had grown up watching nothing but *Project Runway* and *Survivor*.

Sam, Matt and Ethan's faces emitted the kind of free-fall excitement an adrenaline junkie might chase by skydiving. And, although uncertain what my own face was telegraphing, inside I was consumed with pure, unfiltered panic. I was about as far outside my comfort zone as I could imagine. As excited as I was to be with Sam, I looked around and thought, *What the fuck have I gotten myself into?*

Outside the central tent, hundreds of decorated bikes littered the ground. I took careful mental notes as to where I placed my bike, so I wouldn't have to spend twenty minutes trying to find it, as I often did my skis on winter holidays. Entering the tent, I didn't know where to focus first. Two naked people, a man and a woman, crusted in sand, were doing a sort of acrobatic yoga, while beside them a young girl dressed like Pebbles

Flintstone played her guitar and sweetly sang Fleetwood Mac's 'Landslide'. Around the perimeter, colourful people lounged against patterned cushions resting against hand-painted floral walls, while a juggler dressed as a court jester entertained them.

Samantha and I leaned against the colourful mural, taking in the spectacle, while Matt and Ethan fetched coffees. Sam was wearing flared pink floral leggings and a transparent lacy bra, which under any other circumstances was a fashion choice most moms would not approve of. Her colourful bandana and bedazzled goggles were at the ready, like chunky jewellery around her neck, just in case the wind blew up. Most of my clothes were borrowed, as I had not adequately prepared for this unexpected journey. I wore a tattered full-length raccoon scarf I'd picked up from the roadside garment rack, with a men's blue-and-white Aztec-print shirt over my black tank top and my cut-off jeans. Adorning my hair was a plastic flower garland, a gift from Samantha. Matt handed us our coffees. Taking a sip, I looked around and exhaled. Whether I was here to punish Edward, impress my daughter or push my personal limits, make no mistake ... I was here.

A few hours later, after a well-needed nap, I heard a question I never would've thought I'd ever, ever hear from my daughter.

'Mom, we're going off to drop acid. Would you like to come?'

I gave it a moment and let it sink in.

I had done acid once. I was probably Sam's age, and my circumstances involved a mechanical bull at someplace called Cowboys, not in a tent with singing bowls and wind chimes, not that I knew for sure that that was where they were going. *How hypocritical I'd be to oppose it,* I thought, not that Sam was looking for permission. However, I couldn't cross that line of doing drugs with my daughter. I'd struggled enough with her barely-there transparent bra as daywear. I was weirdly honoured by the invitation to partake in this illegal recreational activity, and it certainly did move the bar in our mother–daughter relationship, although I'm uncertain in which direction. I parked my judgement, which wasn't easy, having spent most of the last 21 years saying, 'Don't do drugs.'

'I think I'll go check out some of the art exhibits on the Playa and take some photos,' I said. 'The light is remarkable.'

'OK, Mom,' she smiled. 'Have fun.'

As the three of them rode off on their bikes, it was all I could do to stop myself from screaming at the top of my motherly lungs, 'Make smart choices!' I tucked my iPhone into my small Prada satchel, strapped it across my chest, and got on my bike. I thought I would go and explore this rich photogenic playground and try not to worry, never imagining that the next time I'd see them, it would be four days later, and I would be unable to walk.

It was the magical hour of twilight when I arrived back at the RV. The Playa was transforming itself from the town of Bedrock to Vegas on acid. It had taken me forever to find my way back, and had I not attached a giant Union Jack flag to the back of the RV earlier, I might still be out there. Through the RV's small window I saw two new arrivals struggling to erect a tent. Embracing the ethos of inclusivity, and with beers still cold from the morning's ice, I fished out two cans and introduced myself. Ryan and Bryan were young doctors living in Silicon Valley, both in their mid-thirties, related by marriage, one being married to the other's sister. For the most part, I'd thought Burners were grass-smoking, acid-dropping, VW-dwelling hippies or millennial techno ravers, but actually, that wasn't true. People come to Burning Man from every conceivable corner of the earth, with tech giants, teachers, celebrities, renowned surgeons, doctors, captains of industry and multimillionaires all there for one week a year to let their freak out.

Ryan and Bryan invited me to join them at a Prince retrospective party they had seen on the itinerary. That appealed to them more than the EDM fist-pumping raves that some of the camps were known to favour. I hadn't seen any sign of Sam or the boys, so I thought, *Why not?* I went back to the RV and quickly changed, adapting my wardrobe for the coolness of the upcoming desert night, and went back out to join the boys. Both guys had clearly gotten the fur fashion memo, as they were now wearing oversized raccoon coats and fur hats, looking like extras from *Doctor Zhivago*. With the addition of illuminated neon ropes of hot pink and blue draped around our necks and wrists, we resembled some brightly lit, futuristic aboriginal tribe.

Burning Man at night had all the promise of Alice freefalling down a long, technicoloured rabbit hole. Teetering forth on our bikes, we passed a campsite immersed in colourful fog, with throbbing sounds and pulsing lights so bright I'm pretty sure it could have been seen from space. A serpent-shaped car lit by kaleidoscopic bulbs and a neon caterpillar sprouting electric wings rolled by us. A full-size pirate ship rumoured to belong to Elon Musk housed fist-pumping ravers with music so loud I could feel it reverberating in my chest. Dozens of identically clad chanting lamplighters walked in a slow, religious-seeming *Dawn of the Dead* procession. I had never seen anything like this limitless, psychedelic, untamed wilderness and its most incredible array of colourful human participants.

Cycling amid the distracting cacophony, the temporary road was like a freakish super-highway full of colourful, eye-catching people, art-cars and cyclists making their way to wherever their night was taking them. I saw him about 50 yards in front of me, coming straight towards me.

He's not looking my way … I thought.

He's wobbling on his bike …

He's high … Electric dragons and psychedelic butterflies are pilfering his attention.

Please look forward …

Which way should I move?

Do I go left … or right … left … or right?

I stopped thinking. Aggressively, I swerved to the left. The hard desert floor with its loose sand and gravel gave nothing for my bike to grip onto as its wheels left the ground. I saw a flash of blinding light, this time from behind my eyes as the ground I had embraced at dawn while making angels slammed hard up against my body. Immediately there was a surge of pain … blinding, hot … a fiery explosion beneath my sandy skin.

And then, silence.

I was having trouble hearing the alien faces that were staring down at me, hovering like I was an unfinished, complex puzzle they were looking to solve. My scrambled mind tried to focus on the shadowy outline of their dark backlit faces, pulsing with halos from the lights of the Playa.

Immediately the faces had voices.

'I'm a doctor,' said a man.

'I'm a doctor,' said another.

'I'm a doctor too,' said yet another.

'I'm a healer,' said a woman by my feet.

Once again, I was reluctantly lying in the sand, feeling its warmth. There was no pain, only numbness, and I felt crippled by embarrassment more than anything. 'I'm fine, let me try and get up,' I insisted, as bits of gravel tore into my arms and legs like shards of hot glass. The Burners surrounded me as they tried to help me to my feet. A surge of blinding pain radiated from my pelvis like a lightning strike. I collapsed back onto the ground, squeezing my eyes tight, trying to hold in the tears. I was not OK. A short time later, I found myself inside the emergency medical tent for damaged Burners.

'Good news,' Dr Rick said, dressed in a rainbow-coloured tutu and Day-Glo leg warmers over his scrubs. 'The X-ray doesn't seem to show any fractures.'

As a nurse hooked up an IV of painkillers to my arm, he suggested I had perhaps bruised my hipbone, and said he would try and get me up and moving in a few hours. Dr Rick was an ER doctor from a trauma hospital in Reno who came to Burning Man every year, he told me, and he volunteered his time in exchange for a ticket. He upheld yet another tenet of Burning Man, communal effort and civic responsibility.

Lying on a campbed, I watched the outrageously dressed medical staff treat an endless stream of colourful damaged or super high Burners, full of frenetic energy, like a well-organised Mardi Gras. If I had thought people-watching was fascinating on the Playa, it was nothing compared to the inside of the *M*A*S*H*-style emergency tent. The person occupying the campbed beside me looked like a broken Barbie doll, *Barbarella* edition. Her left leg was sticking out like a sharp 90-degree turn in the road. Selfishly I felt a little less of an idiot, thinking, *At least it's not just me and my prehistoric menopausal bones.*

I kept checking my phone, thinking I needed to get a message to Sam. But my screen just read 'No Service', reminding me that despite my chaotic surroundings, I was in the middle of nowhere. I was exhausted, but it was impossible to sleep. A constant dread rattled inside of me as I kept one eye on the door, terrified that at any second I'd see Sam's limp body being dragged in. What had I been thinking, taking off to Burning Man? What an idiot, believing running away would be met with any kind of spiritual reward. Instead, I was being punished. All I wanted was for Dr Rick to tell me I was all good to go, so I could return to the RV, where Sam and the boys would be hopefully sleeping it off.

Twelve hours after my accident, the ER was quieter, as the evening's surge of stupidity subsided. From the back of an ambulance, I was instructing paramedics to look for the RV with the Union Jack. I desperately needed to know Sam was OK, to let her know what had happened so she wouldn't worry. As I lay strapped to the gurney, one of the paramedics entered the RV, returning to tell me there was no sign of anyone. Grief enveloped me in a way I'd never known before, as the ambulance silently made its three-hour journey to Renown Regional Medical Center in Reno, Nevada. I remember almost none of it.

Twenty-four hours, that was it. My dance on the edge, my life as a Burner, my *Woo-hoo! Let's play outside my fucking comfort zone* lasted a blasted 24 hours. It wouldn't be until two days later that someone would track Sam down to let her know her mother was in the hospital. It turned out my pelvis was fractured in three places, something the X-ray in Burning Man's medical tent hadn't picked up. Sam, Ethan and Matt temporarily left Burning Man on the fourth day of my hospital stay and drove the RV to Reno to bring my clothes, a phone charger and toiletries. I was in the hospital for eight days, most of that time requiring two people to move me from the bed to my new walker, so I could gingerly roll myself to the bathroom. I lay alone on my back for days, unable to move, nauseous from the painkillers, feeling a new level of sorry for myself, like this somehow was my karma, that I had brought this on myself for taking off in a fit of anger to punish Edward.

My only moment of light came from a surprise visit from my friend George. He'd come to Reno to pick up his new girlfriend, rightly concerned that his young relationship wouldn't survive the hedonistic temptations of a week without her at Burning Man. As he walked into my hospital room, I saw George's smiling face and immediately and uncontrollably burst into tears. A double-barrel, snot-bubbling explosion shaking my whole body. Never in my life can I recall being so genuinely thrilled to see anyone as I was George.

'Here, I brought you a present,' George said, smiling, handing me a bag of takeaway sushi and a pocket vibrator.

Laughter now accompanied my tears as I looked at the vibrator.

'You know I broke my pelvis, don't you, George?'

'Ya,' he laughed. 'Think of it as an incentive to get better quickly.'

Behind the scenes, as I lay in a hospital bed, friends tried convincing Edward to board a plane, be by my side, help get me home. He didn't. Citing a pressing workload, he used words like 'inconvenient' and 'bad timing'. I couldn't return to London yet, as I couldn't climb a single step, so Lizzie graciously moved me into her condo in Toronto. I struggled through weeks of torturous physiotherapy, daily nasty shots I self-administered deep into my stomach, overwhelmed with unparalleled sadness. It would be six weeks before I could walk again. This was one of the lowest points of my life, and I didn't know it yet, but it was about to get lower.

During these weeks I only saw Edward a few times, as he bounced between Toronto and London. He was always 'slammed with work', he told me. Each time his visits were chilly, without empathy or compassion. There was no affection or tenderness. I don't recall a single hug, kiss or reassuring word. Maybe all those years with Karina had taught him to detach, or perhaps it was something more. There was what I believed was a certain self-satisfaction on his part, a 'you brought this on yourself' kinda look and feel, not that he ever said those words. And had I? Was I responsible for this? Did Edward have the right to punish me as I'd punished him? I was buried in pain, grief, humiliation and Edward's absence, his lack of warmth surrounded me like damp, thick darkness. We would get past this, but not without some permanent scarring, not just on my broken body, but on my heart, on our relationship.

What's that annoying saying? 'Life doesn't give you anything you can't handle,' like some sort of survival mantra equal to 'What doesn't kill you makes you stronger,' or 'Everything happens for a reason.' I hate those sayings. They're things people optimistically say to you when you find yourself being tossed side to side helplessly in the eye of a relentless shitstorm. Well, I have my own particular survival mantra gifted to me from that time, one that more accurately reflects my life lesson. Simply stated, sometimes, what doesn't kill you makes you undead. Sure, maybe it won't be embroidered onto a cushion anytime soon, but I think it's every bit as profound. For without saying a word, Edward said everything. There was no room in his life for broken, damaged, maimed. I did not work if I was undead … the same way Karina hadn't.

CHAPTER 6

No Good Deed Goes Unpunished

*'Nothing ever goes away until it has taught
us what we need to know.'*
Pema Chödrön

Sometimes you can only make sense of your life by rewind-
ing it, playing the tape backwards from where you're
currently standing to where it all started. Only then can you
see how you could've arrived so far off your intended destination. Because this story, the one you're reading now, wasn't
anywhere remotely close to where I'd been dutifully steering
my ship.

I have experienced/lived/survived the traditional mother–
father parenting duo and single parenting. Both parenting
roles are hard and ripe with challenges, but equally, they're
exceptionally rewarding, made sweeter as you watch your children sleep. But for me, the most difficult role with the least
reward has to be stepparenting. It's brutally difficult attempting
to raise someone else's child. You don't have the same rein with
your stepchildren that you do with your own. There are limitations on discipline, a fundamental imbalance, and variable
discord between the kids, and, of course, the most dangerous
and destructive of all emotions, jealousy.

When I first met Edward, I was drawn to him because of
what he looked like in a sea of moms and nannies: a loving and
strong father. Edward was attracted to me for what I believed
were the same reasons. We both had holes in our lives that

seemed better filled than empty and, unlike John, he was present and engaged. But with all of Edward's many strengths, I could never describe him as strong when it came to his daughter, who I felt knew only too well his weaknesses and how to exploit them, as kids often do.

Edward's love for me, or sometimes lack of it, was always in direct proportion to his daughter's. In those early days when Quinn played with Briar or when Quinn's little body wrapped around mine, she loved me madly. So, then, did Edward. When Quinn was scorching some serious earth, so too was her dad. They were like those identical twins capable of feeling each other's pain or pleasure from miles away. But it wasn't until I ran my tape backwards, from its powerful end to the beginning, that I saw that it was Quinn all along who'd been in charge of my relationship. And Edward, for reasons too complex to fully grasp, had granted her that power.

The morning of my mother's memorial, I was frantically waiting on Edward. I desperately needed a couple of framed photographs of Quinn. The central hall table of the McLean Estate had been set up as a photographic tribute to Elena. Surrounding a large vase of rubrum lilies were photographs of my mother, her life, her family. I knew there was no way Quinn could be left out, nor should she. I also knew the first thing Quinn would do once she arrived was actively scan and look for her picture alongside all the other family members. As Edward arrived, I quickly placed Quinn's photographs alongside those of Sam, Briar and the various other grandchildren. My focus then returned to the heartbreaking task of saying goodbye to my mother, who had finally succumbed to her battle with Non-Hodgkin lymphoma.

I loved my mother immensely, and if she hasn't featured more prominently, it's purely because this story is about the men in my life, not the women. Elena deserves more than a chapter. She deserves her own beautiful book of immense depth and unparalleled kindness. And it would undoubtedly end with everyone happily ever after at the seaside, as that was always Elena's definition of a happy ending.

I'll share this with you about my mother and her final days as a human on earth. She was the happiest palliative care patient that ever inhabited the planet. She'd often answer the question 'How are you feeling today, Elena?' with an exuberant 'I'm as happy as a pig in a poke.' I also will tell you her last words to me were: 'Ah, Christina, my co-conspirator.' I'm still trying hard to decipher their meaning, but it sounds like I should be deeply honoured. I'll also impart the last thing I said to her. Holding her beautiful, still hand, her eyes closed, no longer able to speak, I whispered gently in her ear, my voice catching in my throat, 'I love you, Mamma. Please don't die on my birthday.' I guess she couldn't hear me, because I was born and orphaned the same day. Watching my mother die taught me more about life than death, but wouldn't that be just like Elena, teaching me things right until the very end. Although it's immensely comforting thinking she might be looking over me, on some higher plane, guiding me like she always has, I'm uncertain if I share my mother's beliefs of angels living among us, or life after death. But it would have made Elena and her angels weep looking down on us that weekend, the point where everything began to painfully and irreversibly unravel.

My sister Victoria and I had decided to have a weekend at our cottage immediately following the memorial. Vic's best friend, Tonia, was in from Vancouver, and my girls had a few friends around. With my car packed up for a weekend's respite, a small convoy of nine girls made their way up Highway 400 to Georgian Bay ... and Quinn was not invited.

'I can't take her drama,' I explained to Edward, 'not even a blush.' And drama, like a sinister shadow, always seemed to accompany Quinn, especially when she had to share me with others. Not now, not this weekend. There was nothing left inside of me. I was wholly and utterly hollow. My father had died only four months earlier and the collective loss was tremendous.

'Quinn will want to know why she isn't invited,' Edward said.

'Tell her the truth, Edward,' I insisted.

Poetically, I'd like to think I said something like: 'I can't endure the tiniest ripple from the smallest of pebbles that she could lob into the water, as its disturbance would surely drown me.'

Realistically it was more like: 'She's a drama queen, and I'm too fragile to deal with her shit right now.' Either way, that's not what Edward told her.

He devised his own story, something he thought would be more palatable. He told Quinn she wasn't invited because 'she wasn't family'. Now, this was the worst thing anyone could've said to this young girl who introduced me as 'Mom', and I'm sure the words reverberated in her like a deafening, lonely echo, Not family ... not family ... not family. Of course she was family, as was evident from the photos that had been placed on that table at my absolute insistence. But that was the way Edward felt. He had no emotional connection to my children, feigning almost indifference, which in and of itself was deeply disappointing. So I don't think he was really capable of understanding my connection to his daughter or the effort I always made. She was family. She was my family. But this wasn't a family weekend. This was to be a drama-free weekend, and for that, Quinn did not qualify.

That night at the cottage, as the younger generation were downstairs, Vic, Tonia and I were making dinner. We were nostalgically reminiscing, sometimes crying, but more often laughing, fondly recalling happy memories.

'Hey, Mom,' Sam called, as she came upstairs, 'do you think we can open a bottle of champagne to toast Grandma?'

There have been less important reasons to drink with my daughters, but none more important. I told her to find the bottle of Veuve Clicquot I had chilling in the freezer, and Vic, Tonia and I went downstairs to join the girls. As I descended the stairs, my heart exploded with unparalleled joy and delight. The room was decorated with pink-and-white streamers the girls had strung from the ceiling. Pale pink balloons with black Sharpie letters spelling out 'We Love You' arched above the girl's faces, all beaming up at me. 'Surprise!' they shouted in unison. 'It's an "I Love you" party.' Ecstatic tears brimmed from my eyes. Never in a time of such sadness, such sorrow, had I ever felt so much happiness and genuine love. It was the most joyous, glorious thing anyone had ever done for me. *This is what loving someone looks like,* I remember thinking. *Taking your darkest moments and shining a light so brilliant it chases away the shadows.* To this day, it still stands as the most magnificent gift I've ever received.

But that all slammed into reverse the following day when Quinn saw a photo Briar had posted on Instagram of the 'I Love You' party weekend. A line from an Elton John's song reflected that moment perfectly: 'It's funny how one insect can damage so much grain.'

Edward's texts, like bullets, came in rapid-fire, loaded by his jealous, angry daughter. *Ping. Ping. Ping.* Laced with phrases like 'putting my foot down', 'I will not allow' and 'what were you thinking?', they had the tone of a scolding head teacher. Each message triggered heart-sickening reactions in me, like a soldier jumping with fright at the sound of fireworks. *Ping. Ping. Ping.* It was as if somehow this lovely act of love and kindness, during this excruciatingly painful time of loss and mourning, had turned into some too-hot-to-handle scene from *Project X*, something outrageous and forbidden. Somewhere back in the city, Quinn was spinning out, as if someone had just thrown water on a Gremlin, and in twin-like response, so was Edward. He was being whipped up and was tearing me down by way of his twenty-year-old daughter with an extreme case of FOMO. I was relentlessly reprimanded as he took the saddest time in my life, discovered where the fragments of joy were hiding and bludgeoned them. Oh, how I had underestimated Quinn. She didn't need to be under the same roof, or even in the same city as me to have an impact. Her jealous outrage instantly deafened and destroyed all the joyous quiet space that, for a moment, had swaddled me.

Quinn refused to speak to me for a year.

I stayed at a friend's flat for a few days when I returned to London. I was in so much pain I could feel it in the back of my knees, and I was so very angry at the man who was punishing me, making me feel like crap for uncharacteristically doing what was best for me. Anxiously, I waited for him to call, apologise, admit that his daughter's irrational rage was fuelled by jealousy. I needed him to give me one of those hugs that make you forget everything that's happening around you, just for a moment. I wanted him to remind me in any way whatsoever that his love for me would ease my pain, that his love was stronger than her hate. I desperately needed to hear those three magic words from him, the only words that mattered at that moment, perhaps the only words that had ever really mattered … 'I got you.' I don't recall receiving any such comfort. I was drowning in the lack of things I needed. Instead, Edward had a talent for taking my worst days and increasing the volume, just like he had after Burning

Man. I felt like screaming, with a voice that would throw open the ground like an earthquake, 'What pleasure do you get from making it worse? If you can't see the love in that gift those girls gave me, then something, someone, has really got in your head and fucked it up.' *Is this it?* I thought. *Is there anything left for me to give to this man who only measures my worth by what I am willing to give up?*

A few absolutes surrounded me during that time, when anger and grief were indistinguishable. Sitting in the shadow of my parents' deaths, I knew I shouldn't be making life-altering decisions. I was brittle, fragile, not sure if my bruised heart could sustain one more loss. In fact, I was pretty sure it couldn't. I was almost catatonic in my pain, uncertain how much was attributed to Edward and how much to my new reality: that I was now an orphan, and in that, no longer someone's child. This was the only sorrow I'd ever had to face without my parents, and at 56 years old, with all I had accomplished, it was the first time I'd sat with the uncomfortable realisation that I was now an adult.

Had my mother been alive, I believe she would have told me to still my mind, gather my strength, and give myself some time. Only then could I objectively ascertain the damage. This made for a complicated final year between Edward and me. It damaged us, and it really damaged me. Fatal cracks set in as I felt disillusioned, uncertain, confused about the Man in the Park. How was he so completely paralysed by his daughter's erratic emotions? How was he not capable of seeing beyond the edges of her jealous lens? Who was this man I was living with, and, most importantly, who was I when I was with him? That final year was not without its pleasures, travel, sex, or even hope, but something was broken, something I was praying time would heal. My heart dug through the dirt, turning over rocks, desperately looking for reasons to stay.

Of the thousands of words I have written on these pages, it is the story of my breakup with Edward that has been the most challenging to tell. Not because the details escape me, or the emotion is too raw, but rather because it wasn't just a breakup between two people; this was a breakup of a family, Quinn's family. So, out of concern and respect for her, as I tell this story and how the end unfolded, I will focus on the consequences of her actions, and less on what was said. For the story she told, the words themselves, possessed no ability to dampen the heart, twist the mind or spoliate the soul ... unless someone gave them power, and believed them.

For almost a year Quinn refused to speak to me. She was in pain, and as pain often does, it came dressed as anger. Not just from the exclusion of that weekend, but from what she believed it meant, that she was not my family, that she did not belong. My attempts to talk to her, text her, hug her, were met with an icy, painful resilience. Her father supported this silence. I can't say for certain if she truly hated me during this time, or if perhaps she was mourning my loss, but what she did make abundantly clear to me, and to others around us, was that she was looking to punish me. 'If I am not family ... neither are you.'

At the centre of her efforts to support her well-voiced campaign to break me and her father up, she told a lie. One that cut deep and had one single motive, to obliterate. Now, lies are powerless if they are not believed. And this one – well, based on the absurdity of the story, and the mindset of the storyteller, I honestly gave it little weight, almost dismissing it as trivial. But as she emotionally told her tale, laying her words at her father's feet, it was Edward who gave them strength and power and purpose. Teaching me that one single lie – just one – could have a thousand consequences.

It wasn't Quinn I blamed or held accountable. How could I? How could anyone? She was just the storyteller. And although I couldn't be certain what Edward did or did not believe, what I am completely certain of was that Edward wanted to believe ... more than anything.

I insisted on hugging Quinn hello as she entered the cottage the following summer, one year after my mom's memorial. Her arms lay heavy and lifeless at her sides, greeting me with all the warmth of a scarecrow. I'd often try to love her when she least deserved it, as I knew that was when she needed it most.

Edward had returned to London and he had given her permission to have some friends up for the weekend. I was in the kitchen, out of sight, making a pavlova, when I heard it. Her voice cutting through the quiet as she gossiped with her friends, weaving her story. *She doesn't know I can hear her,* I thought, as her voice pushed against the walls and she wove her story. I didn't think much of it at the time, for what she said had absolutely nothing to do with me. But rather, it would be her denial of saying it that would pull me in and propel me out, for I made a mistake. A big mistake. As casually as tossing a lit cigarette from a moving car, not ever thinking it would start a fire, I repeated the story to a friend. The wrong friend, as it turned out, and with that, the tale and its fiery sparks were released into the world, and all was set alight.

Like a wildfire gathering strength, scorching a path through all that lay in its way, this story and its dangerous sparks landed on another, Quinn's boyfriend, Holden. What fire does not destroy it hardens, and the following morning the fire caught up with Edward, and there was a slew of texts from him, mostly of a 'What the fuck is going on over there?' nature. He informed me Holden had broken up with Quinn and, as he understood it, it was all my fault.

♥

STOP IGNORING ME, Quinn screamed in all-caps over text.

I hadn't picked up her rapid-fire phone calls because I was busy with a repairman.

I'll call you as soon as the repairman is gone, I responded in a text.

NO, she texted back, *YOU WILL TALK TO ME NOW!*

I ignored her demand, and as soon as I was able, I sat down and returned her call. Quinn picked up immediately. She was in an apocalyptic high-octane rage.

'You lied. You lied!' she roared like thunder.

Trying very hard to be calm and gentle, I genuinely apologised for repeating what I had heard. Never did I think for a second this would be the consequence. I was upset for her, angry with my friend, and disappointed with myself.

'You lied, you lied, you've ruined my life,' she screamed, so loudly that I had to distance my ear from the phone. She charged me with fabricating all of this to punish her for her year of steely silence. She accused me of poisoning Holden and his family against her. I apologised over and over again, feeling sick at the horrible role I'd played in this crisis, her breakup, her very raw pain. But through my apologies and my explanations, which went unheard, the one point I kept circling back to was: 'Quinn, I didn't lie, that's what you said.'

'How could I have told you that when I wasn't even speaking to you?' she spat, trying to rationalise.

'Quinn,' I said, 'you haven't spoken to me since my mom died.'

Instantly her anger made way for sadness, and in a giant wave of tears impossible to control, it all spilt out, and the conversation changed.

'You – you ... told me I wasn't family,' she wept.

'Quintana, when did I ever tell you that?' I asked.

Trying to catch her breath, she sobbed, 'That's what Dad said when he told me why I wasn't invited to the cottage.'

I felt the pain and hurt in this child as if she were my own.

'Quinn, you weren't included not because you aren't my family. You've always been my family. You weren't included because you were being a bitch.' There was a calming silence as I heard her exhale, much like the quiet one hears when turning a page.

Relieved, she cried, 'Well, why didn't you ever tell me that?'

Bitch she could handle. She knew she'd been a bitch. But what she'd been told, or what she'd come to understand, was that I didn't love her enough, she didn't belong, and she was not family.

The final few minutes were gentle, calm, like a stupendous storm had passed. I heard the exhaustion in Quinn's voice. There was some light banter, small smiles that seemed to make a quiet, soft sound through the phone. We'd needed this, and I promised her she'd never again not know my truth.

'I didn't mean it,' she said.

'I know you didn't, Quinn, and Holden will believe you too. Just be honest with him. Tell him the truth. I love you, Quinn, and I'm so sorry.'

'I'm sorry too,' she said. 'I love you too.'

I exhaled in the honest belief that it was the most cathartic conversation I had ever had with Quinn. It had started with fire and fury and had ended in love and compassion, coupled with a greater understanding of the importance of truth, or so I believed. Not only could she handle the truth, she required it. We all need to be called out on our bad behaviour. It's essential to our evolution as caring humans. And as parents, that's our responsibility. Had Edward told her the truth about why she wasn't included that weekend, or explained that the 'I Love You' party was a generous act of love, not a deliberate act of omission, perhaps it would have made for a different ending. Maybe. At the very least, it would have helped Quinn understand that her actions needed to change to be included. And isn't that what life is all about, learning from your mistakes?

It was too late to call Edward in London, plus I honestly didn't know if I had the energy to utter one more word. I picked up my phone and texted him. *I spoke to Quinn for over an hour. A lot of shit came up. Let's chat in the morning, but all is good. xo* The rest I'd tell him when we spoke the next day, or so I thought.

I awoke in the morning to an assault of angry texts from Edward. I believed he must have been working with the information from before my conversation with Quinn, but that wasn't true. He'd been talking to her all night.

Accusations came flying at me like bullets from a gun I had loaded, cocked and handed to Quinn. Edward's words – 'liar', 'evil', 'disloyal', 'disgusting', 'unforgivable' – assaulted me and were repeated over and over … and over.

What had just happened?

I phoned Edward immediately, but my call went to voice-mail. I left message after message, urgently asking if we could please talk, assuring him I'd had a great conversation with Quinn and all was good. I used words like 'healing', 'therapeutic' and 'painfully honest'. I assured Edward that Quinn had admitted to everything, all of it, and I'd even got a tiny but believable 'I'm sorry' out of her. Edward didn't call me back. Instead, he mounted a miserable, relentless, punishing character assassination, as told by words blasting across my phone screen. I felt muted, voiceless, rendered virtually silent as Edward adamantly refused to talk, wholly uninterested in hearing my side of this life-changing story, as if the truth might change the outcome. How could he possibly not know who I was after all these years? How did he not want to know? How could he actually think I'd put words in Quinn's mouth? I was gutted. It wasn't until three weeks later when I returned to London that we spoke for the first time. His painful messages, his defiant, deliberate act of refusing my calls had left me broken, vapid. By the time I stood in front of him, sad and exceedingly confused, I had lost fourteen pounds.

Although I was never married to Edward, that didn't make me less of a stepmom to Quinn. I thought about the years of love, affection and attention I had given to the little one who introduced me as 'Mom'. I was in her world for most of her life, and more of a mother to her than sadly Karina could be. But if a stepparent doesn't have the support of the actual parent, the task is daunting. Actually, it's more than that. It's pointless.

I can't answer how a man who balances pros and cons in business, who looks at a deal from every possible perspective, could not do the same when it came to his life or his daughter. Perhaps Edward's inability to stand up for himself made him grossly unqualified to stand up for me. Maybe in parenting we can all be a little blind when it comes to something we don't want to see. But what a disservice we do if we never shine a much-needed light on our children's behaviour. For without light, nothing grows, it only festers.

Through those three weeks of texted insults, accusations, threats, bile and blame, one message stood out from the others, like a screaming child in a silent church. Edward, a C-suite executive, my partner of ten years, my fiancé for five, the man I'd uprooted my life for and changed countries to be with, broke up with me … in a text message, exactly like Quinn had told him to.

CHAPTER 7

The Truth Will Set You Free,
But First it Will Piss You Off

'If I'd observed all the rules, I'd never have got anywhere.'
Marilyn Monroe

I once read somewhere that if you tell a story often enough, it can become a real memory, granting you access to rooms you've never occupied, so I have wondered if that was what happened. There was so much I couldn't understand around my breakup with Edward without access to those rooms that Quinn had created.

There are many reasons people break up, and often it's not because of just one thing, but what I've come to learn is that there's invariably an exit plan. An orchestrated escape, requiring us to psych ourselves up, prepare physically, emotionally and perhaps financially. We amass a tiny army of emotional-support soldiers who sit squarely in our corner. It's not unlike a boxer who needs months to prepare for a heavyweight prize fight, because make no mistake, it's a fight.

Even when confronted with that devastating first piece of evidence – a Visa statement perhaps, with a mysterious hotel charge, or an unfamiliar email-sender speaking of desire and intention – it's rare not to have some sort of methodical exit plan in place before saying, '*Hasta la vista*, baby.' I've been on both the leaving side and the being left side, and honestly, they both suck. In relationships where I've done the leaving, there were always signs it was coming, like warning shots off the bow, signs that I was unhappy, that things needed changing, even if change wasn't possible.

I'm not proud of all my exit plans. My worst 'strategy', and I use that word loosely, was when I wanted to leave Brandon. I basically treated him like crap. Yup, that was the sum of it. So eventually and painfully, he'd be so miserable, hate me so much that he'd be running to break up with me like it had been his idea in the first place. That was unmistakably cowardly and unkind, and clearly, I didn't possess the human decency, emotional intelligence and, most of all, courage to exit gracefully. At 26 years of age, I'll blame this on immaturity.

With Jackson, it was less about looking for a door marked 'exit' and more like trying to find my way out of an escape room. He gift-wrapped me an 'I don't love you anymore' moment, bundled tightly with the harsh smell of smoke and his inability to remove a cashmere jumper. But I didn't leave the following day, bags in hand once the actual smoke had cleared. It took time to dig my way out. My old friend and loyal companion, fear, paralysed me, making the journey from fire to freedom not as simple as packing my bags, grabbing the cat and sashaying my ass out the door. There are often weeks, months, sometimes years that can divide those two life-altering 'aha' moments, the falling out of love, or what I call 'time of death', and leaving, especially if there are kids involved. Seldom are those two moments synchronised. And if they are, I'm going to hazard a guess that it's the landing of the last straw of the many last straws accumulating on that camel's back ... which leads me now to Edward.

What I needed with Edward was a massive emotional catapult, and let me tell you, that's exactly what was delivered to me. Looking back at that relationship, I think I stayed invested so long because I believed our children's (or maybe it was just Quinn's) needs were greater than my own. I threw myself into that family as Anne Sullivan did with Helen Keller, not ever thinking for a second that walking away or quitting was an option. *They need me,* I arrogantly told myself. *Don't you give up on that family.* But if in staying, if in giving of yourself, there is more water coming out of the well than going in, eventually all will run dry.

Edward loved to use the term 'good enough'. It was his universal standard measure for most things in life.

'Was that burger done to your taste, sir?' or 'What did you think of *La La Land*?'

If he was able to get through it, eat it, not return it, his answer would be a resounding, 'Good enough.'

I think that's how he gauged our relationship those last few years: not bad enough to send back to the kitchen or walk out of the theatre, but rather good enough.

There were three painful months from his 'time of death' text message to when I finally moved out of our Chelsea home. They were among the most agonising I had gone through with Edward. There was a decade worth of heartbreaking disentangling that needed doing. As Edward's company paid for the house, it would be me vacating, not him. It's horrible living with someone you used to love madly after you've broken up. I honestly didn't know which way was up. It was as if I had been thrown overboard into a dark body of icy water, upside down, confused, dizzy, disoriented as to which direction the surface was. Did I stay in London? Did I move back to Canada? Where was my home? Where did I even belong anymore? The days were more manageable when Edward was at work, but in the evenings, we'd move around each other like ghosts, wispy sad vapours of our former selves. Even with walls, rooms or floors separating us, I felt his dark energy like an angry spirit, rattling chains and flickering lights to haunt me. There wasn't much dialogue, and if there were words, they were icy, piercing and served one of two purposes: to inform or to harm. The smell of home-cooked meals that had used to fill the house at dinnertime was now replaced with the aromas of tikka masala takeaways.

I was a tiny, tangled knot of cuts and bruises, made to feel wholly responsible for the destruction of our family, and for that, Edward was actively punishing me. I was devastated by two things. First, the horrible debilitating guilt I felt having unintentionally contributed to Quinn's relationship breakup, regardless of who had said what, or how loudly.

The second thing that crushed and confused me was why didn't Edward believe me? He wasn't interested in hearing what I had to say, not even a little. Quinn's suffering rendered me completely voiceless and armed Edward with a bullhorn, blood-hounds, and a royal warrant for my execution. Edward wasn't blind to his daughter's character. Yet his assassination of me was without question ruthless, unjust and deliberate, as though he was morally and ethically obligated to rip me to shreds. This I didn't understand. But I knew that whether he believed me or not, Quinn was trapped under this tale she'd told. One that had lit a fire, scorching an irretrievable path, leaving each of us with the ashes to prove it. Why she did this, I may never know. It's a horrible feeling when you're made to feel wholly responsible for the pain of those you love, and Edward did that exceedingly well.

So ... isn't it interesting how sometimes something bigger than yourself steps in to shine a much-needed light, showing you there is so much more to the story than you know? Some might call what happened next a message from God, but as an atheist, that wouldn't be a word I'd typically use. I've used 'universe' or 'karma' when the actions of some are tempered by something else impossible to rationalise, but I think in this situation, I'll give credit to the spiritual guidance of Elena. While I can't be sure it was my mother's breath behind those words I heard that day, wouldn't it be just like my co-conspirator to whisper in my ear: 'Hey, Christina, have you checked to see if he's changed his password on his old cell phone?'

When I discovered Edward was cheating on me, by way of me hacking into his computer, thanks to that old cell phone, I have to say, in a weird way, I was relieved. Pissed off, but relieved. So many of his actions didn't make sense to me during our breakup. So when the penny dropped, the computer dinged, and that all-telling text message came blindingly into view, I thought, *Of course*. It was the missing puzzle piece. It was the truth he didn't want me to know, as it would rob him of a fabulous, selfless gift he'd given to his daughter: the removal of me.

As I combed through his texts and emails like I was looking for nits – the ones he signed with hearts-for-eyes emojis – something else bubbled up, confirmation I wasn't in love with him. How did this discovery offer substantiation, you might ask? Because my immediate gut reaction to discovering my lover of ten years was cheating on me was: 'Ah-ha! Gotcha!' Had I been in love, my response would've been much like when I'd sat in front of John's computer and made a similar discovery. My heart would've immediately stopped beating and done a freefall dive into the pit of my stomach. My throat would've tightened up, stopped the flow of oxygen to my brain, and I would've had to fight the overwhelming urge not to throw up all over the keyboard. That's a 'love' reaction to cheating. Every part of your body is physically trying to reject the information, as if you've just ingested syrup of ipecac. Your instant gut reaction honestly tells you all you need to know.

This discovery immediately made me less sad. Less sad is good. Conversely, it did piss me off. But I ask you, wouldn't you much rather be angry than sad? Absolutely you would. While sadness can be so debilitating that it can keep you in a catatonic state for months, anger is an empowering, kick-ass, take-no-prisoners, let's-scorch-some-serious-earth emotion.

I traced the start of Edward's messages to his new 'girlfriend' to shortly after my mother had died. The actual moment I had stopped loving him, and perhaps the moment he'd stopped loving me too. Edward had effectually broken my heart that weekend, and you can't re-break something that's already broken. As I continued my cyber-sleuthing, and in what could only be described as a whole new level of 'what the fuck?', I unearthed an online dating profile on a secret email account. I read many flirty conversations with women with names like 2Blonde4U and BubblyBarb, confirming to me that sex isn't the only way to define cheating. If you've got to delete or hide texts or emails from someone you're involved with, then guess what, that's cheating too.

One needs to be very careful when peeking behind the curtain, for what's hiding behind can change things instantly. For I made one final discovery, which ricocheted like bullets between one text bubble to another. There, glowing on the screen, were disturbing messages between Edward and his daughter. Out of everything I'd unearthed, it was these messages that hurt me most: weaponised, hateful words were spoken casually as if malice and vengeance were items you could order from a take-away menu.

In those words sat a promise, from father to daughter. Indulgences and loyalty in return for my extradition. Assurances and a solemn vow that I would pay for my betrayal.

His words read like an epitaph.

Immobilised, I hovered in the stillness, in a garden I'd planted but would never again sit in, allowing the truth to settle in and find me. It wasn't me who'd damaged Quinn, it was her father. In Edward's desperate attempts to show his daughter what love was, he was teaching her the opposite. How had I failed them so completely? I exhaled soundlessly, as I instantly, painfully realised that these messages released me from my guilt and any obligation I might still have felt to love him.

I don't regret the love I gave them. I've never known two people who needed it more. But it was yet another hard lesson learnt, sadly teaching me that love cannot coexist with hate, and in my well-meaning attempt to fix someone else, I nearly broke myself. I couldn't have fixed this broken family. I could not fix what I hadn't broken.

As agonising as it was to read all those texts, they gave me an unexpected gift. They allowed me to stop beating myself up, to stop replaying scenarios over and over in my head, stop asking a question I'd never get an answer to: 'What could I have done differently?' I stopped waiting for an apology that was never coming, I made peace with the fact that I was the villain in someone else's story, and Edward would have to figure out his own injustices. I was incapable of untangling them for him. I walked away from his computer, reassured that I wasn't losing my mind. And even though he'd managed to cancel the automatic top-up on my Starbucks card and my Oyster card before we'd even spoken, he had forgotten about his old cell phone. *You are now free to go,* whispered the voice inside my head, sounding just like Elena. *There's nothing more for you here.*

Now that I officially had zero fucks to give, I did have one last question remaining. Before I walked out the door and slammed it behind me forever, what should I do with these nuggets of intelligence, this generous gift from the universe/ Elena? Should I confront him in a wild rage? Throw plates at his head? Perhaps I should replace his shampoo with hair removal cream? That last one was Victoria's suggestion, and I thought it brilliant and worthy of serious consideration. Another option was not to say a word, leave it silent, unspoken. I considered the moral, less-trodden high ground, where 'no response is a strong response', a tip of the hat and good riddance. That option danced in my brain like a flickering light bulb, alive one second, dead the next. If you've learnt anything about me as you've been following me on this journey, it'll be that I'm not that emotionally evolved. I'm not Elizabeth Gilbert. So, I silently held on to this new intelligence, letting it stew, confident that when the time came, I'd know exactly what to do.

CHAPTER 8

The Exit Plan

'It isn't what we say or think that defines us, but what we do.'
Jane Austen, *Sense and Sensibility*

The following few weeks leading up to my departure, I have to say, were extremely productive. I had a few orders of business that needed tending to. Let's call it a wee bit of karmic housecleaning. The first item on my agenda was to find out who 'she' was. That hadn't taken me any time at all. A special shout out to Facebook and LinkedIn for making creeping people a relatively easy afternoon project, a little like scrapbooking. She was an estate agent in a suburb outside Toronto, and looked every bit the part: navy blazer, head-tilt, big, toothy Crest-whitening-strip smile. For the record, I've no issue with this woman. Let's call her … say … Randi Realtor, and I seriously don't hold her accountable. Or at least I don't have enough information to declare her as an informed, willing accomplice. I'll assume she only knew what Edward told her, and I think we've established he's not the poster boy for living honestly. It's Edward and his Neanderthal need to grab on to one vine before letting go of the other that I have an issue with. But looking back, wasn't that precisely what he did to Karina with me? 'Be careful how you enter a relationship,' my mother used to tell me. 'You'll be leaving it the same way.'

Something else needed doing, or maybe one could call it undoing. It's not that I went out of my way looking for this morally ambiguous, relationship 'righting-of-the-ship' complot, but it does serve as an excellent example of just what can happen when the girlfriend collective starts kicking up dust. Much like how a few gentle gusts of wind can eventually whip up into a kick-ass *Wizard of Oz*-style tornado.

My girlfriend Nicole, like the glorious human she is, had a glass of chilled Chardonnay with a single ice cube waiting for me as I walked in her door. Wine in hand, we sat in the well-appointed reception room of her charming house in South Kensington, as I acquainted her with Randi Realtor, BubblyBarb, and the cruel texts between Edward and his daughter.

One of the many things I love about Nicole is that she can and will get angry for me. She's always been a thorn in the side of the smugly comfortable, and at this moment, Edward, she believed, was overtly smug.

'So let me see if I've got this straight,' Nicole began, giving me a full Queen Latifah head twists. 'Edward has a wife, a fiancé, a girlfriend … aaaand he's cheating on all of them with someone named BubblyBarb? What a total fucker. This I need to see for myself,' she pronounced, reaching for my phone, hoping to see Edward's online dating profile.

'I don't have it,' I said. 'I think you have to be a member.'

Now I can't quite remember exactly whose moment of inspired genius it was, mine or Nicole's. To be honest, it's a bit of a Chardonnay blur. What I can tell you is that even before there was a need to top up our glasses, the two of us were huddled together like teenage girls stalking a celebrity crush as we brought up the dating website. The thinking, if one could call it thinking, was that we'd quickly set up a fake online profile so that I could show Nicole Edward's profile. But the site didn't work like the others I knew, essentially spitting out hundreds of guys at a time like a human man Pez dispenser. A lengthy questionnaire required filling in and a credit card needed to be plopped down. Furthermore, we discovered the site only sent you ten matched profiles a day, meaning we'd have to wait to be matched before we'd be able to see Edward's online persona. Almost discouraged before we began, we noticed a two-week free trial period. So, bubbling up from the part of my brain where weird shit is born and occasionally manifests, it was decided. We'd go online fishing for Edward and would give it no more than two weeks. Out of principle, I wasn't interested in this costing me a blasted shilling, nor was I comfortable with the idea of becoming a serial cyber-stalking ex-lover. So with no real plan beyond that, and fuelled with a bit of white-wine just-ice, we enjoyably went to work customising Edward's dream girl.

It wasn't difficult.

She had to be blonde, pretty, employed, ski and love the Rolling Stones.

'We're going to need some photos,' I said, realising Edward would not poke his head out of his burrow without photographic enticement.

'Hmmm, how are we going to do that?' Nicole asked.

I hadn't thought that far.

Ignoring what my mother would've called 'the better nature of our angels', we turned to Facebook and found an attractive random stranger who fitted Edward's criteria. This would not go down as one of my finest moments. However, it wouldn't prove to be my worst.

'Whatcha think, Nic? Is she someone Edward would be attracted to?'

'Definitely,' she said, then paused. 'So wait, do we just start using this Facebook girl's photos?'

We both sat silently for a moment with that unanswered, ethically grey question hanging in the air.

'The past isn't quite yet over,' I said, paraphrasing Faulkner, looking for literary permission. 'Yes,' I said, 'we'll make peace with the devil later on.'

With glasses raised, we apologised to the woman on Facebook.

'Facebook Girl,' I said, 'we ask forgiveness for using your photos. Please know that God (or the devil) as our witness, this will not last longer than the two-week free trial period.'

'What shall we call her?' Nicole asked.

'How about Amanda?' I said, having absolutely no idea where the name came from.

So just like that, a blonde 40-something gainfully employed Rolling-Stones lover became the newest member of the online dating world.

Amanda was instantly popular. Duh. Profiles would pop into her newly created email account with introductions or invitations to meet. Trite one-liners like 'You're so hot' or 'Hey, sexy' were the most common. Amanda thought it showed a tremendous lack of originality and inherited laziness. If Amanda was going to bide her time waiting to see if Edward would nibble on her online bait, she'd have to sift through what she was now calling the debris of single men.

Two days into Karmic Reset, as we came to call it, there was still no sign of Edward. We found this puzzling, as the match score couldn't have got much higher, since we'd answered every question with him in mind. I mean, we were just one photo of her in a tight Rolling Stones tank-top short of guaranteeing him a lifetime of happiness.

I awoke on day three, and just like the days that had preceded that one, the first question I asked myself was *Do I check my phone before I pee or while peeing?* Up came a new daily crop of men. Immediately I was struck by a bolt of adrenaline, causing my somersaulting heart to free-fall. There was Edward. What had started out as simply sharing Edward's online activity over a glass/bottle of wine was now gathering girl-power momentum, and now had all the makings of an espionage episode of *Charlie's Angels*. Quickly, I shared the news with Nicole, giddy and chuffed with our accomplishment.

'So, what now?' Nicole asked. 'Do we send him a message?'

I thought for a moment. 'I think we sit back and wait, see if Edward comes to Amanda.'

I really wasn't sure whether this was something he'd do. I mean, he had a newish estate-agent girlfriend. I'd read their oozing, flirtatious texts, with Edward's exhaustive use of that heart-eyes emoji. However, by late afternoon, any doubts were obliterated, for there in Amanda's inbox was a message from Edward.

I just want to jump in here for a sec. Perhaps some of you are thinking round about now that this little catfishing escapade should be reason to hang my middle-aged head in shame, and yes, I did feel an occasional twinge of conflict. And sure, we'd stolen the idea from a reality TV programme so ethically challenged that it alone should act as some kind of massive warning for its lack of moral standards. *However*, let us not forget two very inspirational call-to-action words. Bubbly! Barb! Sure, maybe those words alone don't offer complete absolution, but couple that with a grown-ass man old enough to need regular prostate exams who broke up with me over a text message, and well ... it pretty much pardoned me from feeling like a sinner at the threshold of Hell.

Edward's introduction wasn't like Amanda's other suitors, with just a few uninspired words. He wrote a frickin' novella. I laughed out loud reading his first sentence: 'Wow, Amanda, you've got my attention.' His lengthy introduction talked of his passion for skiing, sailing, riding, his prestigious public-school education, and his love of Latin. He confided that his profile had resulted from having too much claret one night at his computer, and ended with the cheery, upbeat, optimistic hope of hearing back from Amanda. With an enthusiasm that would rival tween girls having Harry Styles surprisingly show up as their prom date, we read and reread Edward's lengthy self-introduction. Nicole, absorbing the new intel then asked a question I hadn't yet asked myself.

'What's the endgame, Christina?'

I stopped for a moment and realised we didn't have one.

'Obviously, they won't be meeting,' I laughed.

'Nope,' Nicole said, 'but he could think they will.'

Then Nicole's stupendous 'I could make your death look like an accident' girlfriend loyalty chimed in. With the focused conviction of a human rights activist, Nicole's mind started twisting. 'Say, for instance, Amanda catches Edward in a few untruths or contradictions. Maybe the world is so small that Amanda could know someone who knows someone who knows Edward's story. She can call him out on it, give him just enough rope to hang himself.'

Beaming, I thought, *This is the hallmark of a brilliant friend, someone who hates my ex more than I do.* This light-hearted experiment was now being moulded into a karmic lesson, a little 21st-century justice. We had eleven days left. Eleven days for Edward to get completely enamoured with Amanda, share his life story with her, lie about it, ask her out, then have her call him out on his shit, and dump his ass without giving him a chance to explain.

'Easy-peasy,' Nicole said.

Diligently, the two of us got to work. We'd carefully craft every word and nuance of Amanda's questions and responses. Nicole would often rewrite or delete a sentence or two that I'd written, saying it sounded too much like me, as apparently I have 'a style'. 'Amanda wouldn't use the word "fuck",' Nicole would insist. 'She'd need to know him better,' as if Amanda was a great friend of Nicole's who had graduated with her from a Swiss finishing school. There was friendly, flirty banter between Amanda and Edward, asking and answering questions about life, desires and love. He'd use words like 'rock-solid', 'honest', 'loyal' and 'a real family guy with strong moral values'. She'd use words like 'an annoyingly bubbly morning person', 'playful', 'honest', 'active' and 'a Democrat'. Both grew up riding horses ... both used Red Bull to treat jet lag and, of course, they both agreed The Rolling Stones was the best band ever.

Edward couldn't believe the remarkable, delightful similarities.

I was personally surprised by the detail Edward would share and the time he put into it. I felt only a few pangs of discomfort, as one could imagine hiding behind a fictitious online alias and communicating with your ex-partner might evoke. They came from reading Edward's rose-filtered, creative recounts of his life, or from the direct lies he told, some of which I didn't even understand his need to tell, or in the disparaging disses, like, 'The only thing I miss about my ex is her Soho House membership.' I'm not going to lie. It kind of smarted.

With two days to go, it happened. In a leap of reckless abandon, Edward and Amanda agreed to meet. Amanda picked the spot: 'A lovely quiet place on Marylebone High Street.' She told Edward that she had excitedly shared details about her upcoming date with a friend, telling her about this incredible man, sharing his picture, his story.

'Can I have your phone number?' Edward asked.

'If the date goes well, I'll whisper it in your ear,' Amanda playfully responded.

'I have a million questions,' Edward told her. 'And forgive me, but I'm already optimistically planning our second date.'

The following morning Edward received a carefully worded message from Amanda. 'Dear Edward, I am cancelling our date,' she began. 'You know how they say the world is a small place, well it's so interesting when it's proven to you.' She informed him that in sharing his photo, name and details, her friend thought his story sounded familiar. So her friend had done a little digging and had come back with a truck-load of facts, all contradicting Edward's stories about his wife, his fiancé and rumours of multiple affairs. Amanda reported that, most wrongly, he'd described his character as honest with strong moral values, adding he was more morally messy. She recognised there was always more than one side to every story, but she had heard more than enough to conclude that she had no interest in starting anything up with him, grateful she was finding out the truth now, as opposed to later. Without waiting for a response, a possible explanation or using the word 'fuck', Amanda deleted her dating profile on the last day of the fourteen-day free trial period.

My therapist, Nancy Pope, used to like to say, 'Look for the patterns, and people will show you who they are.' Had Edward not lied to Amanda, not coloured his story, she wouldn't have had anything juicy to throw at him to challenge the moral core of his professed 'character'. Sure, we might all exaggerate our strengths and downplay our weaknesses on a dating website, but this was more than that; he'd lied to her about the things that should have mattered most. Amanda's brief fourteen-day life gave me a tiny pocket of peace, for, seeing her future, I could release the hope that my past could have been any different. So, in the wise words of Amanda's favourite band, let us always remember: 'You can't always get what you want, but if you try sometimes, you just might find ... you get what you need.'

♥

There was now only one last piece of unfinished business, that final push of the broom across an all-but-swept floor. It was time to address the estate-agent mistress in the room.

The weekend of my move, Edward was away for a conference. The night before he flew out, he came into our bedroom, which he'd vacated several months earlier for the guest room. He sat on the end of the bed, much like a parent who wanted talk with their child. He seemed somewhat nostalgic. I can't honestly remember much of his long monologue, even though he was there the better part of an hour, or so it felt. But I interpreted it as him tidying up emotional loose ends. He did most of the talking as I sat in bed, duvet tight around me like it was high-thread-count armour, and a wine glass clutched firmly in hand. I only interrupted him once, to go down to the kitchen and get a much-required refill.

As I sat there listening to him, I silently surveyed the room, which had been filled with promise, sex and storybook romantic hope three years ago. My clothes of that day were draped over a Victorian armchair he'd never liked. Clumps of dust surrounded the TV stand, looking like shed skins of my former life, lying lifeless on the dark hardwood floor. On his bedside table sat some loose change, a book on Winston Churchill I'd given him but didn't recall him having read, and a 5"×7" framed photo of us in Venice, smiling, looking over the Bridge of Sighs. Although I don't remember most of what he said, I remember what went through my mind. Edward was insistent that in a few weeks, after everything had 'settled down', the two of us should have dinner together, that he'd very much like to get together, stay in touch, etc. He was smiling, nothing too big, but seemingly optimistic in his invitation, in the spirit of us moving from this phase of our relationship into, perhaps, the next, reminding me, 'After all, Christina, you were really the only mother my daughter ever knew,' like somehow that meant something now. Using the worst of all breakup clichés, he added, 'I very much want to remain friends.' *He'll be lonely,* I thought, because in his three years back in London, Edward had not reached out to a single friend from before he'd moved to Toronto, nor made any new ones. But what so resoundingly resonated in me from my inner core was the fundamental truth that we would never, ever have that dinner he was so brightly suggesting. Not because I wouldn't have entertained the idea, but because I knew he was so blindly confident he had successfully hidden his unsavoury secrets from me. If the last few months had taught me anything, it was that this very accomplished man sitting on the end of my bed was a coward.

Until I had unearthed the truth, I'd endured the balance of blame around the breakup. It was me who had caused the 'irreparable rift'. It was me who had left him 'no choice'. But the moment light was shone in his direction, evidenced by Randi Realtor and BubblyBarb, it couldn't only be my fault anymore. He'd immediately become that guy, the one who'd cheated on his sick wife, then cheated on his fiancé, whose expectations had permitted her to uproot her life and come with him to London. You learn so much more about someone at the end of a relationship than at the beginning, for how Edward said goodbye told me everything I'd ever need to know about the man. That's why I felt relieved discovering those messages from Randi Realtor and friends. They spoke the truth, which, simply told, was that he was seeing someone else and didn't love me anymore. Quinn and her dramatics were just his exit plan.

Nothing much more stuck with me. He got up to leave the bedroom and asked for a hug, then said goodnight and goodbye.

'End of the month ... dinner,' he reiterated.

'That would be nice,' I smiled, knowing what I knew.

I looked at his face. There was nothing there anymore. The 'ick' factor had settled in and was doing its job nicely. I couldn't see any of it, what I had loved, what I had found so attractive as I looked at him for the very last time in our bedroom. It was gone. It had all been erased, eroded by events that had disfigured him. Weird how that happens, how someone you once found so attractive, so deliciously mouth-watering, becomes someone who ... wait ... have you always made that annoying noise when you chew your meat?

There was a brief moment when I contemplated the idea of revenge sex. It floated up into my consciousness, not from a place of desire, but with rather more of a self-serving purpose of fucking him up just a little, giving him a lasting memento, a 'thank you for playing' parting gift. But as quick as the thought entered my mind, it disappeared. *I don't care enough,* I thought. Again, that voice inside me said with kindness ... *Nothing more for you here, Christina, you're free to go.*

I lay in bed early on the morning of my move, after returning from the kitchen with a much-needed latte. Spotify was playing The Cure, 'Pictures of You' over my speaker. My eyes wandered around the room, settling on the framed photo of Edward and me on his bedside table. As The Cure sang of staring at pictures for so long that they began to feel real, it happened: my moment of blinding brilliance. Had I been a cartoon character, you'd have seen a bright light bulb appear above my head. And if one were going to pair that light bulb with a sound, it would be a deep-bellied laugh, a triumphant 'Ba-ha-ha-ha-ha!' With help from The Cure, I had my Randi

Realtor resolution, and I humbly say it was genius. I knew exactly how I'd address the estate-agent mistress in the room.

I quickly got up and went to Edward's computer, pulling up Randi Realtor's corporate photo. I dragged it onto a memory stick and, within five minutes, was heading down the King's Road to the local stationery store. Standing at the digital photo desk, I said, without hesitation, 'One 5"×7" colour print, please.'

'We're having a special promotion on photo keyrings,' the young sales assistant informed me, and pointed to a display of clear acrylic key fobs with custom photos in them. 'Two for one, they're scratch-resistant.'

The corners of my lips curled up like I was the Grinch, and I beamed with unconcealed joy. 'I'll take two.' Twenty minutes later, I was back home, replacing Edward's bedside photo of the two of us with Randi Realtor and her casually folded arms. Retrieving my house key and the spare, I attached the new keyrings with the smiling suburban realtor photo, sealed tightly in scratch-resistant acrylic. Marvelling at my handiwork, I stepped back. This was bloody perfect.

The movers arrived a short time later, and we walked room to room as I pointed to this and that. 'That table gets shipped back, and this lamp stays in London,' I instructed them. This was hard, standing in a house I'd once loved, dividing my possessions between shipping and storage, the past and the future. Nicole and her husband had graciously offered to house me for a couple of weeks. But beyond that, I had absolutely no idea where I'd be living. The movers spent the day wrapping my china and all things fragile in white newsprint. The windows seemed to rattle from the loud sound of long strips of packing tape being pulled taut over boxes that contained fragments of my decades on the planet. I had purposefully not done any packing before that day, not so much as a butter knife. I wanted Edward to walk into the house on his return and see it in stark contrast to the place he'd left, its soul ripped out, as told by shadowy imprints where family photos had once hung, hitting him all at once between the eyes, like a brilliantly thrown tomahawk.

The house was almost empty of my things, aside from a few packed cardboard boxes surrounded by a menagerie of dust bunnies. Empty picture hooks scarred the soft grey walls. Where candlesticks, vases and wine decanters had once stood, faint, dusty silhouettes softly reminded me I was standing in the middle of relationship rubble. But sitting among the ruins in the bedroom we'd once shared, was a lovely silver-framed 5″×7″ photograph, my glorious exit plan.

I put my coat on and slung a giant yellow Ikea bag over my shoulder, carrying the last things I'd need for the next few weeks at Nicole's. I looked around my bedroom for the last time, feeling bigger than that relationship had ever allowed me to be. *I will not be sad over this anymore,* I thought, feeling the room's emptiness lighten me. I smiled at the photo sitting perfectly poised on his nightstand table. *This will drive him crazy,* I smugly thought, *and that's why it's so perfect.* #humblebrag. There were no words, no confrontation. All I had to say was in one photograph, a thousand words saying, 'You're caught!' And this will come as a surprise to absolutely no one, but that dinner Edward so insistently suggested, the 'let's be friends' scenario … Well, I never heard from him. Who could've predicted?

The black lacquered door closed behind me. The flowers in the window boxes I'd once tended to were wilted, lying on the soil like day-old salad, softly supporting a notion I'd refused to see before: that I had been watering a dead plant. The late-autumn air was crisp, the sun casting long shadows through the colourful trees. I smiled. Some relationships bring you far from where you started and take you somewhere unexpected. Some years ask questions, and some years answer them. After a relationship died, I'd always end up asking myself the same question, the one that effectively glues together all those broken-hearted endings: 'What was the bloody point of that? Squandering some fabulous babe years I won't be getting back?' As I gazed upon the sunlit streets of London, I received my answer immediately. Edward had left me with a parting gift: a new relationship with a fabulous old gal, with ancient secrets, impeccable style, centuries of wisdom and chutzpah. I had embarked on one journey, and it had taken me not where I'd planned on going, but to exactly where I'd needed to be.

I adjusted the large Ikea bag on my shoulder and lowered my sunglasses. *I think I'll walk to Nicole's through the park.* As the English sunshine embraced me with a warm hug, I strutted down the street, and I grinned.

I was a Londoner.

The Book of

Christina

Advice to My Twenty-Year-Old Self, or Shit I Wish I'd Known Sooner

*'You can't go back and make a new start, but you can
start right now and make a brand new ending.'*
James Sherman, *Rejection*

I can't say I wasn't warned. I mean, my dad did say to me, 'Christina, one day you're 35; you blink, and then there you are, flashing your senior's pass, seeing films at half price.' I always thought my father was kidding, as he did about most things in his life, but nope, as I discovered, he was as serious as a case of shingles.

It's an interesting platform, your fifties, from which to reflect on life. There is an abundance of things to look forward to, plenty of runway left, and a ton of life experience to act as guidance. Many of us have children who are young adults and have launched or are well on their way. There are likely some regrets, but hopefully they're few, and perhaps some could even be reframed as life lessons. And likely, like me, there's been at least once instance of heartbreak, when it's been impossible to consider if the tiny fragments would ever find their way back together again.

The weird thing is that emotionally, I still feel like I'm in my twenties ... until I hang out with twenty-years-olds. Then it's like, *Nope, I'm most definitely not twenty.* I get slapped with that reality every time I hang out with my daughters and their friends, or when I take one step inside Soho House. Their language is different, how they communicate is different, and don't get me going on their abundance of energy. As I stretch, yawn, ask for the bill and say, 'Wow, is it that time already?' they're just getting started. They use terms I don't understand, like 'hunty', 'turnt', 'OG', bae', 'ratchet', 'bougie' and 'Netflix and chill', which, by the way, has nothing to do with hanging out and binge-watching *The Crown*. I guess every generation has its own thing, like secret passwords granting you access into a private club. Although the moment I try and throw out a word or two – you know, to show I'm still cool – there's an immediate cringe-worthy look, accompanied by: a 'Mom, don't ever use the word "baller" again.'

So nope, I'm no longer twenty, and I'm not going to lie, not all of it is great, this getting older thing. I honestly fear that every time I eat popcorn, I might crack a tooth on an un-popped kernel, or I sometimes wake up with an unexplained injury just from sleeping weird. And if I had known that the last time I got IDed would be the last time ever, I would've brought along a news crew and documented it. Seriously! I'm a television producer, I can make that shit happen.

But as I sit here writing this, grateful that wrinkles don't hurt (physically), I'll be honest with you, it's not all bad. I'm no longer as vain or concerned about my looks as I was back then. Don't get me wrong, I haven't completely given up. It's not like my iPhone's face recognition, in confusion, doesn't unlock my phone anymore, but I don't worry about my appearance in the same way as I used to. And here's a newsflash for you, it's not because I'm skinnier or hotter in my fifties than I was in my forties or thirties – my neck alone would tell you that. Rather, I am nicer and more accepting and forgiving of who I am and who I am definitely not. I still love squeezing into my sexy Hervé Léger dress and getting a big'n'bouncy blow-out, but it will never be like it once was, and you know what, I'm good with that. My sense of self comes from the inside these days, more than from a sensational pair of Jimmy Choos that I remove the moment I'm in the Uber. Nope, I'm not even waiting until I get home anymore. My eyesight might not be 20/20, but I can see things with a clearer perspective and through a kinder and gentler lens.

It's been said that life's tragedy is that we get old too soon and wise too late. So, as I reflect on my many rotations around the sun, I ask myself, *If I could go back in time, what advice would I give to my twenty-year-old self?* You know, beyond warning her that it'll take a whole week to recover from a hangover, and that hair will grow where it shouldn't.

Here's what I'd say:

* Stop worrying. Ninety-nine per cent of the things you've worried about have never happened.
* Use sunscreen (and look younger than your friends). I know my twenty-year-old self would find it most useful knowing that Hawaiian Tropic coconut tanning oil (SPF 0) and a face reflector board are not her friends.
* Relationships will not make you happy unless you are first happy with yourself. So choose to be happy. You have lots to be happy about but are just too young to realise it yet.
* It's OK to un-choose your choices.
* Not all friendships are meant to last a lifetime, or even past high school.
* You will have your heart shattered into a million pieces, and you will not only survive, but you will thrive.
* Trust your gut feelings. They are your guardian angels.
* Never pluck your eyebrows.
* Meditation works. Oh, wait, sorry, I meant medication.
* Take yourself on, not others. You've got this.

* Find gratitude for what you have. Be aware, humble and grateful. You're so fortunate.
* Tell your parents you love them … often. Take them for dinner, say 'thank you'. They'll never get tired of hearing 'I love you', and one day you would give anything to tell them one more time.
* Don't dread getting older. It is a privilege denied to many.

Here's another thing I would drum into that much younger me. As you go through this road trip we call life, choose your soundtrack wisely. The music surrounding you has frickin' magical powers.

Here is an example of what I mean. Shortly after my breakup with Edward, but before I discovered sweet liberation with Randi Realtor and friends, I found myself wandering miserably, aimlessly through Hyde Park. The soundtrack accompanying me was a playlist cheerfully called 'Antidepressants Optional'. You guessed it, it was a super-sad, curl-up-and-die breakup playlist. Clearly, I wasn't ready to give up feeling crappy. As I limply meandered past the Italian Gardens along the banks of the Serpentine, it dawned on me that I was a pathetic, sad sack of shit. Listening to songs like 'Say Something (I'm Giving Up On You)' or Adele wailing about finding someone like you, I was feeding my misery, note by agonising note. Did I want to continue wallowing in this, become one of misery's great graduates, or was I willing to give up feeling crappy?

So, I dug deep, moved the needle forward and created new playlists, with names like 'Badass Strut' and 'Happy as Shit'. And after only a few songs (and this is not me exaggerating, as I am sometimes accused of doing), I was strutting through Hyde Park like Heidi fucking Klum owning her shit on the Victoria's Secret catwalk. It magically dropped me smack-dab into the middle of my own fabulous musical TV montage, like on *Ally McBeal* or *The Mary Tyler Moore Show*. Those incredible single babes never knew who their supporting characters would be, but they never lost sight of the fact that they were the heroines in their own stories. You need proof? See what happens to your body after you crank David Bowie's 'Rebel Rebel'. Its transformational properties are no less magical than anything Cinderella's fairy godmother can throw your way. So sure, go ahead, my twenty-something self, and lament to Leonard Cohen or wail along to Joni Mitchell; see just how far that gets you when their insanely painful, beautiful lyrics rip your broken heart clear out of your chest and plummet it to the ground. Or ... you can crank up the volume to eleven and let Abba's 'Dancing Queen' decide your fate.

If I was in the mood to ruin my life, I could, if pressed, string together a true ugly-cry mixtape, a musical man melody, in a playlist I'd call 'Advice I Learnt the Hard Way', or perhaps a more fitting tribute title, 'Push That Dagger Deep into My Heart ... and Twist'. Brandon's song would have to be 'Can't Take My Eyes Off You' by Frankie Valli. It was our first dance at our wedding. The advice I'd share from being with Brandon is to silence the noise in my head and listen to my heart, as that's always where the truth is lying. Jackson's song would be 'I Will Always Love You', Dolly's version, not Whitney's. He played that song as we said our final goodbyes. I learnt from him that if you believe in yourself, you're capable of all you can imagine. John's, well, that would have to be Peggy Lee's 'Is That All There Is?', his karaoke go-to song which he sang without irony. I think John's lessons were my hardest, teaching me that my value doesn't come from how others see me but rather how I see myself. What is it they say? It doesn't matter what they call you, it's what you answer to. With Edward, his song could include most of The Rolling Stones' musical library, and I have to tell you it's hard to hide from The Rolling Stones. But if I had to choose one song, it would be 'Satisfaction', his semi-biographical theme song. Being with Edward taught me that regardless of the good intentions or the efforts one can put into someone, there will be things you cannot fix, and that's OK. My younger self could benefit from knowing that we can't fix what we didn't break; all we can try and do is fix ourselves. And recognising what makes *you* happy, not others, is a hell of a start.

I think we can all benefit from an ugly-cry now and again. Wallowing in sad songs that reassure us we aren't alone in our feelings is a rite of passage, granting us permission that it's OK to feel like human garbage for a bit. But continually surrounding yourself with that kind of stockpile of musical triggers is akin to being that cartoon character who walks off the side of a cliff, then looks down to realise the ground is no longer beneath their feet. So, choose your soundtrack wisely, for even if you're certain you've blurred, buried or burned those 'I'm so-over-your-fucking-ass' emotions, the song will always, always pull you back in. The song remembers when.

So, thinking forward (way forward), what advice would my 70-year-old self give to me today? I think she'd start by telling me to live life on my own terms and actively seek out the moments of joy that keep me alive and smiling. It's the only way to truly be happy. She'd remind me that I alone am enough. All I need to be happy I already have, so to carry it proudly, marvel at every sunset, find joy in every day. And during those shitty moments life can sometimes hurl at our heads, she'd remind me that I am my father's daughter, so to find the humour, laugh at the madness, and never let the bastards get me down. Of course, there'd be some skincare advice, but I'm guessing it will again boil down to always wearing sunscreen. She'd say to keep moving. To give away all those shoes taking up space in my closet that I haven't worn in aeons, and to get a pair of fabulous walking shoes and see the world. That one day walking will be an effort. She'd tell me to light those Jo Malone candles and break out the good china, for no other reason than it's a Tuesday. She'd remind me that friendships are as essential as the air you breathe, and to nurture those that feed your soul and release the others and thank them for their service.

But most importantly, and I believe this, she'd trumpet from every rooftop in London:

Love like your heart has never stopped believing.

Love like you've never mourned what might have been.

Love with the belief that you're worthy of every last bit of it.

Love out loud, and love louder.

Love as if your heart has never been broken.

Always, always, always allow yourself to love.

Love is never the mistake.

Epilogue

Flawsome

*'Flawsome: (adj) a woman who fully embraces her
flaws and knows she's awesome regardless.'*
Unknown

Tell me if I've got this straight. A woman shows up at an off-the-hook party in clothes that technically don't belong to her. She's transported by wild and free woodland critters who, without written consent, were transformed into unpaid Uber drivers. And during her early and abrupt departure, she loses a shoe, triggering a nationwide manhunt. I'm just going to go ahead and say it. If you're coming home after a night of partying without a shoe, girl, you aren't a princess, you were hammered. And please tell me that the next morning Cinderella, still rocking the previous night's makeup, *à la* Courtney Love, stared deep into her mirror and said, 'Fuck it, I'm going back to bed.'

If I think about how hard I've been on myself, my body, especially after giving birth to two wonderful healthy children, I want to give myself a swift kick in the ass. As women, we spend so much of our lives focusing on our flaws. We know precisely the wrong angle to have our picture taken, and where that extra ten pounds is stashed, as we lug around every mistake we've ever made. We'd never be that monstrously unkind to any other human being, ever, yet we're so quick to criticise ourselves, entirely without compassion. We're sure the gorgeous size-00 models with flawless faces taunting us from the covers of fashion magazines or the dressed-up-to-the-nines celebrities voguing on the red carpet are all lacking in a healthy dose of self-deprecating loathing. But I know enough of them to say with complete conviction, 'As if!' Before those Louboutins have so much as touched that red carpet, they've assembled a small, elite, lavishly paid army of experts, the beauty dream team. With fairy godmother-like powers, they camouflage their imperfections, dress them in expensive clothing and jewellery they do not own, and although I have no proof of this, I suspect their glowing sun-kissed tans are licked on by kittens. I don't know about you, but to me, that approach no more reeks of reality than Cinderella's late night out with the prince.

Sure, I can tell the difference between fairy tales and real life, most of the time, but with all the stories we've been fed throughout our lives, don't you think we could use fewer fairy tales and more fabulous coming-of-middle-age tales? And maybe a story that doesn't end with riding side-saddle into the sunset, on a white steed, with an impossibly perfect dude. Perhaps it ends with a giant sacrificial bonfire where women over 40 throw their Spanx into the fiery pit and scream-sing in joyous unison 'I Will Survive', 'Ain't Your Mama' and Billie Eilish's 'Get My Pretty Name Out of Your Mouth'. And it celebrates the glorious things we've accomplished, the people we've become, regardless of who may or may not have joined us on the journey. And in my middle-age tale, I'd be surrounded by my incredible soulmates, my girlfriends, my small imperfect army who've kept me sane, alive and believing not only in love but in myself. And if you're reading this, Shonda Rhimes, consider this my elevator pitch. Instead, as I've ranted about before, the stories surrounding us leave us searching for something that may or may not exist, leaving us totally confused as to why we don't all look like Jennifer Lopez at the age of 50. So I don't know who out there needs to hear this, but let that shit go.

I've learnt a hell of a lot about life while searching for Mr Darcy. Some of it has gently wafted into my lap, and some, well, I've almost broken my neck tripping over it. Perhaps I could even throw some of it into that giant heap of advice I'd tell my twenty-year-old self, as advice and life lessons often go hand in hand. But here's the thing, it's the difference between telling my twenty-year-old self, 'Christina, you need to learn to cook,' versus tasting what you've made. Life needs to be tasted. It needs to be devoured and savoured with enthusiastic lip-smacking. So, here's what I've learnt from tasting life:

* Sometimes a one-night stand can fix a specific problem better than years of therapy.
* A scorned woman can do better research than the FBI.
* Karma is a bitch, especially when its schedule doesn't jibe with your own.
* Life's problems are only temporarily solved with assault-eating and day-drinking.
* Pain is just part of the game when you're a baller like me (sorry, girls, Mom's using the word 'baller' again).
* The greater your capacity for love, the greater your capacity for pain.
* And ... whether the glass is half empty or half full, there's always room for wine.

I've also learnt with absolute certainty that I'm a good person. Flawed, yes, erratic at times, perhaps, but fundamentally good and decent. This is more important than I once knew. My current understanding of my moral compass and its true north came with accepting the fundamental truth that being human and flawed doesn't mean being bad. So I'll no longer be googling my symptoms without stopping until I hit the word 'schizophrenic'. And once I realised we are all a little mad, the world made a lot more sense.

I think what screwed me up the most was the picture in my head of how I thought it was supposed to be. We are programmed, pretty much from the start, into wanting something we are supposed to want. Can I blame books and movies for that? Maybe a little. Where I've ended up is far from where I'd thought my destination would be. Regardless of my carefully thought out, brilliantly well-meaning decisions and hard-learnt lessons, they did not equal the mathematically expected outcome of rose gardens, white picket fences and happily ever after. As we pick up those hitchhikers in life and get some mud on the tyres, there are so many unforeseen forces pushing us off in different directions: short-cuts we thought would save time, dead-ends, collisions, joyrides, faulty GPS, rusted detour signs or simply a dreadful sense of direction – all of it taking us further and further off-course. Maybe sometimes you have to get out of that dented shitbox of a car you've been driving for years, leave it at the side of an unfamiliar road, and start running like hell. I believe that's when the real adventure begins.

After my ride with Edward ended, I set a new course. I didn't drop myself in the middle of a Balinese ashram, surviving on nothing but leaves from some holy tree, plant-based stews and tea brewed from sticks. And not a chance would I be seeking internal enlightenment and the secrets of life through sun salutations or sitting for hours in the lotus position while lost in deep meditation. My pilgrimage included sinfully good carbonara, ricotta-stuffed courgette blossoms, beef carpaccio drizzled with local olive oil, carbohydrates in all their various splendid forms and wine. My road to anywhere will always, always include wine.

I carried myself away to my idea of a magical kingdom, a place whose ancient spirits greeted me like a spectacular epicurean seance, the incredible, beguiling Cinque Terre, Italy. The five colourful, ancient seaside villages are perched on the edge of a mountainous precipice cascading down to the Mediterranean Sea. People come from around the world to hike between these villages, through their old vineyards, dense olive groves and breathtaking seaside cliffs. Its unparalleled beauty could make even me question the existence of God.

After a genuinely inspiring hike, starting early in the morning in Vernazza, I ended my day at the edge of a beach in the sleepy seaside town of Levanto. I purchased a bottle of local wine from a tiny shop and took out the cellophane-wrapped plastic cup I'd brought from my hotel room. In front of me was an apricot-coloured beach stretching for miles. Lovers lay on blankets, children chased the surf, and a few dogs were thrilled to be running free, kicking up sand. The air was sweet and sticky like pink cotton candy, and the slowly sinking sun was falling with grace into the sea. Colours of burnt orange, fuchsia and lilac were fighting to keep alive against the impending darkness. *How could anyone ever tire of a sunset,* I thought. Its spectacular celestial light show celebrates the end of a day, a day that is never promised to any of us.

Wait … I know what you must be thinking right about now. She's not going to end this book happily ever after at the seaside, is she?

Well, if my mother can define a happy ending that way, then so can I.

Pouring the wine into my plastic cup, I pulled out my iPhone, ready to capture a little bit of the immense and resounding beauty. I thought it would make an excellent Instagram post or blog entry, so I took a few shots, then stopped. *Not now,* I thought. *This can't be replicated and perhaps never should.* Not only that, I was robbing myself of being present by trying to capture something impossible to capture. It was majestic and glorious, not just the spectacular sunset but absolutely everything.

At that moment, as the seaside offered stillness, there was absolutely nothing standing between myself and me. In the restorative silence, for the first time in my life, I wore no labels that screamed to the world who I was. I was no one's mother, daughter, sister, friend, employer, wife, partner or lover. And this might sound crazy to some, but in my 50-odd years on the planet, this was the first time I'd arrived at a place where nothing was defining me. I wasn't being measured by what I was willing to give up. I wasn't outsourcing my sense of self to others. I'd stopped comparing my insides to everybody's outsides. I was no longer defining myself by roles I'd willingly assumed, all woven together like some sort of technicolour dream coat I'd wrapped myself in. And those guys … they don't get to define me based on the few chapters they helped write. I am the entire book – no, wait. I am the whole encyclopaedia set, from A to glorious Z.

In my enduring pursuit of love over the decades, in my search for Mr Darcy, I've come to appreciate that not all relationships are meant to last forever, but that doesn't mean they didn't do exactly what they were supposed to do: carry me from one chapter of my life to the next. Science tells us our bodies are entirely and cellularly different every seven years, giving life to a new body. Following that science, my body has changed eight times so far, so wouldn't it stand to reason that we need a lot of different lives and a lot of different loves? Each relationship was its own remarkable story with a beginning, middle and end. And there was romance, passion, adventure and love, just like in any Austen tale. Come to think of it, wasn't it Austen who said, 'There are as many forms of love as there are moments in time'?

Society has programmed us to celebrate longevity, an 'ever after', but perhaps we need to look at it in a slightly different way. Maybe instead of years being the measure of relationship success, we should be calibrating it by the moments of happiness, joy, self-discovery and laughter it gives us. Just enduring something for decades can't be the end goal, it needs to sparkle. In what Oprah would describe as an 'aha' moment, I recognised I was the brilliant result of not just everything that had gone right but everything that had with a resounding blast gone *KABOOM!* My failures were a weird-ass portal into something beautiful. Even with my modicum of cynicism, imperfect body and fine lines circling my neck and eyes, I was fucking flawsome.

If I think about all the men I've loved, tried to love, hated, lusted after, cried for, liked enough, tolerated, or shared some intimate sliver of my life with, they were the ones who brought me here, all of them, to that exact moment in time, to that stupendous sunset. And I'd been shown, over and over, that just when you believe everything is finished, that, my friends, is when, magically, something new begins. So, I say with complete and unparalleled gratitude, God bless the broken road.

Who knows, maybe my soulmate got stuck in the reservoir tip of a Trojan condom, or perhaps I'd confused a soulmate for a life lesson. Maybe I'll share my life with someone, maybe not. But when I think back to my loneliest times, it was always with someone sitting next to me. And I know it's still early days, so I don't want to jinx it, but I think *I* just might be 'the one'.

Following my personal credo that sometimes life's moments are worthy of a musical overture, I'd created a Spotify playlist

I aptly named 'Cinque Terre, Ti Amo'. A beautiful selection of Puccini arias, Pavarotti and Andrea Bocelli. I hit 'shuffle' and let the symphonic music envelop me and the sinking sun. Around me, 'Nessun Dorma' was drawing a small crowd of locals. Seamlessly connected by the beauty of an aria and the majestic sun, we silently stood listening to the tenor accompany the fading light. This was absolute magic. The Italian sunshine gave me a gentle, warm kiss as I placed my wine on top of the stone seawall. Blinking into the light, head held high, I put my hands on my hips and heroically summoned Wonder Woman. There she stood beside me, in me, surrounding me, just like my father had taught me so many years ago. As we stood together, Wonder Woman and I, until the last rays of that fiery orange sun dipped below the horizon, my heart said to my mind, in a softly whispered voice that was unmistakably my own, *I got you.*

I smiled. *This is going to be good,* I thought. *Happily ever after at the seaside.* I mean, why else would I be crying?

Acknowledgements

I want to start by acknowledging the extraordinary, unwavering support from my super-rock star friends and family. I know everyone says this, but I really mean it, you're the best. Thank you for drilling into me the unshakable belief that there is nothing gutsier than a woman who believes her story deserves to be told. I am humbled and bursting with gratitude, for without you guys, this book would not exist.

Marie Robertson and Julie Bristow, thank you for a lifelong pattern of laughing and crying in all the right places. I love you more than wine. Linda Atkinson and Lindsey Shaw, you were always at the ready with a chilled bottle of something dry and a 'he had it coming' eye-roll when most needed.

To Elspeth Lynn, for seeing the ending of this book before I even saw the beginning. #CFF, baby.

A shout-out to Leah McLaren. For a wee cottage in Wales and perfectly timed G&Ts.

To my early readers: Leslie White, Deborah Katz, Charlotte Fry, Alyson Feltes, Niki Muller-Gass, Kathryn Abajian, Sharon Boccanfuso, Julie and Marie. Your insight, bluntness and unfiltered enthusiasm kept me going … really.

To my parents, Alan and Elena Dixon. As you're no longer inhabiting this planet, you most likely don't know this (OK, maybe Elena does), but you were with me in every word I wrote. With my eyes still and my heart open, I spoke to you. Your voices are etched on my skin, and your love and belief in me have allowed me to tell my story.

To my agents, Katie Fulford, Helen Edwards and the team at Bell Lomax Moreton, thank you. To the fire squad at Icon Books, you rock. Special shout-out to my wise, youthful editor Ellen Conlon. Not only did you take a chance on this slightly older, first-time author, but you recognised that my story is one for women of all ages.

To my daughters Samantha and Charlotte (still Briar in my heart), you are everything that is good in me.

And finally, to all those men who have danced through my life, whose pages have serendipitously overlapped with mine. A wholehearted, from the bottom of my heart, thank you. Not that I knew it at the time, but wow, what a story you've inspired. Seriously, you just can't make this shit up.